STARVING

TO

DEATH

ON

$200

MILLION

James Ledbetter

STARVING
TO
DEATH
ON
$200
MILLION

The
Short, Absurd Life
of *The Industry Standard*

 PublicAffairs NEW YORK

Book Design by Jenny Dossin.

Library of Congress Cataloging-in-Publication data

Ledbetter, James.

Starving to death on $200 million: the short, absurd life of The industry standard / James Ledbetter.

p. cm.

Includes bibliographical references and index.

ISBN 1-58648-129-0

1. Industry standard (San Francisco, Calif.)—History. 2. Internet industry—Periodicals—Publishing—United States—History. 3. Business—Periodicals—Publishing—United States—History. 4. Business failures—United States—Case studies. I. Title: Starving to death on two hundred million dollars. II. Title.

HD9696.8.A1 I5335 2003

338.7'610045678—dc21

2002031617

First Edition

10 9 8 7 6 5 4 3 2 1

In reading the history of nations, we find that, like individuals, they have their whims and their peculiarities; their seasons of excitement and recklessness, when they care not what they do. We find that whole communities suddenly fix their minds upon one object, and go mad in its pursuit; that millions of people become simultaneously impressed with one delusion, and run after it, till their attention is caught by some new folly more captivating than the first.

—from the 1852 preface to
Extraordinary Popular Delusions
and the Madness of Crowds,
by Charles Mackay,
originally published in 1841

Contents

$50,000 Cocktail Party . . . Fight the Power! . . . Lowering the Standards . . . What's Bamboo.com? . . . Management for Dummies . . . Doesn't Herb Look Like a CFO?

8: THE CASE FOR MURDER   245

Branding *Uber Alles* . . . Who Is David Lauren, Anyway? . . . Live by
the Business Magazine Sword . . . Why No IPO? . . . Death and Taxes
. . . It's Still Alive!

EPILOGUE: WHO DO WE SHOOT?   267

Acknowledgments

Writing any nonfiction book is intrinsically collective; writing a book about a magazine where you've worked is especially so. You can't tell the story of a magazine without the help, formal and informal, of many of the people who joined you in putting the magazine (and Web site) out.

Thus, my first acknowledgment is to the entire staff of *The Industry Standard,* in America and especially in Europe. I have drawn this book from their dedication to a project that at times was crazy but, I still think, worthwhile.

Specifically, for their generous help in recalling their experiences, I am indebted to John Battelle, Sue Davis, David Evans, Jim Evans, Mark Gimein, Thomas Goetz, Jane Goldman, Matt McAlister, Anne-Marie McGowan, Alissa Neil, Michael Parsons, Gary Rivlin, June Sargent, Neil Thackray, Bernhard Warner, Debra Williamson, Matthew Yeomans, and Kerry Zeida. A distinct and profound gratitude goes out to Jonathan Weber, an excellent editor and boss whose recollections were vital.

Sarah Hansen from IDG always answered my questions promptly and professionally, which was greatly appreciated. Some others involved with *The Standard* gave their recollections yet preferred to remain anonymous; I am grateful for their help. Author Gary Wolf shared his insights about *Wired* magazine's early days.

My agent, the sterling Kay McCauley, earned major kudos for scoring the contract for this book within a few hours of *The Standard*'s demise—in August, no less, when getting hold of a New York agent is not easier than getting hold of a New York shrink. Paul Golob, my editor at PublicAffairs, is everything a writer could ask for: smart, engaged, efficient, tough, and completely professional. I am also grateful to Peter Osnos, the publisher of PublicAffairs, for seeing the value of this project and giving it the support it needed. It has been a privilege to work with them and the rest of the PA team.

Some of the most important assistance on the book came in material form. I deeply thank Thomas Goetz and Whitney Wright, Pavia Rosati, Matthew Yeomans, Jowa Coffey, and everyone else who housed me during various research trips. Tim and Jenny Hamilton graciously provided me with access to Vivaio, their magical Tuscan villa, to complete the manuscript; Alexander Hamilton and Gus Park spent the better part of a late summer afternoon helping me chop the wood that would keep me warm while I wrote there.

Lauren Goldstein saw me through some of the harder parts of this book and made helpful comments on portions of the manuscript. Those who read the manuscript in toto prior to publication are best left unnamed, but I am grateful for their insights and suggestions.

Collective though this book may be, it is a personal story, and if I've made mistakes they are surely not the fault of the generous people named above. My first defense is that objects in the retrospective dotcom mirror may be larger than they appear. But in the end, all flaws in this text fall on my shoulders.

London, June 2002

STARVING

TO

DEATH

ON

MILLION

Introduction:
An Overdose, or a Murder?

They say that nothing important ever happens in August, especially in Europe, which is why you should take your holiday then. In
my case, in August 2001, I had no choice. As one of many cost-cutting measures, *The Industry Standard* had mandated that almost all of
its staff take off the middle week of August, without pay. I grumbled
to colleagues that our company, a weekly magazine covering the business of twenty-first-century technology, was acting like a nineteenth-
century shipbuilding factory.

But there was little I could do about it, so I left my London home—
I was the magazine's European executive editor—for a small coastal
town in the British county of Norfolk, which has beautiful beaches if
you overlook the fact that they consist of large black stones.

As my girlfriend, Lauren, and I sunned ourselves, I contemplated
how far things had fallen in twelve months. A year before, *The Industry Standard* was arguably America's most successful magazine. Our
cover story on August 7, 2000—"Stop the Music!"—was a package
on the legal setbacks faced by the music-swapping Web site Napster,
one of the hottest stories of the year. Although August is traditionally
a slow month for advertising, that issue of *The Standard* was a hefty
208 pages thick. By comparison, that week's edition of *Newsweek* contained 96 pages.

The continual flow of advertising had been attracting all sorts of attention—from the press, from our readers, and from Wall Street. We were planning to sell stock in the company through an initial public offering (although no date had been fixed), and a flattering article in the media watchdog magazine *Brill's Content* that summer had estimated that the publication, just two years old, was worth between $300 million and $450 million.[1] By the end of 2000, *The Standard* would sell more than 7,440 ad pages. That was more than 1,000 pages greater than *Fortune* magazine, a title that had nearly a century more publishing experience than *The Standard.* The ad-page figure surpassed that of any other magazine in the country—indeed, it was the highest in American history. We were projecting that we'd bring in $200 million of revenue in a one-year period, not three years into the magazine's existence. At an offsite meeting, the executive team delivered a high-flying "State of *The Standard*" speech. In it, our CEO predicted that by 2005, Standard Media International would have more than 900 employees and annual revenues of a billion dollars. We would become, he pledged, the Dow Jones of the twenty-first century.

This was heady stuff. The company hired consultants to teach us, through elaborate role-playing exercises, how to cope with our stunning success. Stressed-out staffers billed *The Standard* for massages and facials. At our frequent conferences, *Standard* executives traded jokes with the dot-com world's pashas in exotic locales like Aspen and Laguna Niguel.

And success in America was only part of the plan. *The Standard* wanted nothing less than global media domination. Central to that strategy was our European edition, which debuted in October 2000 and gave me, as its editor-in-chief, my own quirky taste of international glamour. I recalled one recruiting trip the previous summer to Stockholm, where I interviewed four candidates for the bureau chief position (we would also have bureaus in Paris and Berlin). There weren't any normal hotel rooms available—inadvertently I had chosen a date during Stockholm's annual Water Festival—and so I had to stay on a moored boat.

I drank beer and smoked on one of the ship's decks, and watched the sun set after 10 P.M. over a beautiful spired church, the 700-year-old Riddarholmskyrkan. Having finished a number of interviews, I was struck by the power of what my magazine had accomplished in just over two years of publishing. Here I was in a city more than 6,000 miles away from our San Francisco headquarters, and there were multiple journalists who were truly eager to work for *The Industry Standard*. And that was in a country where the first language isn't even English!

But no matter how beloved *The Standard* was in Stockholm, we never exactly became Dow Jones.

The magazine began laying off employees in January 2001, and in April the European edition shut down, after not quite six months of publishing. I stayed on as European executive editor, where my principal duties consisted of shedding what little staff remained. Practically the only telephone conversations I had with the editor-in-chief were about exactly which employees had to be let go and when. By the time I went to Norfolk, our European presence was down to just myself and a part-time Web editor—and I'd had to raise a stink to keep his job.

With dot-com gluttony now a quaint memory, the magazine had been successfully losing weight: The July 30 issue had been a slender 64 pages. In addition to the enforced week off, the publication had halted bonus payments in the second quarter, and an across-the-board pay cut of 20 percent was said to be imminent. More layoffs were on the way, and a number of my friends in New York and San Francisco were anxious that they'd be out of work.

But ever confident in the management that had moved me to London, I tried to remain upbeat about the future. The ad slump was hardly our fault; everybody was getting killed, and not just the financial and technical magazines. We were hurting more than most, but that's partly because we had farther to fall. The publication's majority owner, the Boston-based publishing conglomerate International Data Group (IDG), had told *The Standard* that it wanted out. I found that scary but also believed that it could be good in the long term if we could find the right backers. IDG and *The Standard* had never been the best-fitting partners, and I believed that a more mainstream media company could do a better job of promoting *The Standard.* While we were looking for a new buyer, members of our board had, I'd been told, come up with a "bridge financing" package that would keep *The Standard* afloat until the first quarter of 2002.

So when Lauren and I got back to the Norfolk bed-and-breakfast after dinner on the evening of August 16, I was saddened but not entirely surprised to find a somber message on my mobile phone from a colleague in New York; I figured that he'd been laid off. I rang him back but got an answering machine. In the meantime, I'd gotten a message to phone the magazine's editor-in-chief, Jonathan Weber.

Suddenly I thought: *I've* been laid off.

In a way I had been—along with essentially the entire staff. When I phoned Weber, I learned that *The Standard* had announced that it was ceasing publication and was preparing to file for bankruptcy protection. There was no "bridge financing," and IDG had apparently decided that it was time to bail out on a little more than three years of publishing *The Standard.*

I was devastated by the news, but at least I was better off than Weber. The Web site for *The Wall Street Journal* already had the story of our closure, and the various department heads were in the lamentable position of scrambling to find their vacationing staffers to tell them they no longer had jobs.

Back when I had been a media reporter for *The Village Voice,* my experience with dying publications had always been from the other side: that is, phoning the victims and begging them for details. When I awoke on Friday morning, I had half a dozen messages from members of the British press, seeking to glean some kind of grisly anecdote from me so they could write the business equivalent of an obituary. I didn't return most of the calls. I was in no mood to chat, and because I was thousands of miles from where the fatal decisions had been made, I really didn't have much to offer.

Inevitably, the massive coverage that followed, both in the United States and Britain, suggested that *The Standard* died because it had to die. A lead editorial in *The New York Times* struck this note. It was filled with praise and flattery; it singled out my boss, editor-in-chief Jonathan Weber, for emphasizing "journalism over boosterism." It said that *The Standard*'s journalists felt "like entrepreneurs themselves, real players in a generation's hottest story, much like *Rolling Stone* writers must have felt in the heyday of rock 'n' roll." But the magazine's demise, the *Times* said, was "a dizzying reversal of fortune for a publication whose meteoric rise and fall mirrors the euphoric, then harrowing times lived by the dot-com entrepreneurs it covered."[2]

Using the magazine's closure as a metonym for the entire dot-com collapse was irresistible; there was always a running joke at *The Standard* that we were the story we were reporting on. Yet the analogy between *The Standard* and the average failed Web start-up struck me as flawed. Over the course of nearly three years at *The Standard,* I'd covered quite a few failed Web companies, and so I had a fairly good grasp of why most of them had died. Many of the Internet's high-flying failures flopped because they could not function as businesses. Either they misjudged the market (such as broadband prophets ExciteAtHome), or they could not consistently deliver the product they promised (such as the slick clothing retailer Boo.com), or they were following myopic business models (notably those purveyors of lazy gratification, Kozmo.com).

At least on the surface, none of those flaws truly applied to *The Standard.* The weekly magazine is a proven business model dating back more than a century. Compared, say, to a Web publication, a magazine has several advantages that, while obvious, are decisive— starting with the fact that people are willing to pay for it.

Second, *The Standard* met a genuine need in the news marketplace. The publication grasped early on that the Internet was a business story—and almost certainly *the* business story of the late 1990s. Through 1998 and 1999, most big newspapers like *The New York Times* and *The Wall Street Journal* still covered the Internet as a technology story. They knew that the Nasdaq was soaring, but they hadn't yet reorganized their newsrooms to the changed business environment. That left holes in their coverage that *The Standard* could fill, and did, often with flair and class. We were an essential read for the burgeoning class of technology workers and investors.

And most important, we did function successfully as a business. Depending on how the revenue was counted, Standard Media International was taking in between $140 million and $200 million in its best year. That is an astounding amount for a magazine in its second full year of publishing, and we had consistently shown a profit through the middle of 2000—a feat that almost no Internet companies have matched.

So how could it all fall apart so fast? With the media insisting that *The Standard* had to answer for the sins of the dot-com era, many writers strongly hinted that we had spent our way into oblivion—on lavish parties, far-flung offices, and a sizable and well-paid staff. But far more significant were the financial figures that began to emerge toward the end of 2001. In January 2000, Standard Media International had secured a round of investment from a group of prestigious partners that included the investment banks Morgan Stanley and Chase, the media conglomerate Pearson plc, a high-flying New York–based venture capital group called Flatiron Partners, and the French business mogul Bernard Arnault. That move put $30 million into our bank account, in return for about 15 percent of equity in the company. My colleagues and I had always assumed that this was a kind of dedicated rainy-day fund. Of course, it was meant to be spent—specifically on marketing and expanding our business—but as long as the publication was profitable, there was no need to touch it. Obviously, if we were declaring bankruptcy, that money had not only been touched, but it had been completely spent.

Moreover, when the negotiations for bridge financing had begun in the late spring of 2001, the company's books didn't show that *The Standard* was out of cash. They showed that it was, in fact, in debt.

Deeply in debt. According to the company's bankruptcy filing, *The Standard*'s immediate liabilities amounted to about $9.1 million. That figure was about $5.5 million more than the company had in its bank accounts.[3] More troubling were *The Standard*'s long-term obligations, mostly in real estate, which amounted to some $50 million.

And so if you added up the revenue Standard Media International made in 2000–2001, the investment cash, and the debt obligations, the publication had managed to spend or otherwise commit something like $300 million over the course of a year and a half. Where could all of that money possibly have gone?

There were other mysteries as well. Why hadn't the publication been able to find financing? We had hundreds of fans and supporters in banking and venture capital circles. Two of the world's largest investment banks, Morgan Stanley and JP Morgan Chase, had representatives on our board. Banks like that bail out companies every day; surely they could have come up with some kind of plan that would have kept *The Standard* afloat.

Certainly most of the editorial staff believed that the magazine's death was drastic and unnecessary. Even with the free fall in *The Standard*'s advertising that began at the end of 2000, the magazine still brought in approximately $34 million in advertising from January to July 2001. According to the Publishers Information Bureau, that's almost exactly the same as two weekly magazines—*New York* and *The Economist*—which are considered healthy.

Yes, the company had become bloated and even three rounds of layoffs throughout 2001 did not eliminate all the fat. Yes, the bottom fell out of the tech market, as our articles had warned it inevitably would. But none of that eliminated the need for a newsmagazine analyzing technology and business.

A premature death like ours is a story that doesn't make sense—unless there's a villain. And the publication's leaders, John Battelle and Jonathan Weber, were happy to point toward the villain. It was our majority owner, IDG.

True, IDG had backed us from the very beginning and had given us all kinds of support in the lean early days. But it had never been the best relationship, and now, we were told, IDG had become bad parents: They didn't love us like they were meant to. They had the chance to fund us through a bad patch, and they declined. Outside funding from JP Morgan was put in front of them, and they turned it down. IDG, not surprisingly, scoffed at this interpretation and pointed a finger back at *The Standard*'s greed and poor budgeting.

It all seemed like an exercise in business forensics: There's a corpse in the room, but the cause of death is unknown. Did *The Standard* cause its own demise, through lavish overspending and poor financial management? That is, was it an overdose? Or did the death of the publication come about because a onetime partner, IDG, decided that if it couldn't own *The Standard* then no one could? Was it a murder?

1

Impatient with the Present

These new business leaders crave bottom-line information. They scour countless publications and spend hundreds of dollars on conferences for anything that might help them get a clear picture on how to lead in this new economy. But there is always something missing. 　　　　　　　　　　　**—from marketing material, *The Industry Standard***

You'd look at John Battelle, and you'd think: surfer.

If you had to design a man who summed up everyone's image of Californian man, you might well end up with someone resembling Battelle. He was blond, perpetually and improbably tanned, fit, and aggressively casual in his clothing. (In point of fact, Battelle is not much of a surfer, though he does frequently make waves.)

You'd look at Battelle, and you'd think: frat boy. That may seem slightly unfair—except that he was one, Delta Kappa Epsilon. And he retained a whiff of a fraternity's combustible mixture of elitism and bad-boy energy; he favored expensive bourbon, and he was quick to salt his language with expletives, both mild and profound.

But the reason it seems unfair is that frat boys are not generally credited with intellectual ambition, and Battelle certainly had that.

Because he accomplished a great deal at a young age—he was born in 1965—many people have looked at Battelle and thought: visionary. Though he rejected the moniker—"If I'm a visionary, that just shows you how low the threshold is," he once told me—perhaps a more apt description is that Battelle has always instinctively looked to the future as a way to solve problems. Like many Californians, Battelle was impatient with the present.

For all of his professional life, Battelle sought to adapt his chosen profession—media—to the possibilities of technology, or perhaps it's the other way around. It started in a fairly ordinary way. When he graduated from University of California at Berkeley, he went to work as a reporter for *MacWeek* magazine. Not much magic there; a lot of short pieces about incremental computer developments, a lot of trade shows.

Finding the trade format too restrictive, Battelle went back to Berkeley in 1990, enrolling in the graduate journalism program with the stated intent of writing about the intersection of culture and technology. That could have been scripted as an invitation to meet Louis Rossetto, the cofounder of *Wired*.

TO CREATE A REVOLUTION

Rossetto was an itinerant writer and entrepreneur who became a cyberanarchist, and one who did not reject the title of visionary. He was fond of citing Marshall McLuhan and Pierre Teilhard de Chardin, and in the early 1990s he believed, along with many others on the West Coast, that digital technology was the most important human development of the past several hundred years. There was a palpable spark between him and Battelle. "He was a very smart, serious, switched-on guy," Rossetto recalled in a later interview.[1] "He exuded this straightforward competence and confidence."

And thus at the tender age of twenty-six, Battelle became the managing editor of a new magazine that Rossetto and business partner Jane Metcalfe were starting, to be known as *Wired*. Almost immediately after its January 1993 debut, *Wired* became the epicenter of the technology revolution that was spreading from Silicon Valley. Each issue was less a description of the world of technology than it was a kind of serial manifesto. Its writers often saw themselves as prophets or philosophers rather than mere journalists. Its stars included Nicholas Negroponte, who did cutting-edge technology work at the Massachusetts Institute of Technology, and John Perry Barlow, who at a different point in his career had been a lyricist for the Grateful Dead.

Much of the magazine's editorial thrust was fervently antiestablishment, almost militant. Rossetto once proclaimed, "Mass media in the 20th century destroyed community. It is single handedly responsible for destroying neighborhoods and families and creating mass society." But the establishment quickly embraced *Wired*. In fact, the magazine's instant success left a lot of people in the East Coast media industry kicking themselves. Almost every major media company in America had been offered a chance to invest in *Wired* prior to its publication, and they had all turned Rossetto and Metcalfe down. But it conveyed such a sense of urgency from the very start that it made instant converts. Si Newhouse, head of the Condé Nast publishing empire, invested $3.5 million in *Wired* after the third issue. In 1994, the fledgling title won a National Magazine Award for general excellence.

Battelle's duties ranged from reporting and writing stories to the grittier details of making sure that the magazine actually got published every month. He covered topics from national telecommunications policy to the most advanced video games. And while many of Battelle's colleagues were absorbed by arcane technologies or niche culture, Battelle clearly had his eyes trained on how technology would be adopted by big business.

There were times when the magazine seemed more interested in celebrating the companies that popularized technology than in actual journalism. One infamous *Wired* cover story on Viacom featured Beavis and Butthead and Viacom president Sumner Redstone with the cover line: "Viacom Doesn't Suck!" The article predicted that Viacom would be on the cutting edge of all things digital. As it happened, the prediction turned out to be dramatically wrong. Nearly everyone on Viacom's "interactive" team whom it profiled left or was forced out of the company in a couple of years, and the conglomerate was widely perceived to be well behind others in the race to become digital. The piece was written by Battelle, who later told me that it "was not one of my prouder journalistic moments."

Just as Battelle always seemed impatient with the present, *Wired* was impatient with being simply a magazine. Rossetto and Metcalfe envisioned their magazine as the springboard into a multimedia empire: Wired TV, Wired Books, international editions of Wired, CD-ROM publishing. But while Rossetto had a certain genius for inspiring his staff, he was less adept at dealing with the world of finance. Russ Mitchell, who would succeed Battelle as *Wired*'s managing editor, put it succinctly: "Louis wanted to change society, he wanted to create a revolution. That colored his ability to build a business."[2]

Wired tried to take all the right steps. In the spring of 1996, Wired Ventures retained the prestigious investment bank Goldman Sachs to take itself public. The provisional value of the company was placed at an ambitious $450 million. When that number was widely criticized, a new prospectus was issued, valuing the company at $293 million. The company kept ratcheting the number down, but perhaps that sent signs of weakness to Wall Street types, and the venture could not get out the door; Goldman canceled the IPO the day before it was scheduled to take place.

It would be especially painful for *Wired*'s founders to realize that a valuation of $450 million was considered unreasonably high in 1996, whereas two to three years later, a company that had only Wired Digital's Web resources (not even its magazine) might well have been worth more than $500 million on the open market.

In the meantime, *Wired* kept pissing money away at fairly high levels; even in 1996, one of its best years, the company apparently lost $10 million, much of it in expensive expansion plans and Internet projects. Investors signed on and checked out so frequently that *Wired* employees were sometimes confused about who they worked for. By November 1997, some $50 million in capital had disappeared, and Rossetto was forced out of the magazine's central management. In 1998, the magazine (but not its Web division) was sold to Condé Nast for approximately $80 million.

But by that time, Battelle had already flown the coop. He had been dispatched to the company's London office in late 1996, for a reorganization assignment that was intended to last a few weeks. He ended up staying six months, and his task involved shutting down the UK edition.

When he returned from London, Battelle found a company sapped of its morale and in the process of sinking financially. He had frequent disagreements with other managers, and he began thinking about other projects. One was an idea he shared with others on the *Wired* staff, that a weekly magazine was needed to cover the same territory that *Wired* was already covering.

Meet Uncle Pat

Three thousand miles away from *Wired*'s San Francisco headquarters, a very similar idea was being hatched, albeit in a more staid corporate environment. A *Wired* writer might say that a good or useful idea is born because its era requires it, as when Newton and Leibniz invented calculus at roughly the same time in different countries.

But maybe a better way of looking at it is that while Battelle would provide the vision for a weekly technology magazine, the money was to come from a company called IDG. The letters stand for International Data Group, though people use that name about as often as they spell out International Business Machines. IDG is an anomaly: Its products are on practically every newsstand in America, and yet the parent company is nearly anonymous. It may be one of the least-recognized $3 billion companies in the country. IDG was founded in 1964 by Patrick J. McGovern, who, even more than Battelle or Rossetto, was an undisputed technology publishing pioneer. McGovern launched one of the first computer magazines, *ComputerWorld*, in 1967. Since then, hundreds of successful magazines have flowed out of IDG's headquarters. Often IDG titles gave a nod to the original, as in *MacWorld*, *PCWorld*, or *LinuxWorld*, but there were also titles such as *CIO* and *GamePro*.

The IDG approach to technology journalism was about as far as you can get from *Wired* and still be roughly on the same topic. To Rossetto and his *Wired* acolytes, computer technology simultaneously captured an essential form of human intelligence and allowed for its transcendence. It had an almost religious, and certainly mystical, resonance; it was the fire of the gods.

McGovern and IDG saw the fire, too; they just recognized that there was a lot of money to be made by selling lighters. IDG's business was based on a stunningly reductive idea: People, especially people who run businesses, need to buy computers (and software and printers and monitors and so on). If they want to use those products to find the digital godhead, that's fine, so long as they keep buying them. They're always going to want to know which are the best ones to buy, and IDG made billions selling them magazines that helped them decide that.

IDG's master plan, like many successful business propositions, stemmed from the observation that a lot of people are fairly insecure—and that having to deal with technology makes them feel outright stupid. Indeed, the signature IDG product in recent years has been the wildly successful series of books "for dummies." Started as a way for technology novices to overcome their fears without resorting to incomprehensible user manuals—the debut title was *DOS for Dummies*—the series has expanded into nontechnology areas (*Wine for Dummies*, *Bridge for Dummies*) quite successfully.[3]

The company attributed its scope and success to a radically decentralized structure. At the top of the company were four executives. There was no group of middle executives directly managing the publications; instead, IDG's businesses were run as separate units. The company was frequently referred to as a "federation" rather than a top-down corporation. About the only things that linked the units to one another were a weekly internal newsletter and annual gatherings of the unit heads.

As officials at IDG will gleefully tell you, it frequently makes *Fortune* magazine's list of the top 100 companies to work for. And it certainly has a distinct corporate culture. Yet at times IDG seems paternalistic, with an almost cult-like belief in McGovern's power. When McGovern travels, the staff in the company's Boston headquarters can still get a meeting with him. How? There is a life-sized mannequin of him that sits in his office, wearing a dark suit and always available. It has been dubbed McGovern's "vice president of listening."[4]

As one of its nods to corporate loyalty, every employee who has been on the IDG payroll for ten years gets a personal dinner with McGovern in Boston. McGovern personally flies to satellite offices to hand employees their Christmas bonus checks.[5] He thanks each employee, and almost always has some bit of information about them to praise.

People my age and younger are more likely to believe in UFO abductions than in corporate loyalty, and hence these could be painful encounters; staff at IDG magazines referred to him with mild disdain as "Uncle Pat."

THE NEXT ECONOMIC PARADIGM

Creating new magazines—especially titles that focus on new or emerging technologies—was a vital part of what IDG and its competitors did. Typically, IDG would create ten to twelve new magazine titles every year. In the technology field, this task was slightly trickier than it might seem. It's not always apparent which applications will last long enough to retain readers' interest. When, for example, Apple first introduced its Newton Personal Digital Assistant in the mid-1990s, there was a temptation to believe that Newtons would be wildly successful, and that therefore an entire magazine could be shaped around their use, software for them, and the like.

But the product never really worked well and was overthrown by the Palm Pilot, so such a publishing bet would have been wrong and costly. And even if a technology catches on, it may not be able by itself to support a separate magazine. When Microsoft launched Windows in the early 1990s, it was a distinct enough platform that some felt that it warranted a separate magazine; just a few years later Windows was so pervasive that all the larger magazines devoted to PCs simply incorporated Windows into their coverage.

From IDG's perspective, any new title, no matter how exciting or potentially lucrative, was subject to such ruminations. In the spring of 1997, at an offsite planning meeting for future development, IDG's business unit heads floated the idea for four or five new magazines. One of those was for a magazine devoted to the Internet business. Once this idea was deemed viable, IDG officials proceeded by looking to hire someone who could sell them on the idea and then execute it.

As it frequently does when creating a new business unit, IDG retained a headhunting firm, Korn Ferry, to find a project leader for this new publication. Within three days of spelling out exactly what was desired, the recruiter, Vici Wayne, came back with three names, one of which was John Battelle.

Battelle was thirty-one years old and was still working for Wired Ventures. But having worked for a trade magazine in the 1980s, he at least knew enough about IDG to know that it had the resources to back a major magazine. He flew to Boston, interviewed with McGovern, and was invited to assemble a "back-of-the-envelope" business plan: nothing terribly elaborate, but primarily a way of demonstrating to IDG how much money it would have to put in and how promising the market for the new publication truly might be.

Within a few days, Battelle assembled an initial blueprint, dated June 7, 1997, a pitch for a weekly magazine. He began by noting that the Internet support market alone was estimated to reach $100 billion by 1999. "We are speaking of nothing less than the next economic paradigm," he wrote.

And yet, Battelle argued, despite the rush among mainstream and trade press to cover the burgeoning Net phenomenon, "the Internet and the industry of industries it represents has lacked an understanding of itself. The press to date has told the Internet/New Economy story through preset filters of their own readership constraints." Decoded from *Wired*-speak, this means that smart technology executives needed smarter technology coverage than they were getting from the existing media.

With the possible exception of *Wired*, Battelle noted, "no single publication captures the leadership of this new industry, serves as a conduit and amplifier of that leadership's conversations and concerns, or catalyses and crystallizes the power and potential of this new market."

Such words! Conduit, amplifier, catalyse, crystallize, power, potential—all in one sentence! This was no mere call for a new magazine: This was a calling. The economy had created a new creature in mass numbers—call him Digital Man—and Digital Man needs something to read. Thus must a new weekly be born!

"The editorial voice," he said, should be "authoritative, smart, highest common denominator, knowing, inside, analytical, opinionated—more *Variety* than *Entertainment Week* [*sic*], a combination of a *Wired*'s influence with a *Billboard*'s immediacy, news, and targeted marketing."

In retrospect, it seems slightly odd that a technology magazine would look to *Variety* as a model of quality industry coverage. (It seems even odder that if you wanted to create a new *Variety*, you would consider a straitlaced tech outfit like IDG the appropriate place to do it.) For one thing, the writing in *Variety* is often quite poor, and its relationship to the industry it covers is dubious, sometimes to the point of being incestuous.

But the *Variety* example to an extent underlined just how barren the world of good industry reporting is. There was also a bit of northern California envy at work; it's not hard to imagine the technogeeks of Silicon Valley feeling snubbed by the major media, despite the billions of dollars their products created and the way they shaped culture—even Hollywood culture, via the world of video games and special effects. Having one's own *Variety* would be a way of saying: "We're glamorous, too!"

Battelle's initial pitch was sophisticated enough to provide numbers. He assumed a weekly magazine with a circulation of 55,000. He expected an overall staff of 90, of whom 30 would be in editorial and 20 in ad sales. The total expense for staff would be just under $6 million a year, including overhead. And he projected the publication's projected gross revenues at $28.6 million a year.

These were merely top-of-the-head numbers, Battelle insisted, and yet it was part of the IDG system that such preliminary figures, drawn up with a few days research, would become the basis for greenlighting the project. Crucially, that meant that when the road began to get rough, this would be the map that the magazine's financiers would look back at.

That was the audition, and Battelle got the part. After some slight hesitation, Battelle signed with IDG in August 1997. He would later tell an interviewer that he left *Wired* "with my ass on fire."[6] As a parting gift to his *Wired* colleagues, Battelle gave out cloth headbands, with warrior mottoes printed in Japanese characters.

WHAT BUCKET?

Even before he had actually started, Battelle had already done the two things he would end up being best at: selling the prospect of the magazine, and underscoring the importance of its audience. But creating a successful magazine requires a lot more than that. A large number of media players had attempted to capture the energy of the Internet in magazine form and had ended up as litter on the shoulders of the information superhighway. In the mid-1990s, *Newsweek* and *The Washington Post* had made an early stab with a title called *Virtual Cities,* which had failed to find a wide audience. The trade publisher CMG had published a reasonably high-quality but unwieldy magazine called *NetGuide* in 1997, which also failed. And indeed, IDG itself had launched a publication in late 1996 called *The Web,* which would publish its last issue in February 1998.

Perhaps even more threatening was that the trade publishing industry already supported a number of weekly magazines that were adapting themselves to the rapidly changing Internet market. One was IDG's own *InfoWorld*; *Interactive Week,* published by Ziff-Davis, was another. They may not have been especially sexy, nor pillars of literary excellence, but enough insiders read them to make them successful. And so when IDG let it be known that it was launching a weekly magazine focused on the Internet business, recalled IDG president Kelly Conlin, "people thought we were lunatics."

Battelle was undaunted. He moved into IDG offices on 501 Second Street in San Francisco's SOMA (south of Market) neighborhood, a hotbed of digital employment and only a few blocks from where *Wired* was located. He and his staff were to share an area with an unlikely partner, *GamePro* magazine, a title for video-game enthusiasts. The space, as one early employee described it, was "nasty." Still, a magazine needs an office, and IDG provided it, along with all the other vital infrastructure needs, such as payroll and human resources services, and contracts for printing and distribution.

The company's first hire, in September 1997, was Matt McAlister, a twenty-seven-year-old northern Californian who had been producing the Web site for IDG's *MacWorld* magazine but had lost his job when that title merged with *MacUser*. Meeting with Battelle, he recalled later, "I instantly knew that he had a hundred times more charisma and vision than anyone I'd ever met at IDG." (There's that vision thing again.) "He was on another plane."

McAlister had some early desires to work in the film business and was taken with the notion that the Internet business needed its own version of *Variety*. He was hired with the elastic title of "development manager," which meant he did everything from interviewing job candidates to showing the publisher how to respond to e-mail.

Others came on board that autumn, including an associate publisher, a vice president for sales, and a design director. On the editorial side, Battelle hired Debra Aho Williamson, a twenty-nine-year-old writer from *Advertising Age*, as a consultant. Her duties included organizing a detailed database that could be searched on the new publication's Web site. Battelle developed a fairly clear idea for how to segment the magazine into a news section, a section of charts and data about the state of the Internet, and a recruitment section. But IDG didn't seem overly interested in his editorial plan. Not that it made much sense for IDG to carefully monitor every nuance of what was being created at the prepublication stage. In fact, Battelle thought at times that IDG was barely paying attention to anything but the numbers in various columns of a spreadsheet. In November 1997, Battelle met with Kelly Conlin at COMDEX, a sprawling computer trade show held annually in Las Vegas. Conlin praised Battelle's business plan, saying it represented considerable work and would only need a few tweaks. There was, however, one question nagging him (and, by implication, his boss, McGovern).

"I don't understand who the reader is," Conlin said. "What bucket are they in?"

Battelle was befuddled, as he was unaccustomed to thinking about readers in pails. "Bucket?"

Conlin tried to explain. "Are they vendors? Or buyers?"

This was the way that IDG thought about the readers and advertisers of its magazines. Either your reader was in the business of selling technology—and you gave him *InfoWorld*—or buying it—and you gave him *PCWorld*.

But the distinction confused Battelle: "They're both," he said, to no visible effect on his listener. After an unenlightening exchange, he walked outside and found himself in a concrete courtyard filled with wires and servers and generators, a somewhat nightmarish glimpse of the underbelly of the industry he was trying to cover; at the moment, he felt like it was covering him. Everyone standing outside was smoking, and Battelle bummed a cigarette even though he rarely smoked. As he puffed away, he asked himself: "What the fuck am I doing? Do they know something about magazine publishing that I can't see?"

TRADING PLACES

It was a question that would plague Battelle for years to come: Was he or wasn't he publishing a trade magazine?

The question seems straightforward. The distinction between "trade" publications and "consumer" publications is publishing shorthand that everybody thinks he understands. The terminology itself is unique to the magazine publishing business; a "trade paperback" in the book world means something very different than a trade magazine.

Yet when held up close to the light, it looks rather murky. What is a trade magazine, and how does it differ from other kinds of magazines? There's no legal definition, but a few generalizations stick out: First, a trade magazine's readers are all members of the same profession, industry, or interest group. Second, trade publications tend to be small in circulation. In America, a trade publication reaching 100,000 paid subscribers is doing rather well, whereas magazines like *Sports Illustrated, People,* and *Reader's Digest* count their readers by the millions. The small size of the readership is quite intentional: Trade magazines are, by definition, published for people in a particular trade. What they don't earn in newsstand sales they make up by charging advertisers high rates to reach a targeted audience. ("Sure, there are only 15,000 butchers in the United States who really matter, but you can bet that every goddamned one of them reads *Meat Monthly!*")

For the most part, trades tend to spend less on design and artwork than the more successful consumer magazines. And although there are many fine journalists working for specialized business publications, the quality of writing and editing in them often makes more sophisticated journalists wince. In many industries, it's important just for the key players and companies to see their names in print on a regular basis, and so trade publications can fill a lot of pages by running thinly edited press releases. In fact, a lot of people working at technology trade publications don't respect the magazines they work for, or their readers. I've heard them make fun of the product review section as "speeds and feeds" and call their target audience "nose-pickers."

Of course, there's more crossover between the categories than the dichotomy suggests, particularly if a publication tries to blur the lines by calling itself a "business" magazine. But in the tradition of I-know-it-when-I-see-it value distinctions, there is one simple, infallible trade gut test: Would people read this magazine if they didn't have to as part of their job?

The bet that Battelle was making was that a good number of nonspecialists would read his new Internet-business weekly. When he and his top executives said they didn't conceive of it as a trade publication, they were striving to convey several other messages, spoken and unspoken: We're not boring. We're quite cool, actually, because the Internet is cool. We're not going to suck up to our advertisers. And if you think the technology we write about isn't going to affect your life and your business, you need to wake up and smell the Java.

IDG didn't think of "trade" as a dirty word; to the contrary, trade publishing was one of its specialties. But perhaps the bucket would become clearer as the magazine actually began to publish. And in a neat little bit of internal corporate back-scratching, Battelle commissioned a white paper from IDC—the International Data Corporation, the research and consulting arm of IDG—in order to quantify the market he was trying to reach. Using one of Battelle's favorite metaphors, this audience was dubbed the "Architects of the Internet Economy."

The architects were an advertiser's dream, a slice of an emerging vanguard so elite and so powerful that it would transform its generation of business. As Battelle summarized this group:

> A new breed of business leaders has emerged with the rise of the network economy. They are the risktakers, entrepreneurs and innovators of this age. . . . Our reader is an architect of the network economy. Our reader is not responsible, necessarily, for purchasing the equipment. Rather, he or she is responsible for setting the strategy that makes that equipment purchase inevitable. He or she holds, in their own way, a bottom line. They are the venture capitalists, the real estate agents, the consultants, the entrepreneurs, the lawyers, the technologists, the communicators, and the salespeople of the network economy. In short, they are the catalysts of economic change.[7]

How large was this group? The IDC report estimated that in 1997 there were 78,000 such "architects" in the United States and projected that within five years the group would nearly triple, to 226,000.[8] And the power that they held was formidable: 74 percent controlled or significantly influenced their company's Internet strategy; 36 percent controlled or significantly influenced *other* companies' Internet strategies; and a full 24 percent sat on the boards of other companies.

Of course, putting numbers on the size or power of a subdemographic group like this is as much advocacy as it is research. Whether the product is the next generation of microprocessors or just good old-fashioned snake oil, the pitch is always the same: Everybody's doing it! Or they will be by next year! You'd better get on board!

THE ANTI-HYPE

The very exercise of putting numbers on the Internet Economy put Battelle's magazine in a position rather like the flag in the middle of a tug-of-war rope. Pulling on one side would be the advertising and marketing departments (and to some extent editorial): It was their job to explain and exploit the economic benefits that the Internet could bring. Pulling on the other side was the remainder of the editorial mission: the need to say whose technology and business actually worked and to expose the false predictions made by advocates and hucksters.

That task fell largely on the shoulders of Jonathan Weber, a thirty-six-year-old journalist from the *Los Angeles Times* whom Battelle had never met. Weber had floppy dark hair and was almost always in black jeans. His speaking style was a bit laconic, especially compared to Battelle's starry lectures; Weber relied heavily on "um" and "uh-huh" and "you know." When he wanted to emphasize a point, his eyes would open wide. Never quite able to escape his generation, he sprinkled his conversation with slang from the 1970s and early 1980s, like "bummer" and "go for it." He tried hard not to return to the pack of Marlboro Lights, but rarely succeeded for long.

Although Weber had no formal background in science and was not exactly a technology freak, he had covered technology for most of his career and was editing the technology section of the *LA Times* when he met Battelle. This history gave Weber a strange lingo of pseudotechnical understatement. Thus, if something was significant, Weber would say it was "nontrivial"; if something sucked, Weber would call it "suboptimal."

When Weber and Battelle first met in the fall of 1997, they had lunch and a substantive discussion about the project, but Weber was initially hesitant to work with Battelle. Part of this was personal style; Weber, a Jewish philosophy major who'd graduated from Wesleyan, was put off by Battelle's frat-boy demeanor. And he was also concerned that the editor-in-chief position would be his in name only; because Battelle himself had recently come from the editorial side of journalism, Weber feared he'd still want to call the shots.

But his largest objection was that he didn't want to idolize the heroes of the Internet as *Wired* had in its more rhapsodic moments. He wanted to be, in his words, "the anti-hype." Weber, like most American journalists, would always describe his editorial philosophy as being dominated by fairness and evenhandedness—which it is. But in less guarded moments, he would make it clear that much of the magazine's credibility would stem from the fact that it was tough on the companies it covered. "People like to read negative stories," Weber would explain.

As it happened, that vision dovetailed with Battelle's desire to be *Variety*, which can be brutally tough on Hollywood's losers. The pair also negotiated an unusual deal whereby, on purely editorial matters, Battelle actually reported to Weber. That satisfied Weber—as did the generous pay package and the title of editor-in-chief. Weber tried briefly to parlay his job offer into an overseas reporting assignment from the *Times*, but it didn't pan out, so he took the job and moved to

San Francisco. He started in early January 1998. There was already a deadline: a prototype to show advertisers was due at the end of the month.

That's a tight schedule under the best of circumstances—and Weber was not operating under the best of circumstances. He lacked a reporting staff; and more important, the publication lacked a name. Battelle's brainstorming had come up with several potential titles: *Takeaway* (referring, presumably, to the notion that the reader would take something away from reading the magazine, like an attendee at a conference); *Platform* (a mildly clever pun on both computer jargon— a Windows platform, an Internet platform—and the idea of the magazine as a platform); *Ping* (a horrible title deriving from the slang term for e-mailing or phoning someone); *The Business* (which may have worked); and *Catalyst* (very Battelle, but a little too New Age).

It was Denise Caruso from *The New York Times*—part of Battelle's formidable network—who suggested *The Industry Standard.* The phrase, meaning a single set of specifications usually voluntarily adopted by different companies within a trade, was reasonably widespread in the technology business, and it made a nice pun on the idea of a "Standard," which was a common name for a newspaper or magazine. Still, you couldn't easily tell what industry it was referring to, and the average reader was apt to think of something to do with manufacturing. The name was, as Weber might say, "suboptimal." But Battelle and Weber adopted it as the best compromise, though Weber would later say he preferred the more eggheaded *The Internet Economy.*

There was, however, a problem; word came from IDG that the publication had to have "Internet" in its title. Battelle and Weber were opposed. Some technology gurus believed, after all, that what was called the Internet in the 1990s would evolve into a technology so pervasive that it would no longer be associated with phone lines or even computers, and thus "Internet" might sound stale in just a few years. But they had too many other tasks on their hands, and so they settled on the awkward *Internet Industry Standard.* That title adorns the cover of the dummy issue shown to advertisers in January. The name was "just clearly unacceptable," Weber recalled later. "The phone receptionist couldn't say it."

HOW TO HIRE IN A HURRY

Once the dummy issue was put to bed, Weber had only a matter of weeks to produce the first official issue, scheduled for April. He set about hiring a staff at a whirlwind pace. It was a tough sell. After all, the magazine was completely unproven and did not have much in the way of money or reputation to attract journalism's more seasoned veterans. The one exception was Elizabeth Wasserman, a reporter for *The San Jose Mercury News* whose husband had been offered a job in the *Merc*'s Washington bureau. For her a job in D.C. was an ideal opportunity, so she leapt at the chance to become the magazine's Washington bureau chief. But the rest of the recruits were a hodgepodge of reporters with little experience. Some had worked for other trade publications, but others were truly green; one reporter, Jacob Ward, was just twenty-three years old when Weber hired him.

The weeks leading up to the launch of the magazine proceeded like a game of chicken: The IDG people kept expecting *The Standard* staff to say it needed to delay the launch, and *The Standard* staff kept expecting IDG to say the same thing.

To make the situation worse, the staff moved into its proper building, at 315 Pacific Avenue, just a week before the first issue was to appear.[9] Up until a few months before, the building had provided warehouse space for a toy manufacturer, and it did not immediately make the transition to housing a magazine and Web site. The publishing software QPS didn't work, which meant that a number of tasks like copy editing and coordinating editorial changes needed to be done by hand. It soon became clear to the copy desk that Weber would not automatically abide by deadlines, especially if the story was not yet up to his exacting journalistic standards. The greener reporters on staff often required several sessions of re-reporting and rewriting their stories before those standards were met. This meant that the copy and art departments were subject to multiple all-nighters in the days before the launch.

But like at least some of the scrappy start-ups the magazine covered, the staff managed to get the product out the door on schedule. The first issue of *The Industry Standard* appeared on newsstands (well, a few newsstands) on April 20, 1998. Its cover line called it "The Newsmagazine of the Internet Economy." It was 56 pages thick, and its masthead boasted a total of fourteen full-time editorial employees: four top editors and four reporters, with middle-level, assistant, and copy editors making up the remainder.

Like most newsweeklies, each issue of the magazine was broken into distinct sections. The first piece of prose was a lead editorial that was often, but not always, written by the editor-in-chief. The opening editorial, which would later be christened the "Bottom Line," signed by John Battelle and Jonathan Weber, asserted, "The Internet has created the hothouse for a whole new business culture." It defined the phrase "Internet Economy" as "that subset of the global economy in which new computer and communications technologies are driving extraordinarily rapid change." And it established the magazine's goal "to be a touchstone for this emerging business community, an authoritative, entertaining must-read for anyone who is, or wants to be, a part of the Internet Economy story."

Following letters to the editor was a section called "Posts," often the best part of the magazine. The format was quite similar to the "Periscope" formula that *Newsweek* perfected: short, offbeat, or humorous items (in *The Standard*'s case pertaining to the Internet and the culture around it); a section of funny or outrageous quotes; and some regular photo-driven features, such as "Just One Question," in which someone related to the Internet answered a single question.

My favorite "Post" item ever was a collaborative effort between the New York and San Francisco offices. Timed for the beginning of the major league baseball season, it was a full-page seating chart of San Francisco's new baseball park. This was not the park known for decades as Candlestick but now dimly called "3Com Park"; this was the new downtown "Pacific Bell Park." Net companies had taken corporate sponsorship to ridiculous levels; the doomed e-commerce firm Pets.com spent $250,000 to sponsor a team of dive dogs that would fetch home-run balls that landed in the bay. It seemed like no one was going to the ballgames to watch baseball, so the magazine published a chart of where the different Net companies had their corporate season tickets. The headline: "Schmooze on First."

After "Posts" came a full-page column from one of the magazine's regular contributors. In the beginning, this meant *Burn Rate* author Michael Wolff or the formidable cyberlaw professor Lawrence Lessig. By 1999, Wolff had dropped out and was replaced by James Fallows, the author and former *US News & World Report* editor. The next section, originally one page but later expanded to two, was called "The Week." This was a series of a dozen or so brief items summarizing the major developments of the past seven days. (*The Economist* opens with two well-done pages like this, one for politics and one for business news.) Designed as a quickly digestible summary, "The Week" was actually a vital way for the editors to cover their asses if they'd failed to produce a full-length news article on an important story.

Only then did the magazine get into actual news stories. Internally, the news section was broken into "early" and "late" news cycles—although the reader couldn't distinguish them. The final pages of the magazine shipped to the printer on Fridays, so that *The Standard* could, like most newsweeklies, publish on Monday. But most of the magazine had to be shipped well before that, so "early" news was due on Tuesdays and "late" news on Thursdays. Early news stories were often a little more feature-oriented, and late news stories were more directly tied to the week's events.

For the uninitiated reader, the news section could well have been the least comprehensible. There was no sense to the section; a reader couldn't tell why one story ran before or after another. The layout relied heavily on a lot of text, often reducing photos to the size of postage stamps. In the early days, the magazine sometimes ran photos without captions, or the caption would consist solely of someone's name.

These were simply unforgivable errors. Reporters for magazines like *Time* or *Newsweek* have the advantage most weeks of writing about some of the most recognized people in the world; in the fraction of a second during which the reader grasps the photo, the subject of the story has been at least partly explained. In *The Standard*, on some weeks a reader could turn page after page without seeing an easily recognizable face: White-guy-in-a-tie is the CEO of Widget.com, white-guy-without-a-tie is the CEO of eWidget. The layout for the feature stories was a bit better, but it took the magazine nearly a year to rise above typical trade publication design.

The next section was called "Metrics," and although it was shamelessly copied from *The Economist*, it was arguably the most distinctive feature of the magazine. The initial notion was simply to show the Internet's vital signs week by week: how fast or slow the performance was; how many people were logged on that week; how often the words "Internet" or "Web" were used in press releases.

The most gimmicky aspect of the "Metrics" section was a dial gauge that, on a scale from 1 to 10, was meant to indicate how "hot" or "cool" the Internet Economy was that week. Ostensibly, this was calculated by the aggregate of the harder measurements—the speed of the Net, for example—while also taking into consideration the value of any major funding, initial public offering, or acquisition of Net-related companies. In reality, these numbers came primarily from deadline-harried editors, who would pluck them out of the air according to the fine-tuned mechanisms of their guts.

The final section of the magazine—not counting the last-page column by Carl Steadman, a veteran of the cheeky *Suck* Web site and one of the closest things that the Internet culture had to a celebrity—was called "New Gig." As with the magazine's title, "New Gig" had a fairly subtle double meaning. The section tracked the comings and goings of Internet executives, but it also ran longer stories about how technology was transforming the workplace. More practically, it provided the words that surrounded the recruitment advertising, which made up a crucial part of the magazine's business.

THE INDUSTRY STANDARD IS NOT FOR YOU

For the most part, the mainstream media (especially on the East Coast) ignored the magazine's launch. *Newsweek* ran a small "Cyberscope" item, with this condescending opener: "If a cover story about the scramble for not-yet-finalized top-level Internet domain names makes your eyes glaze over, *The Industry Standard* is not for you."

The magazine made its biggest impact on insiders—perhaps more impact than its creators had bargained for. The hardest-hitting story in the debut issue was a twelve-paragraph profile of New York–based Wit Capital, at the time one of the more glamorous companies involved in online finance. Its founder, Andrew Klein, was a media favorite; he had made his name by founding a beer company, which he took public in 1995 largely through a prospectus posted on the World Wide Web.

The piece was written by Mark Gimein, a reporter who would quickly become one of *The Standard*'s stars. Like many of the magazine's early staffers, Gimein was improbably young; he was all of twenty-six years old when he started at *The Standard*. Having nearly failed out of Yale, he had had a wandering journalistic career, working for a time at *MediaWeek* and *Adweek*, and then going to work for State News Service. Like many investigative reporters, Gimein had an odd and complex personality. When he got excited he was prone to a slight stutter; he spoke Russian and favored clothes that looked like they were made from bargain-bin velvet. Weber recalled later that Gimein was "literally foaming at the mouth" during his job interview, and that his writing samples were "unbelievably good."

Gimein was one of the only reporters who had bothered to look beyond Klein's halo of publicity into the messy internal workings of Wit Capital. It had been reported that Wit had brought in an eminence grise, a Wall Street veteran named Robert Lessin. According to Gimein's story, Lessin's arrival foretold that the once-crusading Klein would be quietly pushed aside. The story said that Lessin would bring in a new board of directors, and that Wit was going to move away from Klein's more exotic financial schemes and toward more traditional investment banking activities.

Gimein knew he had an important, and possibly damaging, story. On the Friday that the first issue closed, he was visibly nervous as the staff gathered on the rooftop to celebrate. He was chain smoking, and his leg was shaking. He was afraid that, in the blur of getting out the first issue, some of the final changes he had made to the story at the last minute would not make it onto the printed page. As soon as Weber finished toasting the staff's hard work with champagne, he could be seen huddled with Gimein on the roof, going over the Wit story.

Their apprehension was understandable; when the story appeared, Klein was furious (although probably unaware that his colleague Lessin had been a principal, if largely unquoted, source for the story). He retained attorneys who drafted a full-length libel suit against *The Standard* and sent a copy to the magazine's San Francisco headquarters.

In addition to accusing the magazine of setting out to harm Klein, the suit actually offered a motive. There had been significant financial dealings between Wit and John Battelle's former employer, *Wired*; Wired Ventures was one of the investors in Wit Capital, and in February 1998, *Wired* had begun offering its e-mail newsletter subscribers a month's free use of Wit's online financial services. That same month,

Wired had excerpted Klein's book, entitled *Wallstreet.com: Fat Cat Investing at the Click of a Mouse.*

The suit maintained, therefore, that *The Standard* had essentially put a journalistic hit out on Klein because he was a partner of one of the magazine's chief competitors. Such a line of argument might well be thrown out by a judge, but there are publications that choose their stories out of such relatively base motivations. It was not impossible to imagine that a jury could be led to believe this charge and to conclude that it was a malicious act.

Understandably, the suit put a scare into *The Standard*'s staff. U.S. libel law offers fairly broad protection for any reporter who isn't malicious or severely negligent, and Gimein was certainly neither of those. At the same time, even a frivolous libel suit can sap a publication's resources, and it's about the last thing that the editors of a brand new magazine want to deal with. And so every single issue was published with the threat of Klein's lawsuit hovering above the publication like a sword.

WHEN AM I GOING TO GET MY MONEY BACK?

The reporters and editors knew that the stories they were writing were vital. Sometimes they were writing about household names; a cover package in May, "The Politics of Antitrust," was an examination of the backroom deals behind the Justice Department's case against Microsoft. Sometimes they were writing about technology companies that, though less well-known, were suddenly worth hundreds of millions of dollars.

And sometimes there were stories that simply made one question the sanity of the American populace. The best example was the tale of K-Tel International, a company best known for cheesy compilations of 1970s pop tunes. It had gone bankrupt in the 1980s but had recovered to the point where it was a small-sized company with publicly traded stock—just barely. On April 8, 1998, a typically paltry 300 shares of K-Tel's stock traded at $6⅝ a share. On April 22, more than 6 million shares traded at a closing price of $44⅝. The difference, of course, was that the company had announced that it was going to begin selling music online. Despite *Newsweek*'s insult, a fair number of readers out there were interested in buying Internet stocks—or wanted to know if they should.

But the tiny staff was pushing itself to physical and psychological limits to get the product out the door. Weber's casual approach to deadlines did not change, and the art and copy staffs often found themselves working until midnight or later. As one editor recalled, "I would go home, fall asleep in my clothes, get up, put on new clothes, and go back to work."

Weber knew that the editorial quality of the magazine, while strong, still needed major refinement. But it was all he could do to keep it coming out every week. It didn't help matters when Debra Aho Williamson, one of the key early editorial hires, announced that she had to leave the publication to accompany her husband on a move that would take them out of state. Privately, Weber was furious at losing a top lieutenant only a few months into *The Standard*'s lifetime, but the situation was out of his hands.[10] His one form of revenge was to hang a photo of the original publishing team above his desk; every time someone like Debbie would leave, he would scrawl a large "X" through his or her head.

And the world did not seem to be catching on to *The Industry Standard*. After the first couple of issues, the magazine seemed to be losing momentum. The issues did not increase in size; indeed, the magazine shrank to 48 pages through all of May. The covers seemed rushed and difficult to figure out.

Most important, from a financial point of view, the advertising was not coming in as planned. By summer, the magazine's financial picture looked dismal. One participant recalls a meeting in which Battelle said, with resignation and a little anger, "It looks like we're going to miss our $2.2 million target by $1.75 million."

In magazine publishing, as in so many industries, when you make money you are a genius. When you don't, you're a dolt who has to listen to the geniuses with the money. IDG might boast of how decentralized its business units were, but it naturally had ways of keeping tabs on its investments. The most formal of these was called the Operations Review Board, whose meetings, in keeping with the slightly mystical IDG style, were called ORB meetings. Normally, the publishers of upstarts like *The Standard* had to make a presentation to the ORB every quarter. When the financial situation started to turn sour, the meetings switched to every month.

The ORB for *The Standard* consisted of representatives of other IDG publications, including *CIO* magazine, *InfoWorld*, and *PCWorld*. The latter, with a circulation of well over 1 million, claimed to be the largest computer magazine in the world. It was represented on the ORB by its president, Richard Marino.

It's part of IDG management ideology to allow its business units to run themselves. When its managers make suggestions at meetings, they are simply that: suggestions. Or so they say. Battelle and Weber felt that IDG's managing hand was anything but gentle and that McGovern and IDG were micromanaging by surrogate. And thus when the ad sales were slackening, it weakened their position on every front; the ORB grilled them without mercy. As Battelle recalled, the IDG representatives were constantly trying to rope the magazine back into a strict trade magazine formula: Go back to your bucket.

There was increased pressure to change *The Standard*'s circulation strategy and to restore the word "Internet" in its title. There was even, Weber recalls, a suggestion that *The Standard* create a directories business; that is, that it publish lengthy "who's who" guides to companies and executives within various technology sectors. Battelle and Weber thought this was an odd idea, but if it would allow *The Standard* to keep publishing, then they would do it.

All of these issues came to a head at a meeting in November 1998. McGovern had come out to visit the offices at 315 Pacific, and Battelle and Weber presented him with the directories plan they thought he had suggested. He looked at it and dismissed it: "Why are you doing something out of the 1950s?" They were baffled.

And then McGovern looked at the publication's projected finances and asked, "When am I going to get my money back?" They could not give a ready answer.

IDG officials continued to insist that the word "Internet" had to be in the title; that absence, they said, was at least partly responsible for the magazine's failure to hit its targets.

And so Weber and Battelle cooked up what Weber called a "great ruse." They agreed to change the name, but they argued that the task would require a great deal of groundwork. They would need extra marketing money in order to pull it off, and months of preparation. Why not wait until the one-year anniversary in April?

This satisfied IDG for a few crucial weeks. "We never intended to change it," Weber admitted later. "But we figured that if business had picked up by then, as it looked like it was doing, then the issue would go away."

And it did—for a while.

This Week's Billionaires

Do I understand the valuations for these companies? Absolutely not. Do I own a couple of these stocks? Yes, I do.

—Bill Schaff, chief investment officer at Bay Isle Financial, April 1998

I can recall vividly my first introduction to the culture of the Internet industry. It was early February 1998, and I had a drinks date with my *Village Voice* colleague Hillary Rosner. In addition to editing the recently created technology column, she reviewed bars for the paper, a windfall for friends like me. When we were finished taking notes about some downtown cocktail lounge, we were going to a nightclub on 13th Street. There was a party there to celebrate the fact that an Internet company called Tripod had been bought by another Internet company, Lycos.

You may as well have told me that the planet Typhoo had been taken over by the planet Lork. I had had a home Internet connection since 1994 and was an avid fan of e-mail. I had written about the role of the Web in stories like the Monica Lewinsky imbroglio. But aside from the very best-known brands like America Online, the companies that made the Internet work constituted an unfamiliar galaxy to me.

We walked into the party fairly close to its peak, and I had that unmistakable sensation of there's-something-happening-here-but-you-don't-know-what-it-is. My first impression was of youth: Here were more than 150 people, and at the ripe old age of thirty-three I could plausibly have been the oldest person in the room.

My second impression was the sense of being in a universe that was different, but parallel to my own. That is to say, as a media reporter I had attended several hundred parties and receptions that looked very much like this one: a stylish, attractive crowd in a hip location, professional but in a manner that self-consciously said "creative" rather than "corporate." Yet despite the sense of familiarity, I didn't recognize a single face; clearly I had been sheltered from this particular media subculture.

After a while, I hooked up with Austin Bunn, who wrote the technology column that Hillary edited. Talking to Austin was like talking to a blur; he spoke with the velocity of someone who had been free-basing caffeine. I asked him a bunch of ignorant questions: What is Tripod? Tripod is a company that makes it easy for the everyday person to build a Web site (although in practice the everyday person is often a college student). What is Lycos? Lycos is a Web search engine (at least I had used search engines, but never Lycos).

What did they pay for it? $58 million.

Fifty-eight million dollars? Jesus. I had no way to process that figure. In 1985, a developer and pet-supply peddler named Leonard Stern had bought my paper, *The Village Voice*, for $55 million. At that point, the *Voice* had been publishing for thirty years and had won two Pulitzer Prizes. It attracted more than 100,000 paying readers every week and sold tens of millions of dollars' worth of advertising every year. As best I could tell, everything about Tripod was given away for free; for that matter, everything about Lycos was given away for free.

Why did Lycos buy Tripod? Hillary and Austin dealt with my questions as if they came from a dolt. "Tripod has a million users, most of whom are college students, and they're heavy Internet users, so Lycos wants to make sure they get them."

A million customers was at least something concrete. But why were a million customers worth $58 million as opposed, say, to $20 million?

No one had an answer for this.

There was a guy walking around in a flannel shirt with cowlicked blond hair who seemed to attract a circle of people around him.

"Who's that?" I asked Austin.

"That's Bo Peabody. He founded Tripod."

It's practically redundant to describe Peabody as boyish looking, because at the age of twenty-six, he *was* a boy. Peabody was Internet legend in its purest form; he started Tripod in his college dorm, turned it into a business, and had just flipped that business for tens of millions, plus a seat on Lycos's board of directors. He was smiling, but he didn't look to me as ecstatic as a guy who'd just made tens of millions of dollars just a couple years out of college ought to look. Then I realized: Even though I'd met more investment bankers than I'd ever wanted to, I didn't know what a twenty-six-year-old self-made millionaire should look like. I went up to Peabody, introduced myself, and shook his hand, but I really didn't know what to say.

In less than a year, I would be a recognized media authority on Internet companies, including Lycos. But that night I was thoroughly flummoxed. I left after an awful band began playing (the rumor was that it included Peabody's roommate from Williams College). I grabbed the obligatory goodies bag—Lycos T-shirt, Frisbee, keychain—and got a cab home.

As I tried to describe the evening to my girlfriend, I was practically in tears. I could hardly articulate why I was so upset, but it boiled down to fear—fear that I was losing touch. I was accustomed to the intersection of money and media power: In the 1980s and early 1990s, millions were thrown at people I knew to write books and start magazines. Here were enormous sums floating around to create a medium I didn't understand—but my younger, more energetic colleagues seemed to.

The Internet had invaded my life.

The invasion continued about three months later, when Condé Nast surprised the publishing world by purchasing *Wired* magazine from Louis Rossetto and various investors for about $80 million. *Wired* had been ground zero of the technology revolution, a fervent, sometimes shambolic manifesto preaching the virtues and inevitability of technological change. Rossetto had written in the debut issue in 1993 that digital technology would bring about "social changes so profound their only parallel is probably the discovery of fire." This was not a typical way of speaking for the average editor of a Condé Nast glossy like *Vogue* or *GQ*; it was, as one Condé Nast writer said to me, as if "*Pravda* has been taken over by Prada."

I knew the only way to capture this culture clash was to go to San Francisco myself. I tracked down former and current *Wired* employees and did my best to piece together the fascinating history of that magazine and its Web site. (Curiously, Condé Nast's Si Newhouse purchased only the magazine and left Wired Digital to one side. That company would later be purchased by—who else?—Lycos.)

It's almost hard to recall how much more "digital" San Francisco was than New York in the heady spring of 1998. Everybody seemed to have a Web site, from laundromats to cab drivers. Driving in from the airport along San Francisco's legendary Highway 101, I was amazed that nearly all the billboards advertised dot-com or technology companies (it would be a year before New York's bus shelters and subways would fall under the same spell). It dawned on my smug New Yorker's brain that the companies that, to me, made hard drives and modems were, for Californians, major employers, and thus the subject of speculation and cocktail-party gossip. This was the Internet Economy, stupid.

WHAT'S IT?

But even if I could perceive a world built around the Internet, I didn't think it had anything to do with me—until two months later. In July, I got a call from a woman at a recruitment agency called Howard Sloan Koller, one of the better-known media headhunters. She told me she was looking for a New York bureau chief for a new IT magazine, which she wouldn't name but insisted was excellent.

I wasn't afraid to play dumb, because I was dumb. "What's IT?" I asked.

"Internet technology," she explained patiently, "but it's really more of a business magazine."[1]

My first thought was: Why the hell are you calling me? Do you have any idea what I do? I don't know anything about technology, or about business. I figured that the headhunter got paid simply to assemble a list of names. The fact that headhunters often care so little about matching an actual person to an open slot was the very reason that people hate them.

I decided, however, to find out more. Part of it was reporter's instinct: If a magazine was making an important hire in New York, it might make a good item for my column. Part of it was curiosity, and part of it was the fact that I hadn't been recruited for a job in some time; having an outside job offer is never a bad way to get a raise or a plum assignment.

I didn't focus much on it at the time, but I was feeling a bit stagnated at the *Voice*. On more than one occasion in the previous two years, I had filed a column as usual on Monday, then woken up on Tuesday and thought, "I have a feeling I wrote substantially the same thing in 1993." I'd look it up and, sure enough, I had. This is not a sign of professional growth.

When I went to interview with the headhunter, she told me a bit about the magazine and gave me some of the early copies. It was *The Industry Standard.* It still didn't seem like a fit to me. I read through the issues, and although I saw some pieces that interested me, I didn't understand about half the stories I read. They referred to developments inside companies I'd never heard of, like CommTouch Software and Infoseek, and used phrases I didn't know (like Web page "caching"). I also didn't care much for the layout and overall feel of the magazine.

But when the headhunter said that the editor-in-chief, Jonathan Weber, was going to be in New York to interview candidates, I wanted to talk to him. That interview changed everything. I immediately warmed to Jonathan. He was intelligent and serious, yet with an easy sense of humor. He was more casually dressed than I was, in a pair of faded black jeans. He was only about four years older than I was, and we seemed to look at journalism through a roughly similar lens of experience.

The interview didn't seem to me to be about a job. We gossiped a bit, about the various good and nasty reviews that Michael Wolff's *Burn Rate* had received, and about the bizarre e-mail that Michael Kinsley had recently sent out to friends (a group that encompassed the entire media elite) explaining why he didn't get the job as editor of *The New Yorker.*

The only part of our conversation that really felt like an interview was when we discussed what *The Industry Standard* wanted out of a New York bureau. Essentially, it was someone who could cover the media. He and I agreed immediately on a plan of attack. There are a dozen or so big old-media companies based in or doing substantial business in New York: Time Warner, News Corporation, Hearst, Disney, Viacom, Condé Nast, the television networks, and so on. Each one of those companies either had a big and ambitious Internet strategy (such as Pathfinder, Time Warner's sprawling aggregation of sites) or didn't. Both cases made for good stories.

No newspaper or magazine, we agreed, was defining that intersection of old-media-meets-new-media as a beat unto itself (remember, this was the summer of 1998). I had contacts at all those companies from nearly a decade of covering the editorial side of media, and Jonathan had some friends in the mix as well. In about fifteen minutes, we had mapped out six months' worth of stories for the bureau chief. Suddenly, technology business journalism didn't seem so alien after all.

And so, back to San Francisco for a final interview. Now the billboards on 101 practically taunted me: This could be your future—you want a piece of this? I liked *The Standard*'s building, a funky brick structure on a corner not too far from the Embarcadero. I met a few of the reporters; they seemed cool, though I'd had interns who were older. I was introduced to Michael Parsons, a lanky Englishman who was my age and drove a motorcycle to work.

Perhaps the first thing I noticed about Michael was a paperback book he had on his desk: *Wall Street*, a damning critique of high finance written by Doug Henwood, the radical journalist who edits *Left Business Observer*. I had known Doug for years in New York, and we even shared a book publisher. Having gotten to know Parsons's calculating ways over the next few years, I can almost believe that he bought and displayed that book specifically to make me feel at home; if so, it worked. We had an enjoyable lunch at the Café Macaroni in North Beach and talked about everything from Matt Drudge to Edmund Spenser. He was very open with me about the strengths and weaknesses of the magazine and the organization, a frankness I found refreshing.

I then went to see John Battelle for the first time. Until then, he and I had had just one phone conversation. He had been in New York, staying in a midtown hotel when scaffolding on the unfinished Condé Nast tower collapsed, and so he was wandering around the rubble of midtown talking to me on a cell phone. All I remembered from that conversation was that he continually used metaphors I didn't quite grasp. He kept saying that he wanted a magazine that had "a good top, as well as a good bottom." *The New York Observer,* he said, had a good top, "but I'm not sure if it has a bottom." I feigned some kind of assent.

But given Battelle's exalted status, I wasn't prepared for the man I met. For one thing, he was younger than me (only by a year, but you still notice). And I was momentarily deceived by the surfer looks. Actually, Battelle possessed a forced intensity that one rarely encounters on the East Coast. I would later conclude that there is no such thing as small talk with Battelle. A conversation about the slightest of matters can immediately escalate into a philosophical rant—a legacy, no doubt, of too many years at *Wired.*

I thought the conversation went okay; I told him that analyzing Internet companies did not seem all that different to me than analyzing magazines, and I knew how to do that. He agreed but added, "and evaluating business models," a phrase that I would once have associated with, say, Cindy Crawford. He asked me what I thought *The Standard*'s audience was. Empowered by the headhunter with new jargon, I answered: "People in IT." He said: "What do you mean by IT?"

This threw me off. Surely he knew what it stood for? "Internet technology," I said, losing confidence with every syllable. He acknowledged this, but lectured me that the IT audience was just the core. From that core *The Standard* would build out to reach lawyers, consultants, and businesspeople in general. "We originally thought we'd reach that larger audience in a few years," he told me solemnly. "What we've found is that we're there now." I nodded, because it was the only way to keep my head from spinning.

I must have passed muster, because Weber offered me the job. I tentatively agreed, depending on salary. He balked slightly and said the headhunter would negotiate the money.

I flew back to New York excited but confused. Did I really want to do this? I needed advice. I had already had lunch with Michael Wolff, one of *The Standard*'s columnists. *Burn Rate* had made Wolff the literary star of the Internet, but I had known him back in the 1980s when he'd hired me as a columnist for *Campaigns & Elections,* a magazine that he owned, as I recall, for about ten minutes. Wolff had an almost Zen-like analysis of how I should cover the Internet. "Nobody really knows how this thing is going to play out," Wolff told me. "Maybe Amazon.com becomes the next Wal-Mart, or maybe Barnes & Noble becomes the next Amazon." And, he added, I would have the benefit of bicoastal vision: "You can use San Francisco to make fun of New Yorkers, and you can use New York to make fun of San Francisco."

Aside from Wolff, there was only one name on *The Standard*'s masthead I immediately recognized: Dave Kansas, the editor of TheStreet.com. Thomas Goetz, a former *Voice* colleague and good friend who'd gone to work at *The Wall Street Journal*, had become friends with Kansas over the last couple of years; they were part of a group of Minnesotans who had moved to New York and met up for drinks from time to time. Kansas was very keen on my taking the job and advised me to hold out for a salary figure that floored me: The number he cited was significantly more than twice my *Voice* salary.

Even with that kind of money dangling before me, I didn't want to make a move this dramatic without impartial guidance; the problem was who to ask? Wolff and Kansas certainly knew what they were talking about, but they had a vested interest in the publication. *The Standard* had gotten a little attention in New York when it launched, but it was primarily a West Coast phenomenon. Very few of my friends and contacts were in a position to give me informed counsel. I showed a couple of copies to my father, who said: "I don't know what to tell you. It's always good to get in on the ground floor of something, but I don't understand most of what's in this magazine." My friend Pavia Rosati, the only person I knew who'd worked at three Internet companies, flipped through an issue while sitting at a bar on East 9th Street with me and said, "A weekly? No one wants another weekly," and advised me against going.

Probably the only knowledgeable, enthusiastic adviser I could find was Randall Rothenberg, the onetime advertising columnist for *The New York Times*. His analysis was simple: (1) It was time for me to leave the *Voice*; (2) *The Standard* was a gamble, but a worthwhile gamble; and (3) Weber was a good guy.

Not surprisingly, no one I spoke to made either of the following predictions: (1) In two years this will be, by some measures, the largest magazine in America, or (2) in three years this magazine will fold.

In the end, the calculation I made was largely influenced by my experience at *7 Days,* a much-loved New York weekly that was published for two years until it fell victim to the recession of the early 1990s. Although I still think *7 Days* would have made a fortune if its owner (Leonard Stern, who also owned the *Voice* for fifteen years) had kept it alive, it was also true that nearly everyone who had worked there went on to very prestigious media jobs. I thought there was a good chance that *The Standard*'s owners would close the magazine in six months. By that time, though, I'd have made some decent money, I'd know a lot more about the Internet, and I'd have raised my business journalism and management experience. For a thirty-three-year-old writer with no family obligations and no mortgage, this seemed like a risk worth taking. And while I didn't quite get the salary Kansas urged me to hold out for, I came damn close.

TAKE THE BULLET

Unfortunately, my entrance to *The Standard* was not terribly smooth; even before I started, there was a mess. My conversations with Jonathan had started with the premise that we'd hire a deputy bureau chief after a year. In a time acceleration that would become the norm, he later said we'd hire one in a few months, and then finally told me that he'd essentially already hired one. That was fine by me, especially because he'd hired a star: Adam Penenberg.

Penenberg, who wrote for *Forbes*'s Web site, had helped break one of the biggest and most fascinating media stories of the decade: He had discovered that in a story about computer hackers in *The New Re-*

public, the writer Stephen Glass had clearly made up crucial details. When Penenberg phoned *The New Republic*'s editors about it, they confronted Glass, who eventually admitted his deception. Soon Glass's work for *The New Republic* and others began to unravel; it turned out that he had repeatedly invented sources and scenes and had gone to elaborate lengths—such as building fake Web sites—to convince editors and fact-checkers.

I was excited when Jonathan told me that I'd be working with Penenberg. I assumed it was a done deal, and when the *Observer* and *The New York Post* phoned me about my new job, I boasted that the two of us would make a great team. I should have checked this with Jonathan, but it didn't occur to me. Both papers printed Penenberg's hire.

Whoops. It turned out that Penenberg had yet to tell his bosses at *Forbes*; when they read about it, they squeezed him to stay. They told him he could write for the magazine (considered more prestigious than the Web site), gave him a better office, and threw a big raise at him. Not surprisingly, he stayed put. I met Penenberg at a Net event about a year later; he was still furious with Jonathan, whom he'd assumed had leaked his hire to the papers.

This meant that one of my first priorities was now to hire a deputy bureau chief, and I had a few candidate suggestions from Weber, people who had been considered for my position. Aside from choosing interns at the *Voice* and other jobs, I had never really hired staff before. But a bigger problem than my inexperience was that, aside from certain obvious considerations—Can this person write well? Is this someone I can get along with?—I wasn't especially well positioned to gauge the talent. Not a week into the job, I was interviewing candidates who would say things like, "I don't buy the idea that there will be one line coming into the home for TV, phone, and Internet," or "Java is mostly a triumph of marketing; it's not intrinsically more flexible than HTML or XML." These may have been profound insights or pure nonsense; I had no idea.

There were other pitfalls. One candidate, qualified on paper and energetic in person, dropped the name of a mutual friend as a reference. I called the friend, and he said, word for word: "If you have a choice between hiring [this candidate] and putting a bullet in your head, take the bullet."

I didn't immediately find the reporter I wanted, and in the meantime I had stories to write. *The Standard* had no office space in New York at the time; there was some IDG space on Park Avenue where a few advertising people worked, but it was dingy and Jonathan had insisted that I not work there. Instead, on my first day, September 8, 1998, I took a desk in the Wall Street–area office of TheStreet.com, the financial news Web site. Kansas and Weber had agreed that I could work there for a few weeks while *The Standard* found me an office.

On my second day, I was assigned a profile of Geraldine Laybourne. This intimidated me slightly, since I'd never heard of her before. Once I started researching her, I felt even worse, because I probably should have heard of her. She was generally credited with building Nickelodeon into one of the most successful media companies of the decade. Now she was focused on new media, and her fledgling, New York–based media company, Oxygen, had just bought three women's Web sites—Thrive, Moms Online, and Electra—and it looked like her Internet strategy was beginning to take shape.

The reporting began easily enough. I asked for help during a story meeting, and various colleagues in San Francisco were kind enough to e-mail me names of contacts and sources, even though many of them had never met me. Laybourne's publicist, from the high-flying firm of Robinson Lerer & Montgomery, called me back right away and set up an interview, as if we'd been working together for years—not the kind of treatment I usually got at the *Voice*.

But I remained hampered by my inexperience. How did I know if I was asking the right questions? My goodbye party from the *Voice* was on that Wednesday night, and the piece was due to be filed on Thursday morning, so I got up at around 5:30 to put on the finishing touches, nervous and a bit hung over. I got through to a source at AOL who was an early riser. He gave me the view of Laybourne from inside AOL, where president Bob Pittman apparently thought she was a genius. This gave me confidence about what I was writing.

In my desperation, I loaded the piece with a lot of statistics, mostly about the traffic on women-oriented Web sites, rather akin to discussing magazine circulation figures. The analysis was not especially far-seeing—like so many similar sites, Oxygen would soon prove to be a money-sucking black hole—but as a piece of deadline journalism it held up. Laybourne's face—one of the few easily identifiable female figures of the Internet business—ended up on our cover: "WOMEN ON THE WEB: Geraldine Laybourne of Oxygen Media thinks she knows what they want." In my first week, I got the cover story. Maybe I could do this after all.

CALLING A BLUFF

That first week, Weber gave me what was, in many ways, a tougher assignment. He asked me to revisit the Wit Capital story in a kind of ombudsman capacity. The notion was that I would look at the original story published in April and everything that had happened since, and we would publish a new story that dealt with Wit's substantive complaints.

This was a steep request. Yes, I had experience reporting on the media, but I had never reported on a story at my own publication when there was a threatened libel suit at stake. Moreover, I came to the story completely unfamiliar with its details, and I had never met the reporter, Mark Gimein. But I jumped in with an amateur's enthusiasm. I interviewed Andy Klein in person for more than an hour. He was furious with *The Standard,* practically spitting as he spoke. A persuasive man, he was adamant that the story was thoroughly wrong. I came away from the interview thinking I was going to have to be very hard on my colleague—not the best way to start a new job.

But as I spoke to other interested sources, including Robert Lessin, I realized that more and more of what *The Standard* had reported was rock solid and prescient. There was one factual error: We had reported that Klein's Spring Street Brewery had been sold the week before to a company called Longshore Brewery & Pub. In fact, that sale had not yet been completed.

But everything else about the story held up. Gimein predicted that Lessin would bring in a new board of directors—which happened. And he predicted, accurately, that Klein's brokerless stock-trading system would never get off the ground. Despite Klein's insistence to me that the system was "sixty to ninety days" from launch, it never materialized. I ended up writing a kind of "amplification" of the original story, which was shown to Wit's attorneys. The idea was that they would sign off on it and agree not to sue. They declined to do so, so we never ran the follow-up at all, and the deadline for filing a libel suit came and went. Wit had been bluffing all along.

SUCKED INTO THE NET

When I resigned from the *Voice*, my editor, Don Forst, cautioned me against thinking that my life would change: "You might buy a car, you might move to a bigger apartment, but it's not going to change your life." I knew what he meant, but I felt things were dramatically shifting.

For one thing, my reading habits changed. As the *Voice*'s press critic, it had been my job to read (or at least skim) six or seven newspapers a day. I also had to be intimate with the major New York weeklies *(The New Yorker, New York, The New York Observer)* and a wide variety of liberal and left-wing publications *(The Nation, The New Re-*

public, In These Times, Z). It's true that some Web sites—such as Slate and the Drudge Report—had become common additions to my media diet, but even at the end of my *Voice* tenure I still didn't have my own computer that was hooked up to the Net.

That changed completely. I now spent the vast majority of my day looking at a laptop screen. I began to read the newspapers almost exclusively online. I had always appreciated the journalism of *The Wall Street Journal,* but I now read its tech coverage as my own competition. I started visiting technology news sites I'd never before heard of—primarily ZDNet and CNET's News.com—regularly, often several times a day.

I also learned the incredible value of the Internet as a research tool. To take just one example: A few years before, I had asked a friend to download some Securities and Exchange Commission (SEC) files for me off the Internet; it was an arduous process and took a ridiculously long time. Now I not only knew how to call up documents in a matter of seconds, but a colleague showed me a site, 10kwizard.com, that provided a searchable database of SEC documents. (Today, 10kwizard.com charges for this feature.) This site was hugely useful if, say, I wanted to know all the corporate boards of directors on which a particular individual sat.

I also immersed myself in my new beat. I tried to go to every seminar, press conference, and cocktail party I got invited to, just to get a sense of what was out there. On more than one occasion I described an event to a colleague in San Francisco who would reply, "Why in the world did you go to that?" I was so green I didn't even know which companies were cool.

In short, I was becoming obsessed. In some ways, that was good: If a job is not worth throwing all my energy and passion into, then it's not worth having. At the same time, some undesirable traits were creeping into my personality. I quickly got to the point where I felt I had to check my e-mail at midnight or later. I was jittery and I got unusually stressed by my deadlines (not surprising, as I was hardly accustomed to writing three to five stories a week). This lifestyle took its toll on my relationship. In later conversations about where things had gone wrong for us, Linda frequently pointed to the fall of 1998 as a difficult time.

And as much as I was pleased with the stories I was doing, being a solo act in New York for a San Francisco publication was no easy task. For starters, I had no office. I didn't mind working out of TheStreet.com, and the staff treated me well. But the arrangement made tasks like technical support or getting into the office on a weekend more difficult than they should have been. Moreover, TheStreet was rapidly bulking up, and after a few weeks I could feel the jealous eyeballs trained on my desk.

I also couldn't consistently get my hands on the current issue of *The Standard*. The mailed subscription copy often arrived a week late when it came at all, and finding a current *Standard* on a New York newsstand at that time was close to impossible. I found myself phoning into meetings where editors would urge us to pitch stories, say, to a new section of the magazine called "Net Returns," and I realized that I'd never seen the section. Part of my assignment was to spread the word about *The Standard* in New York; this was difficult to do without copies of the magazine.

And working with *The Standard* staff was trying at times. There were two required news meetings a week, held at hours clearly chosen for West Coast convenience—especially the 6 P.M. Friday meeting. I phoned into these meetings and listened to people squawk and thump the table around an expensive intercom that didn't work. These meetings were almost my only regular contact with my colleagues, yet the noise made them worse than useless. (More than a year later, at an editorial retreat, I wrote a skit depicting the New York bureau during a news meeting. In it, reporters were forced to guess what the hell was being said over the intercom, which repeatedly made only the noise of Charlie Brown's teacher: whah-whah-whah.)

I had never before written for a publication where I didn't get the opportunity to see the edited version of my stories before they went to the printer. It should be obvious why this is important: The writer may get information at the last minute, or the editors may inadvertently twist accurate copy into inaccurate. *The Standard* used a notoriously awful and unreliable publishing software system known as QPS. One of QPS's ostensible virtues is that when you're hooked into its network, you can call up any story in the system and look at every edited version, even down to seeing who made which changes. But there's a catch: With our version of QPS, you couldn't dial into the system from a remote location, such as the New York and Washington bureaus. Hence, things were happening to my stories that I didn't know about until I got an angry phone call.

You'd think that this would be a problem that a professional magazine would want to solve. I told friends at other publications about it and they were aghast. I raised the issue at our retreats, I sent out polite reminders to the copy desk, I begged the editor-in-chief to set up a system where showing writers their edited work was required. Yet throughout *The Standard*'s existence, there was no consistent system; sometimes the copy editors would e-mail me a version, many times they wouldn't. Partly, this was the copy desk guarding its turf; it didn't want nitpicking writers going back into edited stories to fiddle around. But it was also just a groupthink that grew out of bad technology: Because everyone sitting in San Francisco could see every story, they simply couldn't envision the implications of the fact that the rest of us could not.

Indeed, one of the great ironies of *The Industry Standard* is that for all our supposed expertise about technology, we used some of the least reliable equipment known to modern man. We then had it administered by a succession of tech managers whose brevity of tenure was surpassed only by their incompetence. Several times a week, my e-mail system would stop working, with no warning or explanation. The company's optimistically named "help desk" was of course three time zones away, and so if my e-mail went down in the morning I was out of commission for hours. I couldn't seem to convey to my editors how damaging this was; after all, *The Standard* had no listing in the New York phone directory, and so friends and contacts who didn't have my direct dial at TheStreet.com could only reach me through e-mail. The constant technology failures also made me question our mission: How could we argue that the Internet would change the business world if, in practice, the Internet was broken much of the time?

I finally got frustrated enough with these logistical concerns that I sent Jonathan an e-mail entitled "The Whine and Complain Memo." He was appropriately sympathetic; his assistant was assigned the task of FedExing me an issue every week (although as soon as his assistant was promoted to reporter, the same problem reappeared). And he promised me that things would get better when we moved into a proper office (that is, me, my deputy, and the expanding New York–based advertising team).

In November, I left the desk at TheStreet.com and took a single room at a "managed space" office building in the East 50's, a massive cylindrical skyscraper known as the Lipstick Building. It was nice to have my own office where I could shut the door, but the other businesses down my corridor seemed so dodgy that they depressed me; I half expected that I would walk by an open door and see guys with a suitcase full of money and guns. It was also grim being completely alone all day. But I was assured that I would be there only for a month or two.

That same month, I finally decided to hire Bernhard Warner as deputy bureau chief; he was a young, likable writer who was working for *BrandWeek*. In addition to being easy to get along with and a knowledgeable professional, Bernhard had been a crime reporter for the *Asbury Park Press* in New Jersey—he had nonvirtual interests and credentials. Unfortunately, I didn't have any place to put him; he took one look at the room I occupied and decided to work from home.

MANHATTANS ON THE ROOF

Despite the frustrations, I loved my job. In October I visited the San Francisco office for a week to get to know the staff. And on the weekend Linda came out to join me and we spent time in the beautiful hills of Napa and Sonoma. I attended my first *Standard* rooftop party, an institution that had already developed into local legend. It started very humbly just after 5 P.M.; one reporter brought an acoustic guitar up to the roof, an assistant brought her banjo, and we sang Neil Young and Rolling Stones songs while sipping beers. But after about 6, the roof got quite crowded, with hundreds of the Internet Economy's worker bees showing up to network in a hive where they could drink for free.

Without telling me in advance, the staff dedicated that rooftop to my visit, meaning that the theme drinks were Manhattans and Cosmopolitans. Battelle's assistant, Stacey Foreman, had gone out and bought a bowlful of big apples and ordered New York style pizza. I felt honored.

I was consistently impressed with the journalism that we were putting out. The week I arrived in San Francisco, the magazine had had a genuine scoop: We'd gotten advance word of the merger between the two largest Web measurement firms, Media Metrix and Relevant Knowledge. Our "Metrics" editor, Maryann Thompson, was so plugged into the world of Web research that she'd been inadvertently included on an e-mail that mentioned the merger. A small story, to be sure, but it was a classic *Industry Standard* piece, covering companies that *The New York Times* would not start noticing until a few months later. The information superhighway was an overused cliché, but one reason for its endurance is that, in addition to the obvious function of making interstate commerce possible, a highway requires an infrastructure: cement mixers, bulldozers, sign makers, and the like. What *The Standard* understood in those early days was that even the companies that made the Internet's radar guns were an important part of the whole story.

There were quirky stories, too. One of the oddest Internet tales of all time involved a character named Joe Firmage, who had founded USWeb, one of the earliest and largest Internet consulting firms. A devout Mormon, Firmage was never entirely conventional, but in the fall of 1998, he covertly launched a Web site that promoted his belief in extraterrestrial life. His embarrassed colleagues soon managed to shove him out of the spotlight.

While working in the San Francisco newsroom, I overheard Mark Gimein having an increasingly heated phone call. It ended with angry words and the other party hanging up the phone. Mark was working on an inside account of the failed IPO of Healtheon, a medical information systems company that through the summer of 1998 was considered one of the hottest Net companies in the world. It was chaired by Jim Clark, the cofounder of Netscape and one of Silicon Valley's most legendary figures; not only would he publish his own autobiography in 1999, but journalist Michael Lewis would quickly follow with a best-selling book about Clark, *The New New Thing*.[2] Part of Clark's pitch was that the medical market was worth $1.5 trillion, and that doctors would flock to his service because it would eliminate the inefficiencies in their ordering of products, services, and information. The stock offering was going to value the company at a massive $430 million, and if the immediate after-market behaved the way it did in those days, the company would be worth billions.

The IPO derailed after a devastating, front-page article in *The Wall Street Journal* suggested that the company's software did not yet work.[3] But Mark's angle was that the company, its technology, and the IPO market were in many ways irrelevant: They were not the reason why the IPO fell apart, any more than they would have been responsible for its success. His focus was the bankers: Wall Street had for a while perfected the "concept deal," in which investors were asked to pony up cash for little more than an idea. Because every company's business plan was equally utopian, the only way for heavy-hitting early investors to distinguish among the different companies was to judge by the bankers underwriting the deal.

And the universe of big investment banks handling Internet IPOs turned out to be incredibly small. Just two firms, Morgan Stanley Dean Witter and Goldman Sachs, had been lead underwriters for the Net's biggest IPOs to date, such as Netscape (Morgan), Yahoo! (Goldman), AtHome (Morgan), DoubleClick (Goldman), and eBay (Goldman). Indeed, as Mark's story put it: "It wouldn't be a stretch to say that just four people—Rex Golding and Brad Koenig, the respective heads of Morgan and Goldman's West Coast technology units, plus Mary Meeker and Michael Parekh, their senior Internet analysts—are the primary guardians of the doors to the Net stock market."[4]

What was unique about the Healtheon IPO was that it marked the first time that Morgan Stanley and Goldman Sachs had worked together to underwrite an offering, with each getting 40 percent of the stock to sell. Mark's story implied—though it never exactly demonstrated—that the Healtheon deal had fallen apart because the rival firms couldn't get along.[5]

But if Mark's conclusions were essentially unremarkable, what was remarkable was that his story ran at all. The nasty phone encounter I overheard was with an investment banker who was not pleased with Mark's line of questioning. Shortly after that, a representative from Morgan Stanley Dean Witter called *The Standard* and said that the bank would be pulling its advertising from future issues. The figure I heard was that the advertising was worth more than $50,000; it was also said that, at the time, Morgan Stanley was our single largest advertiser.

The bank was making an astonishingly brash power play. Here was a company threatening to harm our magazine financially not because we published an unflattering story, but merely because it didn't like the way a story was being reported. Moreover, it's not like we were *BusinessWeek* and could easily afford to lose the ads; since *The Stan-*

dard was only a few months out of the starting gate, it needed the revenue. The full picture was even uglier: Gimein later recalled that one of the Goldman bankers he interviewed made a point of how much Morgan advertised in *The Standard* and hinted that his bank, Goldman, had phoned the magazine to match it.

"And then he winked," Gimein recalled. "I really didn't have anything to say. It just seemed so bizarre to me."

I was privy to some of the internal discussion that followed Morgan's pullout, but it was very brief. No one on the editorial staff could believe that the bank was behaving so heavy-handedly. And Battelle agreed; his instructions were simple: "Fuck 'em." We ran Mark's story on the cover. I was relieved and proud to be working for a business publication that had the right journalistic values, but it also turned out to be the right business decision: Morgan Stanley was back in our pages a few weeks later.

INVASION OF THE T-SHIRT MODELS

If the two biggest plagues we experienced were threatened libel suits and blackmail from advertisers, surely the third was the onslaught of public relations. There is a broad critique of the public relations industry, associated with Noam Chomsky and others, that discusses the malicious effects that the growth of PR has on the practice of journalism. And there are excellent watchdogs—notably *PR Watch*—who keep tabs on the slimy clients, nationally and internationally, that the bigger PR firms take money from.[6]

I am sympathetic to those critics. At the same time, that critique is practically useless to the business reporter on deadline. You can't say to a company, "I'm not going to write about you because your outside public relations firm used to represent Papa Doc Duvalier."

It's not exactly that I never dealt with PR people when I was at the *Voice*. They were almost always the point of contact with elected officials, and there were a few specialty left-wing PR firms that called from time to time with ideas for my column. And I knew at least the names of the PR people for the various magazines and newspapers I covered; a few were friendly, but mostly they declined to answer any substantive questions I put to them. If I needed a response from a reporter or editor, I'd just call that person directly. Mostly my view of PR people was summed up by the early twentieth-century British journalist Claud Cockburn: "Never believe anything until it's been officially denied."

It's fair to say that a disproportionate amount of the billions in venture and public capital invested in Internet companies during the late 1990s ended up lining the pockets of public relations and marketing firms. For many dot-com companies, paying the PR firm was their largest expense after payroll. At the bigger, nationally known firms— such as Hill & Knowlton, Fleishman Hillard, and Burson Marsteller —standard services began at $35,000 a month, and additional services for conferences or other publicity binges could double that tab.

Despite having no guarantee that spending such staggering sums would actually produce anything, companies were begging to get the better-known PR firms to represent them. During the summer of 1999, the head of a San Francisco PR agency that specialized in dot-coms told me that he was pitched by about a dozen potential clients every day, or about one every forty-five minutes. At best, he explained, his firm could take on three new clients a month. Some firms refused to meet with prospective clients unless they had been recommended by a select group of venture capitalists.

I had no way to prepare for this tidal wave of professional publicity. On my second day at *The Standard,* I had PR people phoning me, using my first name as if we'd been friends for years, and pitching me stories, almost always about companies I'd never heard of.

Their audacity at times astonished me: They thought nothing of asking me to come to their office, sit through a two-hour briefing with the senior staff, and then go to lunch. Obviously they had never bothered to think about the time demands of a reporter writing three to five stories a week.

That said, I concluded over time that PR professionals are a lot like lawyers: There are too many of them, including a number of very bad ones who ruin the sector's reputation. But when you need them, you really need them, and you want to be damn sure you have a good one. About 5–10 percent of the PR people I've worked with have always behaved decently and I don't mind calling them friends.

Unfortunately, the incidents that stick in my head involve the other 90 percent.

I can remember being on the phone in my office in mid-1999 when the models burst into my office. Two women, one black, one white, both busty, wearing matching T-shirts. I felt like I'd been involuntarily cast in a bad bachelor-party movie.

"Something big is about to happen!" they said in husky voices while handing me a T-shirt. They were gone before I could ask what they were doing. I was left holding a T-shirt that cryptically said: "Hello, is anybody out there?"

Actually, it wasn't all that cryptic. By the time the model-delivered T-shirt found its way into my hands, I had already received an e-mail from Hello@isanybodyoutthere.com. I had received a postcard that said only: "Hello, is anybody out there?" I had seen the massive "Hello, is anybody out there?" ads in *The Wall Street Journal,* and the brief TV spots featuring someone shouting into an echoing canyon.

After digging around, I managed to figure out that the entire campaign was meant to publicize the fact that the Mining Company, a New York–based human-guided search engine, was—stop the presses—changing its name to About.com. A few days later, the company's publicist e-mailed to encourage me to write about the name change, saying she was "just hoping to get this on your radar." Unfortunately for her, I was just trying to figure out how to shoot it off my screen.

The "Hello" campaign was the start of a broader advertising and public-relations blitz that ultimately cost About.com $12 million. Put that in perspective: This is a company that, in the quarter before this campaign, had lost more than $20 million on about $3.7 million in revenues. Though "Hello" accounted for only part of the overall campaign, that's still a lot of money spent on bugging reporters.[7]

150 Percent Wrong

No matter how insulting the "Hello" campaign was, it at least had the virtue of being coordinated. In the manic desire to get their stories out, many of the companies I encountered seemed completely disconnected from the publicity firms they hired.

In January 1999, I was asked to work with Mark Gimein on a story about a deal involving a site called Women.com. Based in San Mateo, it was one of the oldest women-based community sites around; indeed, it had been founded in 1992 as an online service called Womens Wire, well before there was a World Wide Web. Mark had a knowledgeable source who'd tipped him off to the fact that Women.com was about to merge with a big New York media company, which Mark had pretty much narrowed down to Hearst. And though I didn't know it at the time, Mark had done something sneaky and brilliant: He called the office of Hearst's CEO and asked the secretary if he could speak with Marleen McDaniel, the CEO of Women.com. The secretary told him McDaniel wasn't there at the moment but offered to take a message—about as close to confirmation of merger talks as you can hope to get.

If Mark was right, it was a big story: Hearst's Home Arts sites and Women.com represented the second and third largest Web sites aimed at women, and their combination would make them number one over their much-hyped rival, iVillage (and far larger than Oxygen Media, my cover topic from a few months earlier). IVillage had already filed with the SEC for a public offering that would net it $46 million and value the company at some $300 million. At the very least, then, our story was about a merger worth tens and probably hundreds of millions of dollars.

To be honest, I didn't have much to contribute to this story. I had written a piece on Hearst's mostly woeful Web sites back in the fall, but Hearst had hated the article so much that no one there was going to tell me anything. Also, I had been brought onto the story on a Friday afternoon, when I had other things on my mind, including getting ready for a trip to New Orleans to report on the annual convention of the National Association of Television Producers and Executives (NATPE).

So I made a few perfunctory phone calls and reached a woman who handled public relations for Women.com through an outside agency called Connors Communications. I put the question to her directly: We hear you're about to merge, is that true? She said it wasn't, but that we had probably misinterpreted an upcoming development that she might be able to tell me about if I was interested. Obviously I said yes, and she called back and said that Women.com was about to sign an "anchor tenancy" (for prime ad space) with AOL, and that it might be announced next week.

This was not exactly news bound to shake the planet; still, as far as I could tell, we had it exclusively, and for a Friday afternoon Web story it would be fine. I phoned AOL for confirmation and no one called back (typical of that company), so we wrote the story up and I flew to New Orleans over the weekend.

Then I heard again from Mark, who said he was sure the merger was still on. Again, I didn't have much to go on, but fortunately, I saw that one of the people appearing on a NATPE panel was Gina Garrubbo, executive vice-president in charge of advertising sales for Women.com. I didn't want to ask about the merger during the public Q&A session, so as soon as it was over, I went up to Garrubbo and asked her about a pending merger. She was wearing a pink suit and an impossibly chunky pearl necklace. She looked down from the stage, gave me a big smile that was practically a wink, and said: "Honey, I just can't comment."

That was a hell of a lot better than a denial. I got back on the phone with the publicist who'd given me the "scoop" on the AOL anchor tenancy. She continued to stonewall. "It's 150 percent wrong," she said. "I don't know who Mark Gimein is talking to, but the story about us merging is not true."

I'm ashamed to admit it, but her adamant denial made me doubt Mark's reporting a little bit. Worse still, a top *Standard* editor who'd worked with someone from Women.com was arguing from the inside that the story was wrong. I knew Mark had a good source, but I didn't know who it was; maybe the person had outdated information. At bottom, I resisted believing that someone would lie so baldly to a reporter.

On Tuesday night, I flew back to New York and worked on my story about the NATPE convention. On Thursday morning, I saw the story in *The Wall Street Journal,* headlined: "Two Popular Web Sites for Women to Merge."[8] No one else had the story, and the wires were attributing it to the *Journal.* The company was making its official announcement later that day.

So not only had the publicist lied to us, but she had done so to protect an exclusive story for the *Journal.* I was embarrassed and livid. Bad enough that were we scooped, but we had been hoodwinked into printing a news story—the one about AOL—that was significantly inaccurate, or at the very least was not news.

I "attended" the press conference that afternoon by dialing into a toll-free number. Despite what one sees real or fictional reporters do on television, most print reporters I know attend very few live press conferences (obviously TV reporters and photographers have to go to get pictures). Any corporation or organization of a given size will have a teleconference call-in, and if you miss that, audio and often video tapes are available almost immediately.

From the comfort of my desk, I listened to Women.com CEO Marleen McDaniel extol the virtues of the newly merged company. When she finished, it was time for questions. If you're dialing in, you push a button, and they ask you to identify yourself and then ask your question. I was first and pulled no punches: "I'd like to know if you think it's a good idea to lie to the press, and if lying to the press is part of Women.com's strategy."

McDaniel was thrown off and said she hadn't lied to anyone. I wouldn't let her off the hook.

"We asked your spokesperson earlier this week if Women.com and Hearst's sites were going to merge, and were told flat out that they weren't. I'd just like to know if you think that's a good strategy."

She apologized. I could picture the grimaces on the faces of the various executives and PR people. In the meantime, reporters from other publications, also working from their desks, began e-mailing me notes of encouragement—while the press conference was still going on! Everyone knew what it was like to be lied to like this, and I was exacting revenge for all of us.

Later I was told that the head of Connors Communications called Jonathan Weber to complain about my question, which was deemed "unprofessional." I took the criticism seriously, but I also stood my ground: How professional was it for them to lie to us? Besides, it's not as if I published a story saying that the company had lied; I asked a question at a press conference and got an answer. As I explained to Weber, I used to cover New York City politics, a realm in which rude questions at press conferences are practically required. If the executives at Women.com couldn't tolerate a mildly adversarial press corps, maybe they shouldn't hold press conferences.

Within a matter of days, the publicist who lied to me was taken off the Women.com account. And a few months later, Connors no longer represented the newly merged Hearst–Women.com.

DÉJÀ VU

This was hardly the only inexplicable, disjointed behavior we encountered. In the spring of 1999, there was a degree of buzz around the Web site then known as Deja News. The site was a very useful database that hearkened back to an earlier Internet era; it allowed for searches within what were once called "news groups," strings of messages posted usually around a given topic. Before the development of the World Wide Web, such groups (often known by labels such as "alt.whatever.news") were one of the principal ways that Netheads communicated with one another, and there was significant intelligence stored in the collective memory of those millions of postings.

Toward the end of 1998, Deja News announced that it was moving its headquarters from Texas to New York and had hired Tom Phillips as its CEO. Phillips was interesting to me because before landing his previous big Internet job with ESPN's Internet ventures, he had been one of the founders of *Spy* magazine, the wicked satirical monthly that helped deflate the celebrity blimps of the 1980s. It seemed like Deja News had plans to evolve into some kind of media firm, so I began an e-mail correspondence with the company's PR person, from the firm of Alexander Ogilvy in Atlanta, in hopes that she might tell me the company's plans.

A few months later, I found out that Deja News had hired Eric Etheridge, a veteran editor who'd worked at *George, Rolling Stone,* and *The New York Observer* and had been my editor at *7 Days.* The company agreed to give me an "exclusive" story about Eric's appointment as head of the site's content. I didn't understand why a site that relied on Internet users' postings would require a "content editor," but that was precisely the story I expected to get.

I arrived at Deja's New York office. As with so many up-and-coming dot-coms, the space was being renovated to accommodate a rash of new employees. I saw Eric and said hello, then went into Tom Phillips's office. I found it irritating that the firm's new, for-hire publicist—who worked for Middleberg Associates, the same firm that represented *The Standard*—sat in on the interview, but I didn't complain. Phillips gave me a canned statement about how talented Eric was, and then I asked what I thought was a benign, and screamingly obvious, question: "What are your plans for transforming Deja News?"

To my amazement, Phillips balked. "We're not prepared to discuss that yet," he said. I was stunned. Whoever heard of a CEO who refused to discuss strategy? An eager—and reasonably friendly—reporter was sitting in the man's office, pen and notebook in hand. How often did Phillips think that was going to happen?

I tried unsuccessfully a few more ways to ask the question, and then I simply walked out, absolutely furious. The publicist was apologetic but explained that the company was not ready to publicly discuss its new direction. (My translation: The company had already decided to give a daily newspaper an exclusive account. It was the Women.com scenario all over again.) I searched back through my e-mail and found a pledge from Deja's publicist that she would tell me about the plans, but it was my contact from the old firm, Alexander Ogilvy. Somehow in the switching of PR firms, the company's message got changed.

I was in a bad spot, because my editors had already scheduled the story for the following week. But I refused to help publicize Deja at that point. I wrote to the PR firm and said that when I covered the 1989 New York mayoral election, if I sat in a candidate's office and he couldn't or wouldn't explain why he was running for mayor, my editor—Eric Etheridge—would have said either to ignore him or skewer him.

The business idea behind Deja, as it turned out, was not a terrible one. The management's plan was to turn the cacophonous news-group postings into something like a Zagat's guide, in which consumers' experiences of various products or services—cars, home electronics, airlines—would be translated into a rating point system. Yet my instinct told me that an Internet company with two media veterans at the very top that nonetheless couldn't figure out how to work with a sympathetic reporter didn't have much of a chance. I was right. Despite filing for an IPO that would have made Phillips a multimillionaire, Deja.com fizzled. It never went public, and in February 2001, the company's technology was acquired by the Web search engine Google. Etheridge had long since abandoned ship.

WHAT DO YOU MEAN BY "WRONG"?

Even the more triumphant moments had a bizarre taste. In early 1999, I added $350 million worth of value to one of the world's largest Internet companies—in a single day.

I did this by publishing the details of a prospective merger that never actually occurred.

The deal was a proposed strategic partnership between Lycos, the Massachusetts-based search engine and Web portal whose party I'd attended a year before, and the NBC television and cable conglomerate. Toward the end of January 1999, it became well known within the Internet industry that Lycos was seeking a buyer or investment partner. After all, the Lycos network had tremendous reach—nearly half of all Web users at the time visited a Lycos site at some point every month—which made it very attractive to traditional media companies scrambling to catch up with the emergence of the Internet. Lycos's power had never translated into profit; nonetheless, its stock was worth more than $5 billion.

Part of my job was to sniff out multibillion-dollar deals like this one. They were occurring on a near-weekly basis; in November 1998, America Online bought the Web browser company Netscape for more than $5 billion. At the end of January 1999, Yahoo bought the Web "community" site GeoCities for the same figure. Such deals became so routine that, in May 1999, *The Standard* ran photos of two Net executives on its cover with the beautifully blasé headline: "This Week's Billionaires."

My colleague Jim Evans, based in the magazine's San Francisco headquarters, had some good sources at Lycos and among its biggest shareholders. My job was to follow the NBC side. I had a source there who, plied with beer and expensive sushi, would occasionally let slip details of the network's pending Internet deals. To my colleagues, I referred to him as Deep Peacock. He had mentioned Lycos to me once before, and when Evans began hearing rumblings about a deal, we hit the phones. Typically, NBC's well-paid spokespeople would say they could not comment on any rumors (which was useless, but better than a denial).

So on February 4, Evans and I prepared a short article to run on *The Standard*'s Web site, laying out what we believed to be true. Executives from the companies were in talks, and Lycos was seeking to sell between 30 and 35 percent of itself. Any such deal was bound to be worth billions; the only question was how many. Lycos would presumably be integrated into NBC's small portal called Snap, and the two together could be the Web's most dominant force. The story was edited and coded to be read over the Web; we were ready to post the story at about 2:45 P.M. East Coast time.

I called Deep Peacock. We exchanged brief pleasantries, and I brought up the Lycos talks. He was slightly evasive but acknowledged that the subject was "super red-hot right now." I asked, "If we were to publish a story saying these talks were going on right now, would that be wrong?"

He responded, "What do you mean by 'wrong'?"

"I mean, would it be inaccurate?"

"Oh. No, it wouldn't."

"Thanks. Gotta go."

I immediately e-mailed this conversation to my editor in San Francisco, and the story, titled "NBC and Lycos Ponder a Deal," was up on the Web instantaneously. Within minutes it was picked up by the Reuters and Dow Jones news services, and the markets responded instantly. And how: Within twenty-four hours, Lycos's stock rose by nearly $8 a share, adding more than $350 million to its overall value. The cable business channel CNBC asked me on the air the next day to discuss the deal; since CNBC is owned by NBC, I considered the invitation a tacit confirmation that our story had been accurate.

Ironically, by the time investors began reacting to our story, the negotiations between NBC and Lycos had apparently stalled, and Lycos had found a new suitor in USA Networks mogul Barry Diller. That deal, which was eventually rejected by the company's shareholders, quickly erased the value our story had created, along with about another billion dollars.

The NBC-Lycos experience raised a number of interesting business and journalistic questions for me. Was it misleading, for example, to publish details of a deal that had not been consummated? To what extent did publishing on the Web exaggerate the role of rumors or uncertainty in stock trading? These were not idle questions, and certainly my appearance on CNBC could be seen as evidence that *The Standard* and I unreasonably hyped the Net economy. The ironic aspect of that charge is that I was badly flamed on the Lycos story by investors who thought that, by being critical of the proposed USA Networks deal, I hadn't done enough to promote the value of their Lycos stock.

But for me, the most fascinating aspect is that merely a year before, I had heard about Lycos for the first time. I certainly could not have given a coherent explanation of what it did. And yet, just a few months into my job, the *Christian Science Monitor* had sought my views on the AOL-Netscape merger; *The New York Times* had published an op-ed I wrote on the taxation of Internet commerce. I was a certified "expert" on the Internet Economy.

All I needed was a real office.

3

The Fat Year Begins

I stop the cab at the side of the road if I have to make a trade. Safety first.

—Carlos Rubino, who daytraded stocks out of his New York taxi, August 1999

At the very end of December 1998, I visited San Francisco for a few days; I had been asked to deliver a paper on radio and literature at the annual conference of the Modern Language Association. On my way there I realized I'd become pessimistic about *The Standard*. A few good things had happened: I had hired a deputy bureau chief and I had published an op-ed on Internet taxation in *The New York Times*. But overall I had the sense that the magazine was going nowhere. Aside from a few friends who worked in related industries, I didn't have the sense that anyone in New York knew or cared about the publication where I worked. We did not appear to be selling any more ad pages per issue than when I joined, and I began to fear that *The Standard* was going to be shut down.

While in San Francisco I worked out of *The Standard*'s office on Pacific Avenue. One evening, Jonathan Weber and I went to the Old Ship Saloon, a sawdust-on-the-floor joint across the street from the office. After a couple of drinks I shared my pessimism with him, and Jonathan gave me this look. First I read it as fear, then I realized it was more along the lines of: Haven't you heard? He said that, yes, the magazine had struggled through the fall, but that fourth-quarter revenues had exceeded their targets, and that we'd brought in $800,000 that quarter. Besides, he said, there had been outside interest in acquiring the publication, and so surely the magazine would be bought before it would be folded.

As I went off to dinner, I was reassured. If we could take in $800,000 in a quarter and we continued to grow, I calculated, then we would soon be at a level of $5 million a year. That seemed a reasonable basis on which to run a weekly magazine.

Later that week I heard that we had visitors in the office: a bunch of bigwigs from Time Warner. I was sitting at some absent reporter's desk when Battelle walked by.

"So I hear that the Time Warner posse is here," I said.

"Yeah, I spent most of the day with them," he said, smiling with confidence.

"What do they want?"

"I think they just want to sniff my butt," Battelle said.

"Oh. Well, that's always good."

Time Inc. is arguably the premier magazine company in America, particularly for weeklies. But it managed to get caught off guard by the growth of the New Economy magazines; that position was reinforced when Condé Nast purchased *Wired* in the beginning of 1998. *Fortune* did its best to beef up technology coverage, hiring a slew of writers based in Silicon Valley. But Time executives believed that they needed a separate magazine and were very keenly watching the New Economy magazines and the advertisers who were beginning to flock there. Indeed, when I interviewed Time Inc.'s editor-in-chief Norman

Pearlstine in October 1998, I was astonished at how familiar he was with *The Standard.* He told me that he and Pat McGovern had been discussing the prospects for a weekly magazine about the Internet since 1995. I later heard that Pearlstine had been seen reading *The Standard* while he worked out on a Stairmaster.

Throughout the end of 1998 and the beginning of 1999, Time officials had meetings with not just *The Standard,* but representatives of all the major Internet business magazines: *Upside, Business 2.0, Red Herring.*[1] Published accounts indicate that negotiations got closest with *Red Herring,* but they certainly got very close with *The Standard.*

The talks between Battelle and Time Inc. went from initial butt-sniffing to full-scale boardroom talks in April 1999. Both Battelle and Weber flew to New York to meet with Time officials. The idea was that *The Standard* would be run as a kind of adjunct to *Fortune* magazine. In part, that was because there was so much overlap between our subject matter and theirs. But it was also because *The Standard* had genuinely captured the eye of *Fortune* editor John Huey.

A Southerner with a fondness for bourbon (he keeps at least one bottle in his office), Huey is perhaps the most prominent business journalist of his generation. And yet his idols, he says, are not traditional news gatherers, but rather the more literary figures of Harold Hayes's *Esquire* of the 1960s and Clay Felker's *New York* magazine of the 1970s. "Huey felt we were a class act," Weber recalled later.[2] "He felt that journalistically we were superior to *Herring, 2.0,* and *Upside.* He came out and said: 'Let's be clear about the agenda. We want to be in this space, so we can either buy or build. I don't want to build; that's too much work. I'm tired; I don't want to do that again.'"

The terms of the deal were that Time would acquire a minority stake of *The Standard* between 40 and 49 percent; it would also have the option to increase that stake at some future point. The value of the company would be placed at $100 million—an extraordinary number, given that its quarterly revenues were just barely a million dollars.

In the end, however, *Fortune*'s business side rejected the deal. For one thing, they didn't like the idea that *The Standard* was a weekly; they wanted to switch to a fortnightly publishing schedule like *Fortune's*. And second, they had genuine doubts about whether it was worthwhile to put so much of their efforts into a publication which, measured by the yardsticks of *Time, People, Sports Illustrated,* and *Entertainment Weekly,* was puny. This was the first of many mating dances that *The Standard* would have with a number of worldwide media organizations as they began to recognize that the publishing landscape was being overhauled.

WE BECOME THE BIBLE

In my first few months at *The Standard,* I encountered a group of self-satisfied skeptics who used to ask me: "Why are you a magazine at all?" After all, wasn't part of the message of the dot-com revolution that print was an obsolescent medium? And so why not take the plunge, like TheStreet.com and CBS MarketWatch, and be a Web-only publication?

By the middle of 1999, fewer and fewer people were asking that question. More than any other medium, a print publication can display its fortunes before the reader has absorbed a single word. They call it the "plop factor"—the sound the magazine makes when you drop it on your desk—and our readers had begun to notice that our issues were plopping louder.

The plop was a consequence of the fact that Internet companies had life cycles that were hyperaccelerated, like those mayflies that experience an entire existence in twenty-four hours. The time lag between a finished business plan and investment from venture capitalists was, for many start-ups, a matter of days. The VCs, in return, demanded maximum return on their initial investment, and they usually wanted it in a year or two. That meant the company had to expand as quickly as humanly possible, the "get big fast" lesson gleaned from Amazon.com. And if a company couldn't actually grow that fast, the next best thing was to make it seem like it had. The only way anyone could see to do that was to advertise.

During this time, Web advertising skyrocketed; the new medium grew faster than any of its older brethren, and its numbers quickly began to rival those of outdoor advertising. Yet a dot-com company that advertised only on the Internet was failing to reach the broader audience, almost a crime against the investors. And thus the Internet did, as promised, transform the media world—just not in the way that its advocates had envisioned. Far from replacing more traditional communications media, the Internet explosion ended up lining the coffers of television stations, radio stations, advertising agencies, and print magazines. One research organization estimates that Internet companies spent $687 million on advertising in 1999, an increase of 347 percent over the previous year.[3]

It wasn't just a question of getting a company's name out; differentiating a dot-com's corporate brand was absolutely vital in getting Wall Street to deem it worthy of investment. As *The Wall Street Journal* put it: "Because the right corporate image these days can mean billions of dollars in stock market value, b-to-b [business-to-business] start-ups feel they can't afford not to advertise. . . . Most b-to-b start-ups' plans call for them to spend 40% to 70% of their total funding on marketing efforts."[4] In the fall of 1999, a local San Francisco business magazine estimated that there were no fewer than twenty-six Bay Area dot-coms expected to spend more than $20 million apiece on advertising in the following year.[5]

Just as tech advertisers clogged the billboards along San Francisco's Route 101 when I visited in 1998, so now in 1999 tech companies—some well-known, some previously obscure—were suddenly ubiquitous throughout the country. In southern California, radio station revenues jumped an astounding 260 percent in 1999, much of which was attributable to Internet start-ups showing off for potential customers and investors.[6]

It sometimes seemed as if every single spot on New York's two all-news radio stations, WCBS and 1010 WINS, was taken up by a dot-com company. Ridiculous gimmick vehicles, like the one in the shape of a giant bean for the online currency Web site Beenz.com, were frequently seen stuck in Manhattan traffic. Bus stops, phone booths, billboards—everywhere you looked, the Internet revolution was hawking its virtues. When I wrote a profile of Jonathan Bulkeley, the CEO of Barnesandnoble.com, he complained about the pervasiveness of ads from his former employer, AOL: "The only thing you see on buses is America Online. They're everywhere! Every bus! I'm sick of it! I wanna get a shotgun. Ch-boom! They're following me!"[7]

And no one was better situated to harness the power of this advertising hurricane than *The Industry Standard.* This was something of a surprise, since many believed that John Battelle's strategy of targeting the magazine to the very top executives of technology businesses was risky and costly. A good portion of the magazine's circulation as of early 1999 was given away for free (known in the publishing business as "controlled circulation"). Traditionally, the gamble is that advertisers will be so enticed by the demographic desirability of a publication's readers that they will overlook the fact that those readers aren't paying for the publication.

But because of *The Standard's* controlled circulation, practically all of our advertisers *were* our readers. So we started hearing from the sales team that they would go on calls to meet the ad buyers for a given company, only to find out that their CEO had already instructed them to buy space in *The Standard,* because that was the magazine the CEO read every week.

And thus we started to gain weight. As late as the May 10 edition, *The Standard* was 64 pages thick, the same size as the average issue in the fall of 1998 (about 25 of those pages were advertising, though some of those were "bartered," that is, traded for some kind of promotional purpose, and thus not paid for). The June 21 edition was 72 pages. Then in July, typically a slow time for magazine advertising, we had two back-to-back issues of 156 pages each. A publication that had cost just a few million dollars to set up was now taking in about $2 million a week in magazine advertising alone.

The Fat Year had begun.

By the late summer of 1999, the media trade publications began to notice what we had noticed: Our ad numbers were rising as fast as anyone's in the publishing business. We hoped it would last forever; it would in fact last through the summer of 2000, one Fat Year. A *Media-Week* article in 1999 quoted an advertising executive who used a phrase we would hear repeatedly throughout the next eighteen months: "It's the bible of the industry."[8] And who wouldn't want to buy space in the Bible?

WHO'S AFRAID OF BOO.COM?

I'd known from the Lycos-NBC experience the kind of impact a story in our Bible could have on a public company. What I hadn't realized is how thoroughly the newer companies relied on us to get their story out. In the early part of 1999, one of our regular free-lance contributors, Michelle Rafter, sent out an e-mail to the staff asking if anyone knew anything about a yet-to-be-launched Web business called Boo.com. I spoke with her, and she mentioned that *Women's Wear Daily* had written a piece about the site indicating that the French fashion and luxury company LVMH was among its investors. I found the story and called LVMH's New York office, which curtly informed me that there was no connection between LVMH and Boo.com.

So I did what had now become a reflexive bit of research; I looked at the "WHOIS" registry section of the Network Solutions Web site. Although Web site registration has since become more fragmented (and democratic), at the time all Web domain names had to be registered with a company called Network Solutions. If you know how to use its database, you can get basic information about anyone who has

registered any given domain name. The name Boo.com was registered, oddly, from an address in Ireland, to a man named Patrik
Hedelin (who, I would later learn, was Boo's CFO). I sent Hedelin an
e-mail saying I was interested in covering the company, although I
didn't expect to hear back from him.

A couple of days later, I got an e-mail from Hedelin saying that the
firm's publicity was being handled by Hill & Knowlton and that he had
forwarded my request there. Sure enough, I soon heard from Jessica
Kogan, who was handling the Boo account; she quickly promised me
an exclusive story on Boo. We even signed a letter of exclusivity,
which I'd never done before. Even though I'd told her that because we
were a newsweekly I could never promise the cover, she'd included a
clause dictating that my story would be a cover; I had to strike that out.

In the meantime, I'd begun to learn a bit more about Boo; it turned
out I had a friend working there. Hugh Garvey, who'd worked at the
Voice's literary supplement, had been hired to edit an online magazine
connected to the Boo site, to be called "Boom." The idea was to create a lifestyle magazine that was unique to the Web and that would
highlight cool clothes in a manner similar to *Details* or *Vogue*. Hugh
was calling it "an interactive playground for your mind" and hiring
our mutual friends as freelance writers and editors.

The Boo story looked better and better to me: Here was a company
being run by two Swedes in their twenties. One was a poetry critic, the
other a former fashion model—we certainly didn't publish too many
articles about either of those. Although they had no revenues, no product, and a business plan put together on the fly, they had managed to
raise, according to one published report, $125 million.[9] They had con-
vinced the old-school bank J. P. Morgan to lead their investors, even
though Morgan had never backed an e-commerce start-up before.
And their project was ridiculously ambitious: to launch a global e-
commerce site, from scratch, simultaneously in thirty-five countries.
Even the best-known Internet retailers, such as Amazon, had been
cautious enough to make sure their service worked in one country

before expanding abroad. Boo.com was either the most dramatic business start-up in decades, or it was the very essence of dot-com madness.

I knew to get the story right I'd have to go to London, and no one at *The Standard* balked. It was a whirlwind trip, only about forty-eight hours, in early May. At Jessica's recommendation I stayed at the Hotel Intercontinental in Mayfair, but I spent little time there. I had been working terribly hard to get the story out the week that Boo was scheduled to launch, and the jet lag so confused my body that for days I could only sleep about two hours at a time, three times a day. I also managed to squeeze in an interview with the British publishing mogul Felix Dennis, who had a chauffeur pick me up in a black Rolls Royce and drive an hour away to his mansion just outside Stratford-on-Avon.

An all-expenses trip to London, riding in limousines—this is about as pampered as a journalist gets. But I was working; I did extensive interviews with the Boo principals and talked to a number of technical staff in the company's chaotic office on Carnaby Street. And though I was skeptical about Boo's ultimate business prospects, I did become convinced that the main players knew what they were doing. They had sewn up their agreements with suppliers, and the Web site demonstrations I saw were very cool and alluring. I came away with two impressions: (1) If Boo failed, it would fail big, and (2) Internet mania had definitely hit Europe—or at least London—and there was no magazine like *The Standard* covering it.

I wrote most of my story on the return flight, politely declining an offer of the sleeping aide Xanax from Boo's cofounder Kajsa Leander. I lobbied the editors to make Boo the cover. I wanted the cover line: "Who's Afraid of Boo.com? Maybe You Should Be." In the end, my editors went with another story, arguing that we had no real way of knowing whether or not Boo would succeed; they didn't want to give it unmerited hype. My piece was relegated to a sideline on the cover that said "Boo.com: A Global Fashion Play."

At the time, I knew I had gotten deeper inside Boo than any other journalist. What I didn't realize was just how important this bit of publicity was for the fledgling company. In his memoir about Boo.com, co-founder Ernst Malmsten called my story "the most accurate and flattering write-up we could have hoped for."[10] After the piece came out, Malmsten recalled, the company's recruiter "could hardly move without tripping over yet someone else who wanted to join the internet revolution." The recruiter was hearing from 700 people a day who wanted a Net job.

TheStreet Goes Wild

I went almost directly from London to San Francisco to attend a day-long editorial retreat that was being held in Half Moon Bay, just south of the city. And so it was that on a Friday in early May, I was again at a rooftop party at *The Standard*. It had been a warm spring afternoon, but in San Francisco the evenings are predictably chilly, and so the recently acquired outdoor heaters were running full blast. Of course, it was so crowded that maneuvering your body to get near a heater could take you fifteen minutes.

Driving into San Francisco, I had heard on the car radio that the United States had just bombed the Chinese embassy in Yugoslavia. I tried to engage my colleagues in conversation about this but got only grimaces and shrugs: That was a disaster story from a place that was far, far away. The topic of the hour was the imminent IPO of TheStreet.com.

There was never a formal relationship between *The Standard* and TheStreet.com (later on we would have some investors in common), but there were plenty of affinities. I had worked out of the firm's New York City office for two months, and its San Francisco bureau chief, Cory Johnson, wrote a weekly column for us and would later join our staff. The two editors, Jonathan Weber and Dave Kansas, had become friends, united by their fatigue and their ulcer-edged drive to make their publications succeed.

For those reasons, the two publications used each other alternately as a yardstick or a crutch. No matter how high TheStreet.com ever flew, Kansas would always say to me, only half-joking, "When I get fired, will you hire me?" Sure, he'd fallen deep into the Kool-Aid vat, but I always thought of him as a friend, a colleague, a peer. You didn't have to spend too much time with him to see the Christian boy from the Midwest. But when he emerged on the roof that evening, Kansas was not in Minnesota anymore. He may have looked understated in his black trench coat, but that night no one could deny he was holding the dot-com mojo. I made a $10 bet with Cory Johnson that the stock of TSCM, initially for sale at about $10 a share, would not go higher than $70 on its first day. I lost by a hair. On the first day of trading the company's stock soared to $71 a share, making it worth $1.4 billion.

What's even more amazing is that TSCM was hardly unique. In January of that year, despite skeptics who said that the IPO market had softened, CBS MarketWatch had served up its stock to the public markets and watched shares zoom to more than $100 apiece. That company, headed by a former *Washington Post* reporter, was ostensibly worth more than $2 billion. CNET, an Internet-based content company that ran the News.com Web site and provided free software downloads, had a market capitalization of more than $3 billion. And in June, even the tiny online magazine Salon.com had an initial offering, ending up with a net worth of about $100 million on its first day.

Deals like those were making Battelle envious and nervous. In the spring of 1999, he used the phrase like a mantra: "I need currency." There were many reasons for *The Standard* to go public, but one crucial purpose was to go on a shopping spree. Battelle believed that if *The Standard* was going to lead in the modern media world, it had to be a multimedia company. Based around a magazine and a Web site, *The Standard* would eventually, in his eyes, become a force in database publishing, in market research, in all the places where technology and business intersected. It was the omnivorous expansion of *Wired* all over again, except this time Battelle believed he could get it right.

We couldn't get there as a magazine owned by IDG, but if we had a big bag filled with high-priced Internet stock, then we could spend it snapping up little companies and make ourselves very big very fast. Battelle summed up the way he was trying to sell this idea to McGovern: "I keep telling him he could own 100 percent of a company worth $40 million, or 50 percent of a company worth $200 million."

But such seductive arithmetic did not necessarily persuade IDG. A man who had built a multibillion-dollar publishing empire over the course of three decades was not easily convinced to change his formula, and the IDG formula involved keeping control of the publications it started. There was but one exception: IDG Books, which offered stock to the public in 1998. (Even in that case, IDG still retained over 75 percent of the company.) While no one claimed to completely understand McGovern's motives for not cheering on Battelle's efforts to take *The Standard* public, he strongly hinted that he did not always trust the valuations of the company that came from outside IDG. His way of putting it was: "Why should I sell ten-dollar bills for five dollars?"

GROWING FAST AND FURIOUS

That summer the New York bureau had really begun to hum. Bernhard and I had finally moved into an office together, on the tenth floor of a building on East 52nd Street, where everyone else worked for the magazine's growing business staff. I got approval to keep hiring, and so after months of cajoling, pleading, and flattery—and the offer of a hefty salary, plus bonus—I persuaded Thomas Goetz to leave *The Wall Street Journal.* I had first met Thomas in early 1994, when he finished his master's degree at the University of Virginia and moved to New York to be my intern at *The Village Voice.* A skinny guy with an impossibly boyish face, he stood out at the *Voice* by occasionally showing up for work with a tie, even a bow tie.

But he also stood out as an intelligent, hardworking colleague. He quickly became an important contributor to the paper, and then a staff writer. In the summer of 1996, we collaborated on a lengthy cover story about the largely secretive Fisher real-estate empire, New York's largest contributors to Bob Dole's foundering presidential campaign. I still consider that story a model of sustained investigative reporting. In 1997, when a *Journal* editor called me for a recommendation, I felt awkward—not because I didn't wish to praise Thomas, but because it dawned on me that he was moving on to one of the world's most influential newspapers and I was staying.

But the *Journal* can be inhospitable to younger talent, and although Thomas did some excellent work there covering the travel industry, I knew he was frustrated. Meeting for drinks, we talked a great deal about the kind of stories we would do if we worked together again. We were out with a programmer friend who explained to us how unbelievably easy it is to shut down the average Web site. We cooked up— but unfortunately never published—an article called "How to Hack a Web Site: What Your Company Needs to Know." Dressed up as business journalism, this was an homage of sorts to two radical moments in postwar magazine publishing: In 1967, *The New York Review of Books* ran a cover illustration of how to build a Molotov cocktail, and in 1979 *The Progressive* published a highly controversial recipe for building a nuclear weapon.[11] By February 2000, some of the largest Web sites in the world—including Amazon, eBay, and Yahoo—found themselves the victims of "denial of service" attacks of the kind we had wanted to describe.

Lured by such creative ideas, Thomas agreed to come join me at *The Standard.* Weber was thrilled; he took a unique pleasure in poaching from the *Journal*. He told me I could expense a welcoming dinner, and so over champagne and excellent food at Gotham Bar and Grill, Thomas and I plotted our future.

Shortly thereafter, I hired Kenneth Li, a reporter from *The Daily News* who had also once been a *Voice* intern. It's a mercenary observation, but I've consistently found that the most fertile places to recruit journalists are operations where there's low morale and a lot of stagnant talent; for better or worse, the *Voice* and the *News* fit the bill. The *News*'s editors took the view that its working-class readership wasn't terribly interested in the Internet and technology, and so Ken's *News* stories usually ended up being chopped to a paragraph or two, when they ran at all. I also liked that Ken was interested in the world outside the Net; a feature story he wrote for *Vibe* about teenage drag-racing in Queens became the partial basis for the hit movie *The Fast and the Furious*. He was later heard to remark that he paid more tax on that Hollywood windfall than he made from *The Standard* in a year.

THE $9 MILLION MAN

One of the things about getting fat is that it goes to your head. Yes, I had been working my butt off, still writing at least three stories a week, plus the occasional feature story, like the one on Boo. But I found that my view of the business world had changed, without my taking the time to notice. This became stunningly clear one summer afternoon. For years, I'd rented a summer house on Long Island with a group of writers and editors; one of the signature activities of this crowd was sitting around the porch on Sundays dissecting the day's newspapers. In this case, it was a Monday holiday, Memorial Day, and *The New York Times* had published a front-page story about how Internet stock options had suddenly made a lot of people in Manhattan rich, at least on paper.

The story was written by Amy Harmon, a reporter I'd gotten to know a little while covering stories. Inevitably, her story featured Dave Kansas from TheStreet.com. TheStreet had gone public earlier that month, and the story said that the paper value of Dave's stock was worth $9 million, which "has in recent days served as a somewhat obsessive topic of conversation in *The Wall Street Journal*'s newsroom, where he used to be a reporter." Asked if he thought he'd earned that money, Kansas, who was thirty-two at the time, said: "I've sacrificed a lot over the last three years. Can I value it at $9 million? I don't know."[12]

This was too much for my friend and housemate Chris Calhoun, a literary agent. "He doesn't know? How could he not know? Of course it's not worth $9 million."

I reminded Chris that Kansas was an officer of TheStreet.com, as well as one of its larger shareholders. It would be irresponsible, and perhaps technically illegal, for him to say in *The New York Times* that the company's stock was overvalued or that he was overpaid.

I couldn't exactly say that the $9 million figure was justified, but I found it hard to say definitively that it was wrong. After all, at that point, the total market value of TheStreet.com was more than a billion dollars. Who's to say that the editor-in-chief of a vastly successful publication isn't entitled to about 1 percent of its worth? Certainly if Dave had been one of Chris's clients, Chris would argue that he was worth more.

My response was, "He's being rewarded for taking a risk. Who's to say how to put a value on risk?"

Chris was simply incredulous: "What risk? He left *The Wall Street Journal* to go work with James Cramer. Where's the risk in that? I'll tell you what's a risk: working in a coal mine. That's really risky, but you don't see anybody saying a coal miner should be worth $9 million."

There wasn't much I could say.

DHARMA, GREG, AND DAYTRADING

But if I'd been sucked into the culture of stock ownership, I was hardly alone. Because stock trading is a place where real-time transactions and economies of scale genuinely matter, it was one of the most obvious areas of change that the Internet had accelerated. By 1999, much of the American public had become familiar with the concept of the "daytrader," the individual who tries to make gains based on short-term developments in the prices of individual stocks. Such people existed in small numbers well before the widespread adoption of the Internet, but the Net and the explosion of on-line brokerages made this into a mass phenomenon. Even the ABC sitcom *Dharma and Greg* featured a daytrading plot.

In reality, though, actual daytraders were never that ubiquitous. My personal estimate is that there were never more than 100,000 individuals who executed multiple stock transactions every business day. And it was always clear to me that the phenomenon was a handmaiden of the extraordinary Nasdaq boom, which died in the spring of 2000; there are only a tiny number of individuals who can use a daytrading strategy to consistently make money in a bear market.

Nonetheless, there are excellent reasons why daytrading became such a powerful symbol of late 1990s America. First of all, a higher percentage of Americans owned stock than at any point in the country's history; most estimates were that, if you included retirement plans, approximately half of American households now owned stock in some form. And you could simply feel it in the air: When I went home to see my family on holidays, the dinner-table conversations that once would have concerned sports, television, or politics were now frequently about buying stock, especially Internet stocks.

Not just the number of people owning stock had changed, but the way they owned it had changed, too. Although the traditional strategy of finding undervalued stocks and holding on to them for the long term will always have important advocates, in the CNBC-dominated era of The Fat Year, it seemed quaint, even moribund. A study produced by the Boston-based consultancy Bain & Co. pronounced the buy-and-hold philosophy essentially dead. In the split-second world of online trading, stocks became hot potatoes: Investors ought to hold on to them for as short a period as possible, lest they drop in value. According to Bain, the average share of Lycos's stock, for example, stayed in an investor's portfolio for just four days.[13]

Even the mammoth, clunky stocks of the buy-and-hold era did not look all that permanent. A share of AT&T—the kind of rock-solid stock that historically middle-class grandparents would pass on as inheritance—was held for just 1.1 years, according to Bain, down from 3.1 years in 1992, and the average share in General Motors for just 51 weeks.

Moreover, the concept of discount stockbrokers had apparently foreshadowed the death of stockbrokers themselves. The original discounters, like Charles Schwab, had been outpaced by a slew of online brokers offering commissions of under $10 a trade: Ameritrade, e*Trade, Datek, Mydiscountbroker.com. This trend was, for many Americans, the very essence of the New Economy: Use the Internet to find out about Internet companies, then buy stock in them—over the Internet. Investors were even encouraged to buy stock in the online brokerages (like e*Trade) that executed the stock trades. (And in the vicious cycle of business publishing, some media outlets had a big stake in the success of these online brokers; when TheStreet.com first filed for its initial public offering in late 1998, a whopping 40 percent of its advertising revenues came from Datek Online, a company with a history of unsavory encounters with the SEC.)

But in business, many innovations carry the seed of their own destruction. For decades, the tobacco industry resisted manufacturing low-tar and -nicotine cigarettes; its top executives feared that sending the message that smoking was unhealthy would lead many people to stop smoking altogether. In a similar way, encouraging everyday investors to execute regular, cheap stock trades over the Internet foreshadowed the death of the stockbroker. During The Fat Year, one began hearing a great deal about electronic communication networks (ECNs), which could match would-be buyers and sellers of stock on-line, and the trade would be executed without the middleman of a stockbroker. Despite skepticism about the viability of such networks, they caught on rapidly—at least during the bull market. By 2001 some 25 percent of all Nasdaq trades (by volume) were executed by ECN.

EVERYBODY WANTS TO BE DRUDGE

There's an argument to be made that, even more than the stockbroking industry, the business being most ripped apart by Internet technology was my own: the media business.

I found myself covering the media at a moment when the Internet had created genuine ferment. In my traditional niche of left and liberal writing, *Slate* and *Salon* in many ways had taken the place, respectively, of *The New Republic* and *The Nation*—often using those publications' same writers. More widely, the Web had created an explosion of unique, sometimes idiosyncratic journalism roughly akin to the rise of the underground press in the 1960s. The best-known apostle of this media revolution was Matt Drudge, who ran a notorious Web site out of his Los Angeles apartment.

Though Drudge had been an important media character for years, he was thrust onto the main stage in January 1998 by breaking crucial parts of the Monica Lewinsky saga. Drudge managed to scoop *Newsweek* on the story it had been developing for months, and one that it knew was a bombshell.

Yet when Drudge's material about Lewinsky first appeared on a Sunday morning, *Newsweek*—which publishes on Mondays—had no way of responding to its own story. It seems impossible to imagine now, but in January 1998, *Newsweek* did not have its own Web site; Newsweek.com did not launch until the following October. (Instead, *Newsweek* scrambled to catch up with Drudge in the middle of that week by placing a story by its investigative veteran Michael Isikoff on the page it maintained with America Online.)

To many, Drudge was a digital gadfly. But to *The Standard,* he was a legitimate business model, albeit on a modest scale. In January 1999, as a result of late-night Web surfing, I broke the story on our Web site that Drudge had begun to accept banner advertising, after years of pledging to his readers that he wouldn't. A year earlier, Drudge had told a court that his only income was the $3,000 a month he received from AOL. Now, as a result of the banners on his site, his advertising agency estimated that he was receiving $2,000 a day.[14] Not bad for a guy with essentially no overhead.

Could others reproduce Drudge's Internet riches? During The Fat Year, it seemed possible. After all, even in the height of Matt Drudge's fame—the summer of 1998—his Web site was only the 228th most visited, according to the Internet measurement firm Media Metrix.[15]

And there were Web sites everywhere, pushing every imaginable form of content. Never before had there been a medium with global reach, no spectrum limitations (as with radio and television), and a start-up cost of a few hundred dollars a year. In San Francisco, a feisty, funny site called Suck.com published several daily attacks on mainstream culture, some funny and frivolous, some quite penetrating. In New York, Feed.com catered to an intellectual crowd with an interest in technology and culture, while Nerve.com aspired to be the thinking person's source for erotica. A generously funded start-up called APB Online believed that there was a sufficient audience for reporting on crime to make a viable business.

Several months after I started at *The Standard,* some of the most dyed-in-the-wool, old-school journalists began abandoning decades of experience in older media for the untamed frontier of the Web.

When I had announced back in the summer of 1998 that I was joining *The Standard*, I got a call from *New York Post* columnist Gersh Kuntzman, who chided me for leaving the world of New York newspapers. Now he was calling for career advice, specifically whether he should go work for a Web-television hybrid called Pseudo.com. Even the industry's most seasoned veterans could not resist the Web's siren call (which of course carried the promise of money with it). APB Online snagged Sydney Schanberg, a Pulitzer Prize–winning journalist who'd made his name at *The New York Times* and *New York Newsday*. In June 1999, Lou Dobbs, probably television's best-known business journalist, left his position at CNN to head a specialized Web site for enthusiasts of outer space.

And like Drudge, these tiny Web 'zines could occasionally have genuine impact. My former *Voice* colleague William Bastone had founded a site in 1997 called The Smoking Gun that published raw documents obtained from court dockets or requests through the Freedom of Information Act. In February 2000, after 23 million Americans watched a bizarre Fox television spectacle called *Who Wants to Marry a Multimillionaire?*, The Smoking Gun dredged up court documents indicating that the program's designated millionaire, Rick Rockwell, had a history of domestic violence. For two consecutive days, The Smoking Gun's site recorded more than 2 million page views.[16] Fox canceled the program, even though it had been one of the most watched television programs of the year. This was a journalistic coup by a Web site so small it didn't have an office.

The Web offered several advantages to media companies, besides merely being nimble. As an interactive medium, the Web could allow a publication to talk to its audience in ways that could not easily be done in print or broadcast media. On one level, this meant that readers could more or less instantly respond to published stories, either by sending e-mail to the writer or by posting a comment on a message board. But the possibilities extended well beyond mere feedback. One promising area of interactivity was in customizing content.

MSNBC had pursued this strategy aggressively. In 1997, the NBC network program *Dateline* aired a program about especially dangerous highways in America. It then encouraged viewers to log on to the MSNBC Web site, where they could enter their ZIP code and learn about traffic fatalities and dangerous roads in their own neighborhoods. Within twelve hours, some 68,000 people visited this section of the site—an impressive number, especially given the overall size of the Web audience at that time. As Columbia journalism professor John Pavlik has written: "Journalism is undergoing a fundamental transformation, perhaps the most fundamental since the rise of the penny press of the mid-nineteenth century."[17]

RISE OF THE WEB, SORT OF

In the spring and summer of 1999, *The Standard*'s Web producer, Matt McAlister, was frustrated. Every week he would read in *The Standard* about how the Web was radically transforming every business in the world. Yet in more than a year of operation, *The Standard* had not turned its own Web site into much more than a news site, and not an especially popular one at that. On top of that, McAlister was beginning to feel like an administrative ping-pong ball; he was now reporting to the third boss since he'd started, and he had waning faith in the company's commitment. A freelance project he'd worked on evolved into a job offer, and so he went to see Battelle, intending to quit.

Suddenly, everything changed. Battelle matched the money McAlister had been offered, changed the reporting structure, and pledged to put a new spotlight on the Web. "I was given free rein to do whatever I wanted, spend as much as I wanted, and hire whomever I wanted," McAlister recalled later. An outside consultant, ModemMedia, was hired to design and code a raft of new web functions. Internally, the Web team would balloon from 3 people in the spring of 1999 to 35 by the beginning of 2000.

Building such a mammoth Web staff was highly risky. Unlike the weekly magazine—which people will pay to subscribe to and advertise in—it was impossible to know for sure which Web strategies would bring in revenues and which wouldn't. Certainly *The Standard* was thinking big. In addition to the obvious function of serving as an outlet for breaking news, and an electronic archive for everything published in the magazine, the Web team had big plans.

One fairly obvious plan was e-commerce. Due especially to its "Metrics" section, *The Standard* had established itself as an authoritative source of information about the Internet business, and the "Metrics" charts, which could be downloaded as PowerPoint slides, became one of the most popular features on the site. (Over lunch one afternoon, Netscape inventor Marc Andreessen told me that the PowerPoint downloads were the single smartest thing *The Standard* had ever done.)

But typically, the attempts to extract a business out of the Web created an administrative logjam. The Web designers believed the information should be available for free. The business development staff insisted this was a necessary revenue source; they wanted to charge a few dollars per download, but with several thousand transactions a week, that could add up to a real sum. The editorial department was worried that the sources for the "Metrics" section would be offended. And no one had tackled the thorniest issue: In almost all circumstances, *The Standard* didn't actually own the statistics it produced for "Metrics." We simply collated numbers that came from the various research companies. Charging for that material raised a fairly obvious copyright issue. After a few weeks of charging for the downloads in the fall of 1999, the site decided to reinstate their free status.

Despite that setback, the company was convinced that *The Standard* could make money by selling information over the Web. And so in the fall of 1999, the company began operating "The Intelligence

Store," a portion of the Web site where readers could purchase industry reports that had been produced by other companies. *The Standard* would get a piece of each sale. Because these reports were ridiculously expensive—often thousands of dollars a shot—this strategy actually generated sizable revenue.

A less successful plan was for online recruitment. As with many trade magazines, writing about who's getting what job where was a very important part of *The Standard*'s formula; it conveniently went hand-in-hand with the magazine's recruitment advertising. Months were spent trying to figure out how to make job recruitment into a Web-friendly business, with little to show.

"GROK" AROUND THE CLOCK

If *The Standard*'s Internet strategy had one thing that could be called a hidden weapon, it was the e-mail newsletters. While *The Standard* by no means invented the idea of sending out its content via e-mail, it did figure out how to make money off of it (at least for a while). The first *Standard* newsletter, a weekly news summary called "Intelligencer," had actually preceded the launch of the magazine.

But the best-known was a daily e-mail called "Media Grok." ("Grok," a made-up word that comes from Robert Heinlein's science fiction novel *Stranger in a Strange Land,* is now actually a dictionary-accepted verb meaning to fully understand something.)

The origin of "Media Grok" is simple: It was a stolen idea that *The Standard* took to a slightly more sophisticated plane. Since 1997, *Slate* had published a daily feature called "Today's Papers," in which a Los Angeles–based contributor, the late Scott Shuger, summarized the biggest stories in the major papers, usually adding quick, snarky comments about individual or collective mistakes. In a conversation with *Standard* contributor Dan Akst, Weber realized that a similar newsletter could be done focusing simply on technology business stories. He contacted Mark Glaser, a freelancer who'd written for him at the *LA Times,* and "Media Grok" was born.

"Media Grok" had two tiny innovations that made it successful. One was that it contained links to the stories that it criticized. This feature might seem negligible outside the fishbowl world of American media. But because of the links, the reporters at the daily papers didn't perceive "Grok" as their competition; they saw it as a way to widen their readership. Almost immediately, we began getting e-mails from beat reporters at the major papers who demanded to know why their stories hadn't been included in that day's "Grok." They were practically begging to be beat up.

Add that to the fact that reporters and editors would send around "Grok"s to their list of contacts, and you have a genuine example of that much-hyped Internet phenomenon: viral growth. When I first interviewed with Weber in the summer of 1998, I remember him boasting that "Media Grok" had just signed up its 10,000th subscriber. A year later, it had more than 100,000 subscribers, a readership that rivaled that of the magazine. Indeed, we sometimes encountered bemused readers who thought that "Media Grok" was the only service *The Industry Standard* offered.

For a few months in 1999, I volunteered to edit and write part of "Media Grok" one day a week. It meant getting up earlier in the morning than I would have liked, but in many ways it was worth it. I would scan the news sites the night before, trying to identify the breaking stories that would obviously be central to the next day's media coverage. This process was repeated the next morning, when I would gather links and choose which stories to promote or lampoon. By the time I filed the final product at around 8 A.M. East Coast time, I felt incredibly well-informed.

Pulling together "Grok" was an ideal way to grasp the seduction of tech stocks that we were offering our readers. I remember well the morning of June 29, 1999, when the Web was flooded with stories that the computer giant Compaq was going to sell its interest in the search engine AltaVista to the Massachusetts-based Internet consortium CMGI (it was announced the following day, a deal of more than $2 billion). The consensus that emerged from my reading was that this transaction could have tremendous impact on the leading interactive advertising firm, DoubleClick. More of DoubleClick's business came from serving the ads on AltaVista's site than from any other source; the assumption was that AltaVista's ad business would soon be taken from DoubleClick and awarded to Engage, a rival advertising firm that was, conveniently, a unit of CMGI, AltaVista's new owner. Since I was doing my work a couple of hours before the stock market opened, I remember thinking: This would be a really good morning to sell short shares in DoubleClick. (I was, of course, prohibited from any such trading by *The Standard*'s editorial ethics policy.) As it happened, DoubleClick stock ended the day up a bit, but because it dropped several points that morning, in a few hours a "Grok" reader with a strong stomach could have made a nice pile of cash.

At the height of The Fat Year, *The Standard* was issuing nineteen e-mail newsletters, most of them weekly. The topics ranged from "Beat Sheet" (covering developments in the online music arena) to "Net Law" to "Food, Web, and Wine." By the end of 1999, *The Standard* had begun hiring staff whose sole responsibility was producing, editing, and mailing out the e-mail newsletters—because though not all of the newsletters were especially well read, the more popular ones were tremendously lucrative.

And this was "Media Grok"'s second innovation: Sell advertising inside the e-mail. One crucial way that advertisers measure the effectiveness of reaching an audience is cost per thousand readers or viewers (abbreviated as CPM): How many dollars will you spend to get a thousand people to see your ad? Despite the ubiquity of CPM in the industry, it's not a definitive measure of anything. (If you're a beef advertiser who's spent money targeting the 300,000 readers of *Vegetar-*

ian Times, the CPM is probably irrelevant.) The usefulness of this sta-
tistic is that it allows for comparisons across different advertising
media: television versus print versus outdoor advertising, and so on.

It follows that advertisers are happy when CPMs are as low as possible, and publishers and broadcast executives are happy when they
are as high as possible. For large circulation print magazines, if you're
getting a CPM of $60–$70, you're pretty happy.

Every day's "Media Grok" carried two or three ads within the body
of the e-mail. In the beginning (and toward the end) of *The Standard's*
existence, those ads were in-house promotions for various aspects of
The Standard's own business. But during The Fat Year, everyone
wanted to be part of "Media Grok." The CPM reached an impressive
$120, and that was for an advertisement in the primitive ASCII for-
mat, rather inelegantly separated from "Grok" text by a series of
dashes.

The other less-than-obvious benefit of the e-mail newsletters was
that they genuinely drove traffic to the magazine's Web site. Almost all
of the newsletters contained links that readers could click on to take
them to a page on Thestandard.com. In the case of the "Daily News"
newsletter (a summary of that day's stories on our site) and a few
others, a surprisingly large number of readers did. By the spring of
2000, a hefty 20 percent of Thestandard.com's traffic came from
people who'd clicked on a link in an e-mail newsletter. And of course
the more traffic to the site, the more we could charge advertisers, and
the more likely it was people would subscribe to the magazine. A comforting circle of synergy had been established.

Compared to the average radio station, television station, newspaper, or magazine, we possessed an amazing amount of information
about a large number of our Web readers: We knew which e-mail
newsletters made them click on which stories, plus how long they
stayed on the site. And we had their e-mail addresses—the kind of
data that makes advertisers drool. During The Fat Year, we genuinely
believed we'd figured Web publishing out. I described the process at

a conference of Web editors and publishers, and one woman suggested to me afterward that *The Standard* should go into the business of custom-publishing e-mail newsletters for other Web sites.

This did not strike me as a stupid idea.

SELLING THE $50,000 COCKTAIL PARTY

Another part of *The Standard* that exploded during The Fat Year was its conference business. Battelle was a consummate networker who'd built a database of thousands of technology CEOs, advertising and marketing gurus, bankers, and media executives. He knew how to call in favors and could thus attract some of the biggest names in the Internet universe to the *Standard*'s conferences: Jeff Bezos of Amazon.com, Meg Whitman of eBay, Jay Walker of Priceline, plus the legions who wanted a piece of their success.

The Standard's conferences were always done with an emphasis on first class: The Internet Summit in 1999 took place at the Ritz-Carlton hotel in Laguna Niguel, California, a resort with a breathtaking view of the Pacific, where the cheapest room is $325 a night. A *Washington Post* reporter sniffed that the Internet Summit represented the technology business in its "full Gatsby-esque" mode.[18]

And the conferences usually exhibited a kind of show-business flair; at the end of one 1999 conference in Aspen, for example, *The Standard* paid for an elaborate fireworks display, more spectacular than any I'd seen outside of Fourth of July in New York City.

Despite the considerable expense of these events, they could be wildly profitable. That's partly because there were enough executives willing to cough up the $4,000 for the ticket. But the real key to the conferences was the sponsorships. Battelle believed every little slice of a conference could be sponsored, from the first morning coffee session to the favor bags that attendees carried away on the last day. During The Fat Year, there was an endless queue of companies dying to spend $50,000 or more to "sponsor" a *Standard* conference cocktail party, which essentially meant they bought the booze and got to hang signs by the door. "We'd get these calls from the larger tech companies," recalled David Evans, vice president of conferences and events. "And they'd say: 'You don't understand. We have to be there. What do we need to get our name in there?'"

Thus, a really big event like the annual Internet Summit could bring in between $2.5 and $3 million, with gross margins as high as 40 percent.[19] In the height of The Fat Year, *The Standard* was hosting eight conferences a year, and the conference staff grew from one person in 1999 to more than twenty a year later.

FIGHT THE POWER!

It was during The Fat Year that I began to notice that *The Standard*'s attitude toward money was beginning to change.

It's not so much that people wasted money; more that they acted as if every problem or challenge was best solved by spending money. The facilities and business staff would often say, "We have more money than time," using our need for rapid growth to justify any particular expense. Personally, I always tried to be frugal and encouraged my staff to do the same. Well, okay, I entertained business sources in some fairly expensive restaurants, but I never flew business class, for example, even to and from London.

But in other parts of the company, freewheeling spending was accepted, or even expected. Sometimes this took grand form. After the Web site relaunched in late 1999, Matt McAlister asked for permission to do something nice as a reward for his team of about fifteen producers and engineers. He was told yes, please do. He asked his supervisor whether he could take them on a ski weekend in New Mexico, "basically as a kind of goof," he recalled later. He was told yes. Joe Walowski, who headed our business development, told several colleagues that it was his personal goal to visit 100 countries across the globe at *The Standard*'s expense. People would roll their eyes when they told you this, but it's not like he was fired for saying it—or trying to do it. (He left the company after visiting a few dozen nations.)

But it's the little instances that are more telling. At *The Standard*'s apogee, it owned thirty-six photocopiers, or approximately one photocopier for every ten employees. Women on the marketing staff complaining about high levels of stress were told to go get a facial and charge it to the company. During a "Net Returns" conference in Aspen in 1999, I spent a lot of time hanging out with members of the conference staff. We all agreed that our maddening expense forms, which for some reason had to be filled out in Microsoft Excel, were too complicated. The conference team, however, had come up with a solution: hiring temps to fill them out.

And then there were the parties. *The Standard* took a lot of flak for throwing so many parties at such an ostentatious level. Some of the criticism was deserved, although what many outsiders failed to understand was that Battelle was serious about making *Standard* parties into a business, a smaller version of the conferences. And, at least during The Fat Year, we succeeded.[20] The reason *The Standard* could afford to give away free booze and snacks on its rooftop every Friday was that companies were lining up to sponsor the rooftop parties at approximately $3,000 a pop. From the marketing staff's point of view, the rooftop parties were an innovative way both to build *The Standard*'s name and to reward key companies who wanted to do business with us.

From the editorial staff's point of view, however, the sponsored rooftop party was a prison sentence. Inevitably, the sponsoring company felt it could use the rooftop party as an efficient way to pitch its corporate message to *The Standard*'s reporters and editors. Since we spent all week trying to avoid the dozens of unsolicited—and usually unwarranted—story pitches from those types of companies, the last thing anyone wanted was further harassment on a Friday night. Sure, the reporters wanted the publication to make money, but many of them felt—not incorrectly—that their cool little staff party had been sold to the highest bidder. Many writers and editors stopped showing up— and if you can't get a journalist to come to an event with free alcohol you've really got a problem. (Later, a compromise was reached whereby sponsored rooftops alternated with those only for staff and friends.)

Thus, the rooftop was a crucible for the clash between the magazine's culture and that of the companies we were supposed to cover. I saw it at full tilt at a rooftop in October 1999. The sponsoring company was a dot-com start-up that sold vitamins and health-care products (at least I think it did; I had never heard of it and no one seems able to recall its name). When I came up to the roof there was a spread of lavish food, including jumbo shrimp, and, of course, the open bar. The company had set up a small table on one corner of the roof and strewn a few of its T-shirts over the ledge; overall, a fairly restrained example of corporate promotion.

The crowd had thickened to the bump-and-pass stage by the time Jonathan Weber got up to the roof; I watched him head toward me and the bar, so I ordered him a Dewars on the rocks. A reporter colleague, Jim Evans, and I were chatting about various things: He'd split up with his girlfriend that week, and we also debated which was the best Pretenders song. After a few minutes, an effervescent female publicist came up to Jonathan and grabbed him by the arm, saying she really wanted to introduce him to the sponsor's CEO. Jonathan made a pained face and reluctantly agreed to talk to him for a couple of minutes. I followed him for moral support.

When that was finished, the same publicist showed up a few minutes later, saying: "Can I introduce you to our head of marketing?" Jonathan made the same face and said: "Um, no, actually. I'm sorry, but I've had a really tough week and I use this party to unwind and to spend some time with my staff." She looked crestfallen.

About half an hour later the sponsor's CEO decided to address the crowd—with a bullhorn. This was such a crass move that even *The Standard* would not have thought of it. He hadn't gotten very far in his pitch when, during a slight pause, I heard a shout from behind me: "Fight the Power!" It was Evans, standing near the bar, ordering another beer in disgust. I was looking at Jonathan: At first he appeared alarmed, then when he saw who had done the shouting, he started laughing. The head of the Web sales team put her head in her hands. The CEO with the bullhorn restarted his pitch from the top.

LOWERING THE STANDARDS

It might seem that a magazine experiencing triple-digit growth in ad pages, renowned for constant parties, and courted by the likes of Time Inc. would be the happiest place in the world to work. The reality, however, is that rapid growth cannot be done without pain, and the editorial side absorbed a lot of pain that summer.

The simple mathematics of the situation nearly slayed us. In April 1999, approximately twelve full-time writers and two executive-level editors filled a weekly news hole of 12 pages and a total editorial well of 36 pages. By July, just three months later, the news hole had grown by 50 percent, to 18 pages, and the overall editorial well to 62 pages. And we still had just twelve full-time writers. The situation was intolerable. We had more pages to fill than *BusinessWeek*, yet we had less than half the staff.

Under those circumstances, we made a lot of compromises on quality. One story I turned in for the "Net Returns" section was intended to run at 2 pages, or a maximum of 2.5 pages. But we ended up stretching it out to 5 pages by sticking in a group of essentially redundant photos: Here's the staff in a meeting! And here's the CEO on the phone! Stories made it into the magazine that had received, at best, a lackluster edit. One seasoned journalist I tried to recruit for the New

York bureau said he respected what *The Standard* was trying to do but thought some of our stories were "sub-wire copy." (At least we never stooped as low as our similarly expanding rivals *Business 2.0* and *Red Herring*. During 2000, both those magazines on a few occasions responded to their growing girth by simply republishing stories from earlier issues.)

One of the most creative ways that *The Standard*'s staff found to cope with its excruciating growing pains was never seen by the outside world. There was a regular internal, Web-based newsletter called *The Substandard*; its motto was "Lowering the Standards of the Internet Economy." In theory, it represented all departments, and no one was meant to know exactly who wrote and edited its satirical items; in practice, it was produced almost entirely by a handful of people in the editorial department. You had to subscribe by sending an e-mail to a not-very-secret address, and when it arrived it would be the URL to a fully developed Web site. The rule was that if you subscribed you also had to contribute. Some of it, like the fashion section, called "Strut," was rather innocuous office gossip, but much of it was wicked parody along the lines of *Mad* magazine.

An obvious *Substandard* target was the nonsensical corporate speak that had begun to envelop our company. One item, entitled "Join Me in Congratulating," managed to satirize ass-kissing, motivational jargon, and inflated job titles all in one go. It was designed as an office-wide e-mail, and began:

> Hi Everyone! Please join me in congratulating Blah Blah on his completely undeserved promotion to Senior Vice Deputy Manager of Editorial Online Sales Development Design for *The Standard*. In his new and expanded role, Blah will be in charge of people who deeply resent the speed of his rise up the corporate ladder, a rise that has no correlation to the time he has spent with the organization. However, because of a competing offer from *eCompany*, coupled with the key corporate intelligence Blah has been

exposed to in his relatively brief time here that would be disastrous in the hands of the competitors, we feel it's high time Blah
was publicly recognized for his efforts re-energizing the brand research redesign conference push and making it a real win-win situation for everyone involved.

Responses were tagged onto the bottom, such as: "Congratulations,
Blah! You're a real team player."

Although *The Substandard*'s humor was usually gentle, at times it
could genuinely shock. One Friday afternoon I received the latest
issue, clicked on the URL, and guffawed at the front-page image. It
was a doctored photograph, almost certainly from *High Times* magazine, depicting two men standing in front of an enormous greenhouse
filled with tall marijuana plants. In a fairly sophisticated bit of Photoshop editing, *The Substandard* editors had replaced the heads on the
photograph with those of John Battelle and Jonathan Weber. I found it
hilarious but also began thinking: If we become a public company,
could we really risk keeping an inside joke like this alive? What
would investors think?

At times *The Substandard* invoked more extreme reactions. In the
spring of 2000, *The Standard* was having one of its constant technology crises. E-mail wasn't working, and the staff was complaining.
During this, Matt Francis, the head of the Internet technology department, was overheard saying, "Fuck it, let's go have a smoke." This
quote ended up in *The Substandard,* and Francis was furious. He confronted Battelle, saying he planned to sue *The Substandard* for libel.
Battelle told him he'd rather lose his technology chief than lose *The
Substandard.* Francis did not stay with the company much longer.

WHAT'S BAMBOO.COM?

There were moments that summer when I was stretched so thin I felt like a walking *Substandard* item. During my later days at the *Voice*, I had come up with a rule of thumb for television interviews: The only TV worth doing is broadcast TV, except for CNN and CNBC. All the other cable channels have audiences that are so small that it's really a waste of time to go to a studio and sit around until you get your three minutes on camera.

I tried to stick to this rule while at *The Standard* but found myself agreeing to appear on smaller cable channels, mostly because the magazine could use whatever East Coast promotion it could get. Our PR firm was constantly trying to cultivate a permanent weekly or even daily relationship with CNNfn. Of course, this was using virtue's makeup to make necessity look good: CNBC already had an alliance with *The Wall Street Journal,* and aside from commenting on individual stories we broke, there was little chance for *Standard* reporters to get on CNBC.

In August 1999, I had agreed to cut short a summer weekend to appear early Monday morning on CNNfn. The publicist told me we'd be discussing IPOs; I told him that I could discuss the state of the IPO market in general, and some specific upcoming Internet IPOs, but that I wasn't an expert on IPOs. He said that would be fine, he'd convey this to the producer.

There are a few rules about television that may or may not be apparent to those who've not been on it. One is that TV needs bodies. It doesn't matter if the on-screen observation is something blindingly banal, like "The IPO market today is a lot slower than it was a few months ago"; they need a body to say it.

That morning, I was the body. Despite what I'd said, the on-screen title they used for me was "IPO Analyst," a stretch of my abilities on a good day. They started asking me about the IPOs of companies I had never heard of. Another rule of television: You can't say "I don't know what that is." You just can't; so you engage in what might charitably be called improvisation. I cringe when I reach this point in the transcript:

> SCHAFFLER: I just love the name Bamboo.com. What do they do?
> LEDBETTER: Bamboo.com is a specialized technology and Internet company that does certain kind of currency exchanges, Internet currency exchanges, I should say, come up with a specialized currency just for the Internet and it's one that people are looking at. I'm not convinced that's an absolute winner.[21]

This was just completely wrong. Bamboo.com was an online real-estate company that specialized in a technology that allowed for 360-degree images on the computer screen.[22] To this day, I really don't know what I was talking about. I was angry at the PR firm for setting me up to look stupid on television, and at myself for saying something I knew was wrong.

The most telling angle of the story, however, is that no one ever bothered to point out my error. Even the people handling the IPO for Bamboo.com (whose stock doubled on its first day of trading later that week) couldn't be bothered to track what was said about the company on CNNfn.

MANAGEMENT FOR DUMMIES

In the late summer of 1999, my frustration with *The Standard* had become acute. When I had been simply a humble writer, most of my contact at the *Voice* was with fellow writers and editors. And for the most part, I always believed that people on the editorial side told the truth. Sure, writers may tell editors they'll turn in a piece on Tuesday that actually comes in on Thursday; editors may tell writers their piece will run at a longer length than it eventually does. Generally, however, there's a sense that you're all trying to reach the same goals.

The unpleasant lesson I learned as a manager is that on the business side, they lie. They lie to get you off their backs, then they lie to cover up their mistakes.

We had outgrown the New York office space allotted for editorial employees on East 52nd Street. As a stopgap measure, we began leasing space from a marketing company across the hall. In the beginning, we used just a couple of desks in the company's main area. But as we continued to grow, we eventually took up almost all of its largest space, forcing a few of the company's actual employees to share a side office. Not only was this obnoxious, but our heavy bandwidth use slowed down their computer network.

We had known for months that the only solution was to find more office space, but the San Francisco executives were addressing this need at a glacial pace. (They of course had more pressing real-estate concerns at home.) Through the summer of 1999, we had been told that *The Standard* was negotiating with our current landlord to obtain a suite on the building's second floor. Yet this lease was held up for weeks by IDG's corporate lawyer in Boston. In the end the two sides couldn't come to terms, and so months were wasted while we continued to work under cramped circumstances.

The reaction of *The Standard*'s San Francisco facilities staff was to begin a search for New York real estate—without telling us. The facilities manager, Sabrina Johnson, came to New York for several days to work out of our office. I thought she was there to pursue the lease for the second floor. I saw her walking by my door one Friday afternoon and began exchanging some pleasantries with her. Then I asked her how the negotiations were going.

"Have you talked to Chris Patelis?" she asked, nervously referring to her boss.

"No. Was I supposed to?"

"You need to have a conversation with Chris Patelis."

"Okay. What's he going to tell me?"

"You need to have a conversation with Chris Patelis."

I didn't know whether to scream or laugh. What kind of juvenile evasion was this? Here was a colleague (part of *The Standard* "team") whose job description included finding and negotiating space for the New York bureau, standing in the office of the New York bureau chief, and she was incapable of disclosing the status of the lease negotiations.

I phoned Patelis and left a voice mail for him. A few hours later, he hadn't responded, so I sent him an e-mail trying to figure out what was going on. He didn't respond to that, either, so I complained to my boss. I found out the following week that, as baffling as Sabrina's behavior was, it wasn't exactly her fault. It turns out that Patelis had specifically given her instructions not to tell me that she had begun looking for real estate elsewhere.

That same summer, I had a similar run-in with Patelis. Our office had grown to the point where the technology glitches were increasing, both in frequency and in seriousness. We called in some local tech consultants from time to time, but they were unreliable and extremely expensive; one guy charged $350 an hour and spent most of his time calling the same 800 number I had called. Again, the obvious solution was to have a full-time information systems (IS) person in the New York office, and after some lobbying on my part, the San Francisco office approved the hire. Patelis himself sent me an e-mail telling me he was "accelerating" the hire.

About six weeks later, I hadn't heard anything about the New York IS hire, so I sent Patelis an e-mail asking him when we could expect to hire the full-time technology assistant, plus one other editorial position he'd told me he was "accelerating." He responded that he had decided not to make these hires. I was perplexed and livid; I dug up his previous e-mail and sent it back to him, asking if he had ever, in fact, "accelerated" the hires. No response. I phoned him and left an e-mail; no returned call.

I had to get Weber to intervene; eventually, we got what we needed.

DOESN'T HERB LOOK LIKE A CFO?

By the fall of 1999, it was no secret that *The Standard* wanted to go public. A *BusinessWeek* article about us said as much, and Battelle didn't deny it. But we needed someone to handle the process, and so in late 1999, Battelle made a crucial hire: a chief financial officer. Battelle found his man in Herbert D. Montgomery, a fifty-six-year-old executive who had most recently served as a vice president and CFO of Cotelligent, a San Francisco–based Internet consulting firm.

Formally, it was always understood that Montgomery's principal task was to coordinate *The Standard*'s public offering. Informally, his role was to be the designated grown-up. Even Battelle's most ardent fans agree that he is not a financial nuts-and-bolts type. His strength was primarily to articulate the mission of *The Standard*; the day-to-day operations of the business were best left to someone else. Montgomery's age and experience—literally the fact that he had gray hair—were his apparent credentials for that role. For weeks after his hire, Battelle walked around saying things like: "Doesn't Herb look like a CFO?" and "Is Herb from central casting, or what?" (As it happens, Montgomery had done some modeling in his younger days.)

These self-mocking remarks were meant to be reassuring. But in retrospect, it's not clear what Montgomery had to offer *The Standard* besides the fact that Battelle thought he looked the part. The publishing industry may not be the most complicated trade on the planet, but it is a distinct business with unique attributes and challenges. Montgomery had little relevant experience with magazine publishing, a shortcoming that was quickly apparent to his colleagues and to *The Standard*'s board.

More significant than Montgomery's lack of publishing experience was the experience that he did have. Prior to joining Cotelligent, Montgomery had been the CFO of a construction company in San Bruno, California, called Guy F. Atkinson. Atkinson had a proud history; founded in 1926, it had cemented its reputation by providing some of the work on the Grand Coulee Dam and the United Nations headquarters in New York. The company went public in 1984—although it was always closely held and thinly traded—and in 1986, *The San Francisco Chronicle* ranked Atkinson as the thirtieth largest business in the Bay Area. As late as 1996, the company's market capitalization was a sizable $125 million.

In June 1994, the company announced that Montgomery had joined as its chief financial officer. Its finances were already teetering. One of its projects, a retirement facility in La Jolla, got embroiled in a nasty dispute involving one of the great early 1990s institutions: the failed savings and loan. The developers then went bankrupt, leaving Atkinson with a debt it claimed was tens of millions of dollars. Another massive project, a pulp mill in Indonesia, was shut down for months by rioting workers protesting inadequate accommodations.[23] Atkinson may have lost as much as $40 million on that project.

Following a spat in which bankers froze a crucial Atkinson account, the company filed for bankruptcy on August 10, 1997—at 10 P.M. on a Sunday night. Atkinson attempted a merger with another construction giant, Morrison Knudsen, but the bankruptcy court would not allow it. In February 1998, Atkinson's assets were sold to a massive construction firm called Clark.

No one would assert that Atkinson's financial failures were solely, or even primarily, the fault of its CFO. At the same time, Montgomery signed off on financial practices at Atkinson that raised quite a few eyebrows among the company's bankers. One partner at Ernst & Young told the court that Atkinson had "been significantly less than forthcoming to me and the banks in providing financial information." He specifically flagged the fact that Montgomery and another official said they had "generated 'internal financing' by not paying trade payables and subcontractors."[24] Essentially, Atkinson's financial strategy in the few months before it filed for bankruptcy was to stiff the people to whom it owed money, to the tune of more than $100 million.

A company like *The Standard* preparing to offer itself up to the public for the first time needed the cleanest possible team. To have the IPO spearheaded by a financial officer with a very recent bankruptcy on his resume would send out a distressing signal to potential investors.

What's remarkable about Montgomery's involvement with Atkinson is that plentiful information about it was publicly available when he was hired (some of the bankruptcy proceedings remain sealed, but the company's saga was well covered in trade publications). Any of *The Standard*'s reporters could have obtained the relevant facts about Montgomery in a matter of minutes.

Yet no one at *The Standard* will say that they knew about Montgomery's experience at the time. The board did not know; Battelle says he did not know. The best explanation that Battelle offers for Montgomery's hire is that he "presented really well," and that qualified, available CFOs in San Francisco during The Fat Year were an endangered species. "Most guys capable of taking [*The Standard*] public wanted to be paid three to four times what I could afford to pay," Battelle said in an interview. "Either that, or they wanted 2 percent of the company. I barely had 2 percent of the company, and that was only in options."

4

We Need More Buckets!

I'm out to redefine business publishing. The story is that we are not a traditional media company. We are a company that understands how to be a media company in this new economy. I go back to the last time a story this big broke, and by that I mean a story that fundamentally changed the economy—of course, that's the period of 1850 to 1950. What happened in business publishing during that period? Time Inc. was created, Reuters was created, Dow Jones, McGraw-Hill . . . all created out of a need for information about a transformative time, when cities rose up, and mass media rose up, and distribution systems were radically altered because of highways and trains and planes. I believe that fundamentally the same thing's happening now: New media companies will rise up, companies that understand how to execute their business models in a way consistent with this new era.   —John Battelle, June 2000[1]

A funny thing happened on the way to *The Industry Standard*'s revolution: We ran out of space. By mid-1999, the home office at 315 Pacific Avenue in San Francisco was getting cramped. By the fall of 1999, with more than 100 employees on board, the building was downright overcrowded. High-ranking executives accustomed to corner offices grumbled as they were asked to share space with colleagues. Engineers from PacBell refused to install more phone lines, citing fire regulations. On the editorial floor, what was once a TV and nap room gave way to desks, as did the hallway space outside the bathroom. The constant human and occasional canine presence gave the floor a distinct funky smell; a *Substandard* joke was that the odor was going to be "spun off as a separate business unit."

To ease the burden, the company began leasing space in piecemeal fashion from buildings in the surrounding area. It made some sense to put entire departments in separate buildings, though everyone recognized that this was a temporary fix. The ultimate goal was a contiguous building, and since *The Standard* was in this game for the long haul, we were in the market to buy.

But then, who wasn't? The explosion of technology companies in San Francisco, the Bay Area, and Silicon Valley in the 1990s created what one property trade association called "unprecedented, unsustainable, hyper-growth." During the height of The Fat Year, the first three months of 2000, the vacancy rate for office space in San Francisco was a minuscule 1.7 percent. Given that a certain number of companies are always moving from one location to another, a 1.7 percent vacancy rate effectively meant that there was no available office real estate within the San Francisco city limits. The aggressive demand naturally pushed prices into the stratosphere; even as late as early 2001, the average asking rent for San Francisco office space was $66.02 per square foot, and the average effective rent was $57.11 per square foot.[2] Those prices were easily 50 percent higher than they had been just a few years before.

But *The Standard* thought it had found the solution. There was a building in San Francisco's Marina District, at 3250 Van Ness, on the eastern border of Fort Mason, that housed about 220,000 square feet on multiple floors. Hearkening back to its purpose in the nineteenth century, it was called the Icehouse. To *The Standard,* it represented a Holy Grail of real estate, one of the precious locations in San Francisco where a company of more than 150 people could hope to place all of its employees in the same place.

Buying a chunk of real estate that large, however, is not like installing a Web server or hiring a reporter. It can take months of negotiations, especially if IDG is involved. To smooth over the nerves of employees tired of working on top of one another, Battelle launched a benefits offensive. From now on, all full-time employees would re-

ceive a free breakfast on Monday mornings, plus snacks throughout
every work day. A massage therapist would be on the premises two
days a week, and everyone was entitled to a fifteen-minute back massage. And the company would pay for personal memberships at a local
gym, provided that employees visited frequently enough (as Battelle
noted, you didn't even have to exercise; you could just check in and
take a steam bath). These moves were hugely popular with the staff.
Some outsiders sniffed that the company was acting like a pampered
dot-com and began referring to *The Standard* as "the country club."
But the benefits were hardly unique. After all, at *Wired*, where a good
number of *Standard* employees had previously worked, back massages had long been a staple, and an in-house chef provided an elaborate discount lunch every day.

WE MIGHT BE GIANTS

As 1999 came to a close, *The Standard*'s recent confidence
had grown ripe; it had begun to look a bit like smugness.
There were plenty of times when the magazine's lead editorial
seemed silently but slyly self-referential. But in the year-end issue of
1999, there was a rare instance where Weber inserted *The Standard*'s
fate into his "Bottom Line" column. "It might seem insane to spend
$7.5 million for a domain name, as the Los Angeles incubator eCom-
panies did last week—the address, Business.com, sold for $150,000
three years earlier—or to spend $2 million for 30 seconds of Super
Bowl advertising, as scads of dot-com companies are doing."[3] (*Might*
seem insane? It did seem insane.) Weber carried on: "But if there's a
global recession, well, we're all screwed anyway. And if there isn't, the
price of getting in the game will probably keep going up."

That sounds an awful lot like a justification of the dot-com madness
from which Weber had always tried to separate us. Weber continued:

"In our own business, for example, we're figuring the advertising will stay pretty strong, and we're working on ways to make the magazine more readable at its new, larger size. The consequences of planning for a slowdown that doesn't happen are just as bad—or worse—than the inverse. . . . Of course, we've got our eyes open to what could be, but we don't really see any reasons to slow down now."

Could this optimism have stemmed from the fact that our stock-option packages had been handed out, and Weber was looking at a possible 600,000 shares in the company? Possibly; I know the first thing I did when I got my package was to divide the number into 1 million to see what price the shares would have to hit to be worth $1 million. But regardless, with more than 200 pages to follow this editorial, who was going to argue with him? Damn the torpedoes!

And giddy optimism was everywhere. In that same issue, I had written the first substantial article about a new project being cooked up by two former *New York* magazine editors, Kurt Andersen and Michael Hirschorn. It was a Web site to be called Inside.com, and they were recruiting top journalistic talent to cover all aspects of the media business: film, music, television, radio, print, and interactive. Like Battelle when he set his original goal of a digital *Variety,* they focused on the fact that most of the media trade publications—*Billboard, Variety, Advertising Age*—were mediocre in quality but charged hundreds of dollars a year for subscriptions. A high-quality Web site, they believed, could take a chunk of business from all of them. They called themselves a "b-to-b" publication and cited as their examples TheStreet.com and *The Industry Standard.* (That was a red flag for me, because I knew that the finances at TheStreet were actually rather dim.) And they had no trouble getting funding for this idea. In an interview with *The Washington Post,* Andersen quipped that getting $28 million in investment capital that year was as easy as "getting laid in 1969."[4]

I was skeptical of Inside.com as a business because the Web market had almost universally rejected any attempt to charge people for

Web content. But I was intrigued with their plans for interactive media data, largely because I'd thought of something similar myself. I had a terrific idea in the late spring of 1999 that I was convinced could make *The Standard* a leading industry brand for decades. (It's still a good idea, and to my knowledge no one is yet doing it comprehensively.) It was very simple: Reproduce the famous *Billboard* chart, except rank digital downloads instead of record sales.

There are a number of ways to code and compress music so that it can be easily transferred over the Internet. By 1999, it was clear that the MP3 format was going to be the market leader for the foreseeable future (despite some well-funded attempts to push rival formats). A single company, MP3.com, had a massive IPO valuing the company at $344 million, even though it had minuscule revenues and no actual ownership of the MP3 format. Sites offering music were attracting millions: In the spring of 1999 Broadcast.com could boast 3.4 million unique visitors, followed by MTV.com's 2.2 million. So everyone knew that millions of songs a month were being downloaded all over the world, and everyone thought they knew that college students and teenagers were doing the majority of the downloading.

But what, exactly, were they downloading? No one knew for sure. That's what I wanted *The Standard* to find out and publish—every week. Of course, you can't track all downloading all across the Internet, but with a reasonable sample from the more prominent MP3 download sites you could produce a respectable chart.

My bosses liked the idea, but they were too distracted with other duties to really put any muscle behind it. The research department pledged some assistance, and we were able to put together a reasonable e-mail list of sites and arrange for regular updates from them about their most popular downloads. We published some partial charts in the summer of 1999 as a kind of first draft,[5] and these charts had some fascinating implications. For the week of July 5, 1999, the most-listened-to band on the popular Web site Listen.com was not some new California punk band or hip-hop act: It was the Grateful

Dead. And of the sites that gave us information about paid downloads, the third most downloaded song was a track from They Might Be Giants, a band that had put out its first album back in 1986. Those did not seem to me to be the choices of today's college students; they suggested that a good portion of the audience for downloaded music was older and more affluent than the stereotype. (Appropriately, the hit track from They Might Be Giants was called "Older.")

But we ran up against one of the classic sticking points of the Internet Economy: The sites considered such data proprietary. Some sites, such as Amazon.com (which was one of the first big sites to feature musical downloads, though they would digitally disappear off one's computer after a couple of weeks) wouldn't give out any information at all. Others were willing to divulge a ranking of their five most-downloaded songs but not to provide the raw numbers; this made comparison between sites impossible. After one or two experiments, we gave up on the idea of the list. In order to make it work, it would really have to be done as a business development project, requiring partnerships and probably cash paid to the bigger sites. But perhaps Inside.com would be able to focus intently enough on such data to make it work.

THE LURE OF CRM

But if mere editorial midgets like Kurt Andersen, Michael Hirschorn, and me could generate overly ambitious Web dreams, imagine what a real visionary could cook up. *The Standard* was never entirely certain how the Internet was going to make our business better and more efficient. Viewed strictly as an advertising vehicle, it probably never did. Yes, we were able to sell a substantial portion of the Web site's ad inventory and fill the larger e-mail newsletters with advertising, but this was not necessarily enough to justify the millions spent on building and staffing the site. As a free-standing business—that is, without magazine content that could be reproduced electronically for free—our Web operation would have been a flop.

But that, a visionary would tell you, is a very narrow way of looking at what the Web does. From the very early days of *The Standard,* when the Web site was unsophisticated at best, Battelle and others realized that it made a huge difference in the way *The Standard* reached out to the world. Every year, American magazines spend untold billions on some of the dullest tasks imaginable: trying to get new readers to subscribe; trying to get current subscribers to resubscribe; trying to get people who've said they'll subscribe to actually pay up. Depending on the publication, even a loyal reader may require as many as six or seven pieces of mail a year to complete a single transaction. And that's the most efficient case; most of those letters end up unopened in the trash.

Theoretically, the Web cuts through the mountain of junk mail. It even reverses the process of finding ideal potential readers; they find you. The vast majority of visitors to Thestandard.com could be assumed to be at least somewhat interested in the content of *The Industry Standard.* So we put up big flashing signs on the home page: "Get 8 free issues!" And people would actually click on them, and some would end up subscribing. Best of all, the site was set up for the customer to pay with a credit card, meaning that we didn't have to pester them with postal demands for checks. One reason why *The Standard* did so few direct-mail campaigns in its first year of existence is that the "conversion rate" of Web subscribers was dramatically higher than the norm for those contacted by mail.

To Battelle, this success was but a seed. He wanted *The Standard* to pioneer what was beginning to be known by the inelegant abbreviation CRM: customer relations management. CRM is a fantasy imagined by direct marketers; it is the notion that a company will possess so much information about the people who want its product or services that it can tailor business offerings down to the individual level.

Battelle had been thinking about CRM for half a decade, at least since a *Wired* cover story[6] had touched on the burgeoning concepts of CRM back in 1994. He never let it go. His pitch went like this: Let's say you're considering starting a high-level, e-mail newsletter about marketing that will also allow its subscribers to attend an exclusive annual conference featuring marketing guru John Smith. How do you find out if there is sufficient demand to make this work? You could reach out through traditional direct-mail methods, but you'll end up spending a lot doing that, and depending on how broadly you've targeted, you may not know more than when you started.

Imagine, though, a database that gives you the e-mail address of every person known to have read a marketing story on Thestandard.com. And the e-mail address of everyone who's ever bought a marketing report through Thestandard.com. And people who've responded to e-mail saying their company spends more than $1 million a year in marketing. And you can correlate those names with somebody else's list in the marketing business. And in the end you've got 10,000 names. You can send a pitch to all 10,000 people, or just a sample of 100, saying: We're thinking of starting this business; the newsletter will cost $15,000 to subscribe to, would you be interested? If two people say yes, then you don't start it. If twenty people say yes, then you start that business, and it's cost you nothing. (Unsurprisingly, Battelle's vision of what *The Standard* was going to become by 2002 included eight to ten spin-off businesses of this type, each of which would bring in a minimum of $1 million a year in revenue.)

Many businesspeople would look at the premise of CRM and say: "Stay away from it; it's pie in the sky." It was part of Battelle's creative energy that his response was: "How did the pie get in the sky? And what if we could make the pie a lot bigger?" Believing in technology at this level is what gets you called a "visionary." To Battelle, always impatient with the present, the impetus to invest in CRM was obvious. If there was one place where a magazine about cutting-edge technology could make a difference, surely CRM was that place. And there were dynamic, growing companies like Corio and Peoplesoft that were all too eager to help us get there.

And to give Battelle his due, he was hardly alone. Nearly everyone in the publishing business was prone to be seduced by CRM—especially those who'd spent tens of millions on Web sites and hadn't figured out how to justify that expense to their bosses or shareholders. In the mid-1990s, every Web publisher believed advertising would allow them to make money. It didn't. So in the late 1990s, they all embraced e-commerce. When that didn't work either, there was a lot of talk about how to "monetize the eyeballs," and that's when CRM became a leading industry mantra.

But to IDG's executives in Boston, the case for CRM was far less obvious. Perhaps this was because they had never fully embraced a Web strategy; their all-title site IDG.net was unambitious at best and lost its potential market position to rival ZDnet. When Battelle would make his pitches to move *The Standard* toward being a CRM-based business, they would politely try to poke holes in his arguments. But during The Fat Year, no one ever said no. Hence Battelle was given a multimillion-dollar green light to follow the CRM dream.

ROADRUNNER, NOT BUGS BUNNY

There were two events in January 2000 that demonstrated just how vast *The Standard*'s world had become. On the morning of January 10, I woke up with a bolt. For reasons I no longer recall, I had set the radio to go off ridiculously early: 5:45 A.M. A bulletin from National Public Radio was just trailing off, something about the new company being run jointly by Steve Case and Gerald Levin. I sat straight up in bed and said: "Holy shit!" AOL and Time Warner merging? No longer did we have to predict to people that the New

Economy would drive the old one: Here it was at the center of one of the largest corporate mergers of all time.

This was an instance where having the right source really paid off. I had a longtime contact at AOL whom I'd known from the days when I was at the *Voice* and he was an editor elsewhere. I knew two things from experience: (1) I could use anything he said as long as I never put his name into my articles in any fashion, and (2) he was a morning guy and would be up right now, just as he had been when I wrote the Geraldine Laybourne profile my first week. I made coffee and sent him an e-mail; he e-mailed right back saying I should phone him.

I was still half asleep, and I actually had a nasty case of bronchitis. I managed to ask some very obvious question about AOL seeking to get its mitts on Time Warner's content. This line of questioning set my source off into a kind of lecture. "AOL doesn't care about content," he declared contemptuously. "It never has and it never will. Any Time Warner content it wants it can buy or trade for."

As the coffee began to kick in, what my source was saying began to make sense. He was trying to tell me that AOL had its acquisitive eyes not on Time Warner's movies, magazines, and music, but on its widespread cable holdings. Why cable? Through aggressive marketing and an ability to adapt to shifting technologies, AOL had managed to dominate what could be called the first wave of Internet use, that is, when the consumer dials in from a computer over a standard phone line.[7] But at the time, everyone who mattered believed that a second wave was imminent, in the form of "broadband" Internet connections. Broadband was something of a mantra in those days. It's a catchall phrase that means any Internet connection that is: (1) significantly faster than the 56k modem speed common in today's computers, and (2) "always on," meaning that the connection doesn't require dialing in.

There are many technologies that can provide broadband access, but the leading contenders in the United States have been via a digital phone line (usually called DSL for digital subscriber line) or a modem coming through the cable television connection. Once using the Internet became as fast and easy as turning on a television, according to the broadband mantra, then e-commerce and music and video-on-demand would skyrocket.

I have long been a broadband skeptic. I believe that the technologies do not work as smoothly as promised, that the companies delivering them do not have sufficient service and marketing skills, and that American consumers have yet to show themselves willing to pay the high price of broadband. But the week the merger was announced, a report from two prestigious financial institutions predicted that 30 million American households would have broadband connections by 2004.[8] Since fewer than 2 million households had high-speed connections when the merger was announced, that projection represented a massive 1,400 percent increase in four years.

For AOL, the growth of broadband was a tremendous potential threat, especially since cable operators were clearly leading the land grab. (Many consumers don't live close enough to a main phone trunk line to get DSL service, and many phone lines in America are inadequate to provide DSL.) AOL had worked assiduously for years with phone companies like AT&T and the regional Bell operators to provide various tie-ins; that's one of the ways it became the king of dial-in access. But it had no comparable relationships with cable companies. That meant that if a broadband provider like AtHome started to become a significant provider of Internet services, it would use its clout to promote its corporate sibling, the Excite portal—and not AOL.

AOL knew it couldn't afford to be left behind in the next wave, and with a market capitalization of about $200 billion, it didn't need to partner with a broadband company: It could afford to simply snap one up. Time Warner, over the years the largest or second-largest cable provider in the United States, was a significant player in broadband, having created the Roadrunner service back in the early 1990s.

There was a teleconference for financial analysts scheduled for early that morning, which I dialed into. I phoned Thomas Goetz at home, and we had a story up on our Web site by about 8 A.M. East Coast time, which was quite a coup. I didn't go to the superficial press conference that afternoon, with its celebrated sartorial semiotics of Steve Case in a tie and Gerald Levin wearing an open collar. I didn't have time, because I was too busy making my own statements to the press. I had my spin: This merger isn't about Bugs Bunny, it's about Roadrunner. I did an on-camera interview for CNN. I was interviewed by Howard Kurtz, the veteran media writer for *The Washington Post*. I gave an interview to the BBC, and I spent at least half an hour on the phone with a producer from ABC's *Nightline*. In the end, I didn't do *Nightline*, but I did go on public television's *Newshour with Jim Lehrer*.

Part of me feels ashamed for not having done more reporting that first day, but quite honestly I didn't have to. (The lower-level people I talked to at AOL and various Time publications didn't know anything anyway; they were too busy trying to figure out the effect on their stock portfolios.) I used to have a self-mocking saying when I wrote for the *Voice*: Reporting is what you do when you don't know what to say. At this point, I knew what to say. I had become the required cyber-sound-bite; I had become a digital pundit.

THAT'S A FUCK-UP

The second January milestone involved our own little corporate funding scheme. There are few assignments in journalism more thankless than the assignment to write about your own publication. Whatever you produce will be scrutinized at a microscopic level. If it makes the publication look good, your colleagues will be convinced that you're a management stooge; if it makes the publication look bad, you could be putting the brakes on your career.

I had some experience of this at the *Voice*, where I wrote about firings at the paper, labor negotiations, and the controversial decision in 1996 to distribute the *Voice* for free. There were times when I thought I would lose my job over what I had written (which to varying degrees had been the fate of my predecessors, the media critics Alexander Cockburn and Doug Ireland).

But media was my beat, and so in January, when *The Standard* announced that it had closed a round of outside investment, it was up to me to cover the story.

It was by no means a great or hard-hitting piece of reporting. It did have one tiny but significant piece of information that was not part of the official announcement: Their $30 million had bought the investors approximately 15 percent of the company. Put differently, that meant our company had been professionally valued at $200 million—not bad for a magazine that was not two years old.

And then, after noting that the company's anticipated $85 million in revenues for 2000 was impressive, I wrote: "Still, *The Standard* faces formidable challenges. Some media observers believe that the spate of dot-com advertising that has fattened *The Standard* and other magazines is a temporary phenomenon. And for the moment, there is an upper limit on how much *The Standard* can charge advertisers. That's because its magazine circulation—about 125,000 readers—is significantly smaller than that of such titles as *Forbes, Fortune* and *BusinessWeek*, which have readerships of 800,000, 944,000 and 1.1 million, respectively."[9]

We posted the story on the morning of January 19, the day that the investment was to be announced publicly. Before noon that day—still pretty early on the West Coast—I got a phone call from Weber.

A little proud of our speed, I said: "The story's up."

"What story?"

"The story about the investment. It's up on the site."

"Already?" There was a pause. "Well, that's a fuck-up. I was supposed to see that story before it went up."

I didn't know what to say. Jonathan had never spoken to me that way before. All I had understood was that there was a priority to get the piece on the site as soon as possible, and that it was to be treated like any other story. Since Jonathan rarely read Web stories before they were posted (especially stories written in the New York bureau), I didn't see where I'd done anything wrong. I transferred the call to Thomas, who actually had thought about this issue and believed Weber should not see the story, because he was an officer of the company we were writing about. There were, in fact, a couple of small things that needed changing, and we changed them, and I didn't have the sense that Jonathan was trying to enforce a particular pro-*Standard* spin. But both of us felt rebuked and had at least a faint sense that our boss was no longer purely a journalist; part of his role now was as a corporate overseer.

WHERE'S DULUTH?

Jonathan wasn't the only one whose temper was being worn thin by stress. There had been a snag in the search for real estate. The owner of the Icehouse was a pillar of the West Coast economy but decidedly pre–dot-com: It was the Levi Strauss clothing company. Having more than a century of business under its belt, it was not about to sell out to some fly-by-night start-up. Levi Strauss demanded that any buyer must have a credit record of at least ten years. It didn't matter if *The Industry Standard* was America's most successful magazine launch in decades; real estate is the ultimate commitment, and we couldn't measure up.

In the end, the Icehouse sold to the up-market kitchen retailer Williams-Sonoma for $80 million. This came out to an astronomical $364 per square foot. Using that measurement, this was the second-largest real-estate transaction during the first quarter of 2000—in the entire country.

Losing the Icehouse was a bad omen. The practical effect for the staff was additional months of working in an overcrowded office, followed by more months of having the San Francisco staff scattered amid half a dozen different locations.

But there was a broader, less tangible sense that maybe we just couldn't pull off what we were trying to do. Too many plans were pulling us in too many diverging directions. And there was considerable glamour attached to being the hottest magazine in America. *Columbia Journalism Review* had named Weber one of a very few "editors to watch" at the end of 1999, and he'd snagged an invitation to the elite World Economic Forum in Davos, Switzerland. Fixing all the little things just seemed so mundane.

For all of *The Standard*'s financial largesse, there were still significant gaps in the quality of our journalism. As New York bureau chief, I considered it a personal failure that we didn't cover the interactive advertising business as well as we might have. We ran some good stories on the topic, but we never were able to land a truly experienced advertising reporter. (I came close twice, but both candidates chose to stay at major national daily newspapers.)

And the publication never completely worked out the bugs in its system. In March I got a disturbing note from James Fallows. Fallows had begun writing a *Standard* column every other week in the summer of 1999, and I knew that Weber considered Fallows's connection to the publication to be one of his greatest coups. In addition to his tremendous experience—Fallows had been the editor-in-chief of *US News & World Report* and Washington editor of *The Atlantic*—he was also something of a geek, and his ability to write seamlessly about technology, politics, and economics was an elegant addition to our pages.

I, too, had been impressed when Fallows started writing for us, though slightly apprehensive. Back in 1996, I had written a negative review in *Newsday* of his book *Breaking the News*; when a reporter asked him about the review he replied that I should "get a life." I had also written some very tough items in the *Voice* about his tenure at *US News*. But when he began at *The Standard*, it was as if we'd been colleagues all along: nothing but mutual displays of respect.

Still, it was unusual for Fallows to contact me, and he clearly wanted to have a conversation that he couldn't have by e-mail. Although he always speaks in very measured tones, I could tell on the phone that he was livid with *The Standard* because of changes that copy editors had made in a recent column. This was the offending sentence: "Over the last year, I have reported on the saga of Cirrus Design, a small manufacturing firm in Duluth, Ga., that is a spunky high-tech startup in the air transport industry."[10]

The sentence is not only not what Fallows wrote, but it's inaccurate: The company is located in Duluth, Minnesota. Dozens of readers, some friendly and some hostile, had e-mailed Fallows upon the column's publication, essentially saying: You've done a year's worth of reporting on this company and you still don't know where it is based?

How had this happened? In his original copy, Fallows had simply written "Duluth." As he explained later, "I assumed that 'Duluth' meant 'Duluth, Minnesota'—after all, Gore Vidal wrote a novel called simply *Duluth*, and that's the one it was about." And the edited version that Fallows had been shown also said merely Duluth. But at the last minute, the copy desk decided to enforce a style rule dictating that all towns must have identifying states unless they're obvious (i.e., you don't have to say "New York, New York"). And without asking anyone knowledgeable, a copy editor then made the curious assumption that Cirrus was more probably based in Duluth, Georgia (population: 22,122), than Duluth, Minnesota (population: 86,918).

This may be a small grievance, but it's not insignificant. Factual accuracy has to be part of a newsweekly's mission. And this was hardly the first time that errors had been inserted into writers' stories. My reporters and I complained about the problem constantly; Fallows himself said this had happened to him three or four other times in less than a year.

And thus for want of a rational system that allowed writers to see the final version of their stories, we were on the verge of losing our star columnist. I asked Fallows if he wanted me to speak to Weber on his behalf, and he agreed. I didn't have to explain the gravity of the situation to Weber; he immediately made apologetic noises to Fallows and crisis was averted. Some pressure was put on the copy editors, and they came up with an improved scheme, but the copy desk still refused to say it would allow reporters to sign off on the final version of their material.

YOU GET WHAT YOU PAY FOR

Other screw-ups had more serious consequences. Just as I had had my battles with PR companies, my deputy, Bernhard Warner, was known for the occasional testy phone call. We created a mock competition between us to see who could get the most PR people fired or taken off accounts. I resigned from the contest in awe, however, after one of Bernhard's stories led to the firing of *The Standard*'s own PR firm.

Beginning in the fall of 1998, *The Standard* had begun working with Middleberg & Associates, a medium-sized firm based in New York that represented a large number of dot-com media companies, including CBS MarketWatch and MTV Interactive. Because I was in New York, I had met with the staffers who handled our account, and I liked them. To assuage my fears about conflicts of interest, they had promised me they wouldn't pitch me stories about their other clients. They routinely violated that policy, but I didn't mind too much because I needed to talk to some of their companies, and I found it as easy to say no to them as to anyone else.

Internally, *The Standard* had mixed feelings about Middleberg. Weber had an intrinsic dislike for just about anyone associated with PR, and so he had complaints about Middleberg. John Battelle's wife, Michelle, had worked in and around PR and had some firm views about how things should work; I think she made the people from Middleberg pretty unhappy at times. In an offhand remark to me in early 1999, Battelle himself said of Middleberg, "You get what you pay for," implying that we would get a better PR firm when we could afford one.

We hired our own PR person, Alissa Neil, in the fall of 1999; she, too, had been a colleague of Thomas's and mine at the *Voice*. But the PR burden had grown to the point where the company felt it needed an in-house PR staff and an outside agency. We were shelling out as much as $20,000 a month to Middleberg in fees and expenses.

We had a weekly telephone call arranged for Fridays in which we would brief the Middleberg publicist on the stories from the upcoming issue that we thought had the most potential to get picked up by other media. That way, the publicist could begin making phone calls on Friday, and we could get a jump on the following week's news cycle.

Bernhard had written a terrific story—months ahead of its time—about Webhouse, the discount service started by the boisterous founder of Priceline, Jay Walker. At its base, Webhouse was nothing more than an online coupon-clipping service, but like so many of Walker's ideas, the seduction was in the marketing: Shoppers could "name their own price" for all their everyday supermarket needs. Typically, this meant that on selected grocery store products shoppers could save between 30 and 50 percent. The allure was obvious and had won the company some amazing publicity; a *New York Times* writer dropped any pretense of objectivity and simply gushed: "I loved it."[11]

Bernhard tried the service out at his local grocery and confirmed that, from the consumer's perspective, Webhouse worked well and provided significant savings. But Bernhard was smart enough to know there's no such thing as free groceries. Thus he asked a simple question that had somehow eluded everyone else who had covered Webhouse: Supermarket profit margins are notoriously thin, so if the Webhouse consumer is getting discounts of 50 percent or more, who is making up the price difference?

Jay Walker gave him a response: It's the grocery manufacturers themselves who subsidized Webhouse's customers, in return for important demographic information. It was a plausible answer; such manufacturers have historically spent billions on coupons to get a select number of consumers to try their products at a discount or loss.

But which manufacturers had actually signed up? Bernhard contacted the eight top consumer manufacturers: Unilever, Kraft Foods, Coca-Cola, Procter & Gamble, Kimberly-Clark, Johnson & Johnson, General Mills, and Colgate-Palmolive. Six denied that they had made a deal with Webhouse and two declined to comment. Walker's company insisted that it had signed up major manufacturers, but it declined to provide Bernhard with the name of a single one.

This made for probably the toughest early piece written about Webhouse, although it was eminently fair; if anything, Bernhard and I felt that the story's final edit probably didn't do enough to spotlight the hole in Webhouse's business model that we had identified.

But that's in part where the publicist can make up the difference. When we had our next telephone conference with the Middleberg publicist, we made it clear that we felt we had a juicy story about Webhouse. We assumed that he would follow up on this and that at least someone would pick up on Bernhard's diligent reporting.

Instead, about five minutes later, Bernhard got a phone call from a different Middleberg publicist, who also happened to work on the Priceline account. This was a surprise, because Bernhard had not had any contact with her in weeks. She was nervous—on the verge of tears, Bernhard said—and peppered him with anxious questions about just how negative his story was. Bernhard, who'd cut his teeth as a cop reporter, wouldn't budge.

Ten minutes later, Bernhard got another phone call, this time from Kevin Goldman, a former *Wall Street Journal* reporter who had become Priceline's in-house PR person. Again, Goldman and Bernhard had not spoken for days, but now he demanded to know what Bernhard had written. Bernhard told him the story was fair, the reporter's equivalent of giving his name, rank, and serial number, but nothing more. In minutes, the Middleberg publicist called a second time, asking more questions. Bernhard asked her if she'd spoken to Goldman; she denied it, but unconvincingly.

I was dumbfounded. In addition to violating an obvious understanding of confidentiality, Middleberg had actually diluted the power
of our story by giving Priceline more than forty-eight hours to figure
out what kind of spin it wanted to use to refute *The Standard*'s story. I
immediately let Weber know what had happened; he was even more
angry than I was. We'll never know with absolute certainty that Middleberg publicists leaked our details to their client, but the coinci-
dences were too much for us to handle. Not long after this incident,
Middleberg ceased to represent *The Standard*.

DON'T LET IT FALL INTO THE WRONG HANDS

A man rushes to catch an empty elevator. As it goes up, he
pulls out a copy of a magazine and begins reading it; it is an
issue of *The Industry Standard*. He begins to feel the presence of the
elevator's security camera and backs up out of its range. Then he
whips out a can of spray paint and blackens over the camera's lens. A
voice-over says: "Read it. Learn from it. Don't let it fall into the wrong
hands. *The Industry Standard*: your weekly intelligence report on the
Internet Economy."

This was one of three television commercials that *The Standard*
began airing in April 2000. As freestanding ads, the spots were
creative, cheeky, and well-produced, from the ad agency TBWA/
Chiat/Day. They captured the sense of insider knowledge that was
making us irresistible to a certain class of reader.

Yet it's debatable whether it makes sense for small- to medium-sized
magazines to advertise on television. When they do, most such publications buy time on cable stations, which are relatively cheap because
they rarely capture more than 1 percent of the viewing households.
These advertisements often use a tailored deal, whereby the fee that
publications pay to the cable channel depends on how many subscription orders the ad attracts (a unique toll-free number is used for

the TV spot so that the number can be precisely measured). To me, it made no sense for *The Standard* to have advertised on television without even telling viewers how to subscribe. (The closest the spot came to a "call to action" was giving the Web address.)

But it was all done in the name of brand-building, perhaps Battelle's strongest professional belief. It was like a virus: There was so much social and professional overlap between the people on *The Standard*'s business side and the executives of erstwhile billion-dollar companies who advertised with us that inevitably dot-com spending habits infected us. One of the more ironic tenets of the dot-com ad boom was: You had to be outdoors. And so beginning in April 2000, *The Standard* sponsored an electronic ticker billboard overlooking the incoming lanes of the Bay Bridge. Every morning, commuters coming into San Francisco could see news briefs from the Internet business right next to a massive masthead of *The Standard.* Until we bought the space, it had been used to show the size of lottery jackpots. Now, we were the jackpot.

For time-zone reasons, it made sense to program the news headline out of the New York bureau; that way we could guarantee the most topical news items. Hence, one of the duties assigned to my staff was to program a headline into an ancient, DOS-based PC that would then run continuously 3,000 miles away. Sometimes this was done so early in the morning that we figured no one was seeing it. Often it didn't matter what we programmed into the PC, because the sign didn't work about 20 percent of the time.

Battelle considered these purchases a marketing coup. Sure, the cost was high. The television spots cost as much as $5 million to produce and air; about $1 million of that went to produce a video about the making of the spot,[12] which was intended to boost staff morale. The bridge billboard cost the company another $1 million.

But we had the money to spend, and we intended to keep on spending it. For fiscal year 2001, *The Standard* had budgeted a breathtaking $7.5 million for corporate marketing. Of that, $1.8 million was scheduled to go to payroll—enough to employ twenty people with an average salary of $60,000 a year, plus benefits.[13] The public-relations budget was even more top-heavy; of the $1.26 million budgeted for fiscal year 2001, nearly half was meant to go toward payroll. Another $108,000 was budgeted for travel, and $170,000 was for the preparation of PR kits, stationery, and other "collateral" material. If *The Standard* was a principal beneficiary of the boom in dot-com advertising, it was also in some ways its victim.

PARTIES AND PICKET LINES

The *Industry Standard*'s second anniversary party was an extravagant affair held in San Francisco's massive City Hall. Each floor featured a different luxury buffet, with jumbo shrimp and bays of fresh oysters. Not one band but two performed, each in a separate wing of the cavernous building. The guest list had 2,500 names on it; an additional 5,000 people had requested tickets but were told not to show up—by e-mail, of course. Ironically, because this was The Fat Year, the anniversary party was not necessarily the hippest ticket in the dot-com world that evening. At a nightclub called Ruby Skye, Elvis Costello and Nick Lowe performed at a party hosted by the search engine AskJeeves.

The Standard was one of the biggest publishing success stories in years, and the signs of self-congratulation were everywhere. Yet not everyone was happy. Weber recalled meeting Pat McGovern's wife at the affair, who noted that none of the signs or banners mentioned IDG. "Why wasn't IDG acknowledged?" she asked the editor. There was no honest way to respond.

Another milestone of self-congratulation that spring was an event in New York that became known, rather pompously, as the Media Summit. The idea had been hatched between Weber and Michael

Wolff, who wrote the media column for *New York* magazine. They had wanted to do a conference in a place that was swankier and more intellectual than some soulless midtown hotel, and so they settled on New York's Museum of Modern Art (MOMA). This choice created enormous difficulties for the conference staff, which quickly discovered that its usual way of making money on such events—corporate sponsorship for every moment—would not be allowed. MOMA—can you believe it?—considered itself a fine arts institution and had strict rules about allowing indoor billboards to be hung. The conference team wanted us to move the event, but Weber stood firm. In order to make money on the event, we would simply charge attendees some ridiculous amount, like $1,200 apiece.

Working with Michael Wolff is not for the weak of heart. He was creative, smart, and very plugged in, but he has little sense of follow-through. We'd be planning the panels, and Wolff would say: "Do you know who would be perfect for this? [Time Warner chairman] Gerald Levin. We should get Jerry Levin." And Jonathan and I would respond, "Uh, yeah. He'd be great." Then Wolff would turn to me and say: "Do you know him? I know him. I'll call him." Inevitably, in a meeting two weeks later, Wolff would admit that he'd not made the call. At times you couldn't tell if the purpose of the meetings was to plan the sessions or to give Wolff an opportunity to brag about his formidable Rolodex. (To Wolff's credit, we did get top people to commit; we had Michael Armstrong from AT&T, Arthur Sulzberger, Jr., of *The New York Times,* and Charlie Rose to do a wrap-up.)

Because I was in New York, Weber in San Francisco, and Wolff in a world of his own, it fell upon me to reach out to a number of the potential speakers. Never again will I spend that much time sucking up to Martha Stewart. As a reward, I was scheduled to do an onstage interview with Henry Louis ("Skip") Gates, Jr., one of America's leading literary critics and arguably the most prominent African-American academic.

I'd helped organize some events like this before, primarily in politics, and it's an unpleasant task, an endless maze of PR people, assistants, and assistants to PR people all asking the same questions that you've already answered: How long does s/he have to speak? Do we need to submit text in advance? Does s/he have to be there the whole day? And, most important: Who else is definitely coming?

I remember going through all of this trying to get Steve Case to commit to us. Normally, I'd say AOL press people would return about one out of every three or four of my phone calls. I don't think that was because I'd written something that made the company especially angry; it's just a very aloof organization. The essence of its press strategy was to talk to Kara Swisher at *The Wall Street Journal*; everyone else could fend for themselves.

But now, with big names on board with the Media Summit, and Case very much at the top of the invitation list, my calls were getting returned. Indeed, the publicist tried to hit me up for a ticket for herself (the correct response: You get me Case, and you can have all the tickets you want).

I liked the notion of having access, though it's not as if I was getting any actual inside information. And I had to ask myself: If someone came to me right now with a story that put AOL in a bad light, how much incentive would I have to pursue it? I hated that feeling and resolved to remove myself from any future conference planning.

That, however, was not the worst of it. A few days before the Summit, some of the unionized workers at MOMA voted to go on strike. This meant that all of our attendees and speakers would be forced to cross a picket line. And this wasn't just any union: It was Local 2110 of the United Auto Workers. I had been a member of that very union when I worked at the *Voice*; for several years I was even a shop steward.

The Media Summit had involved months of planning, and it was far too late to find an alternative venue. I felt awful, but I knew I had to tell Skip Gates so he would have fair warning. To my surprise, he didn't hesitate at all. He didn't want to cross a picket line, but he also said that this was too important an audience for him to pass up. I walked away from that conversation and said to myself: "You sure earned your thirty pieces of silver today."

Of course, we had our excuses. We weren't, after all, encouraging anyone to go into the museum itself; we were having a private event in a room that was adjacent to the actual public museum. And we promised to give the union members a few minutes on stage to explain to the attendees why they had chosen to strike.

But I couldn't help feeling like a heel. It was bad enough that I had decided I was willing to cross a picket line. The worst part was that I had become so immersed in this glittering world of online media that I hadn't heard anything about the strike and didn't know what the issues were. I felt still more guilty when my former colleague Bill Bastone, who edited The Smoking Gun Web site, regretfully said he couldn't attend; as a *Voice* staff member, he was a member of the union and could not cross the line. Quite unexpectedly, Inside.com cofounder Kurt Andersen also declined to show up, citing union pressure. Deirdre Hussey, a onetime *Voice* intern of mine who was now doing publicity for *The Standard,* refused to work that day. (I had recruited so many *Voice* people that there were no fewer than five former members of Local 2110 now on *The Standard*'s payroll.)

As it happened, I had to be at the museum at about 7:00 A.M. Since the museum wasn't open to the public until 10:00, there was no picket line, not even anyone handing out leaflets.

HOW FAT IS TOO FAT?

And through it all, the money kept pouring in. On the macro level, on March 9, 2000, the Nasdaq composite index hit 5000 for the first time in its history, a gain of nearly 50 percent in just six months. On the micro level, my bonuses were more or less automatically paid, and I got a raise in the fall of 1999. Reasonable but generous expenses were reimbursed, no questions asked. The New York bureau was scheduled to move in the spring of 2000 into a beautiful, large space that I had helped choose on a stylish Soho block. I had a package of stock options that I reasonably believed would have a six-figure value when the company went public. Indeed, when *The New York Times* contacted me about a possible job, I stopped the interview process, in part because I'd have to take a pay cut. I bought a car—well, half a car, split with Linda—for the first time in my life.

And meanwhile *The Standard* wasn't just expanding, it was exploding. In the spring of 2000, the magazine took the unusual step of capping the number of advertisements it would accept for each issue. With the issues running well over 200 pages every week, media observers were running a small competition trying to figure out how best to describe our absurd girth. Some press critics would weigh a copy of each issue, and we were described alternatively as "a phone book" and "thick as a fashion magazine and heavy enough to shatter a plate glass window." My favorite was "a personal defense system"—that is, if you rolled the magazine up it made a formidable truncheon.

I always maintained that no one wants a 300-page weekly magazine; it arrives in the mail, and it's too intimidating to read, so the reader puts it aside. Within a few days, another one arrives, and suddenly you've got a magazine that's too big to digest. Although advertisers were the sole cause of our obesity, they resented it, because they feared their message would be lost in the bulk.

And so, paradoxically, our ad sales staff determined that if we didn't maintain a consistent ratio of 60 percent editorial to 40 percent advertising, we would actually lose advertisers. (There was a more practical reason as well to limit the page count of the magazine: Our printer could no longer handle the size of the issues.) The psychology of running a hot magazine is thus like controlling the velvet rope at a trendy nightclub; the fewer people you allow inside, the harder everyone else will try to get in. One San Francisco–based advertising executive joked that *The Standard* "can walk around town with a wheel-barrow and have insertion orders thrown in. . . . [I]f the worst problem is having too many advertisers, I'd say they have the best problem in the business."[14]

Indeed, it seemed that no matter what *The Standard* did that might impede or drain its overall business, the print ads kept pouring in. In the fall of 1999, *The Standard* raised its "rate base" (the number of readers a publication guarantees to advertisers it will reach) from 100,000 to 125,000, with a corresponding boost in advertising rates. That didn't dent the number of ads that ran in the magazine.

Even when the Nasdaq began to crater, the advertising kept flowing. On Monday, March 13, the Nasdaq composite fell 150 points, to 4907, and by early April it was down to 4224. The Nasdaq index represented, actually and symbolically, a good portion of our advertising base. But the companies kept spending. Our smallest issue in April 2000 took in nearly $2.2 million in advertising, and one issue almost hit $3 million. The following month had five issues, all of which were more than $2.5 million apiece, and two of which topped $3 million. That month, even though the revenues from online sales and conferences were below the forecasts made for them three months before, the publication's overall revenues were well above forecast. The operating profit for that month had been projected at $100,000. Instead, it was $3.1 million—all because of print ad sales.[15] Even given seasonal fluctuations in the advertising market, *The Standard* was well on its way to breaking $200 million in its second full year of publishing, with a hefty profit to boot.

And so what do you do when the money is coming in faster than anyone can count it? You expand. If one magazine is too puny to handle all the companies who want to advertise in it, you split it into multiple magazines. Weber and I, among others, had been talking about different ways to expand *The Standard.* My idea was to follow the way that *AdWeek*, one of the leading publications of the advertising trade, had split itself in the early 1990s into *AdWeek*, *MediaWeek*, and *BrandWeek*. In a memo, I argued that *The Standard* could split into four: *The Business Standard* (focusing on business applications); *The Media Standard* (focusing on the Internet's role in media, advertising, and marketing); *The Retail Standard* (focusing on e-commerce, both in start-ups and in traditional businesses); and *The Industry Standard* (which would function in some ways as a "greatest hits" collection from the other titles and continue to cover technology, telecommunications, and important developments elsewhere).

This was a superficial suggestion; obviously splitting the magazine into four would multiply production and postage costs. Admittedly, it was also self-serving; if my superiors liked this idea, I was going to argue that *The Media Standard* should be based in New York and edited . . . by me. Battelle's brief response to my memo was to endorse the idea of emphasizing "verticals," the jargon du jour for concentrating on a single topic.

What the company came up with was a monthly publication called *Grok.* The idea was based on something *The Standard* had already been doing: On a regular basis, it would publish a "special report" on a single topic, such as the role of the Internet in health care, travel, advertising and marketing, and the like. Because these were scheduled months in advance, the ad department could sell to businesses in those fields; during The Fat Year the special reports became huge moneymakers. Essentially, the idea behind *Grok* was to isolate the special reports and make them into their own magazine. Hence, the first issue of *Grok,* to debut in September 2000, was devoted to the entertainment industry, the second to education, and so on.

Like too many magazine ideas cooked up by already-successful publications, the motivation for *Grok* seemed entirely ad-driven. And in fact, Battelle had told people that we were creating it "because we need another bucket," adopting the lingo of IDG without any apparent irony. In retrospect, *Grok* seems like a profoundly stupid idea. The newsstand is a jungle of competition, and magazines must be able to communicate what they're about in a fraction of a second. That's hard enough to do when your magazine's theme is the same with every issue. If you're a brand new magazine with a nonsense word for a title, and a different theme for every issue, the task of communicating with would-be readers is essentially impossible.

Battelle would later insist that his plan for *Grok* was misinterpreted and that he never intended it to be a separate publication. But that was not Fat Year thinking.

In addition to *Grok*, the *Standard* planned to launch a magazine called *Build*. Although its content would almost certainly be duller, *Build*'s concept at least made some sense. Again, it was a spin-off of a section of *The Standard* that had been added in the fall of 1998 called "Net Returns." It highlighted very specific applications of the Internet that allowed companies to achieve greater efficiencies.

GLOBAL DOMINATION

It wasn't just *Grok* and *Build*. *The Standard* had signed an agreement with Inside.com, the Web site I'd written about at the end of 1999, to produce a magazine based around the site, and there were rumors we'd do the same for TheStreet.com. Suddenly printing on paper was hip again, and everybody was trying to get in on The Fat Year's ad bonanza. *The Standard* was to be their ticket.

And finally, the publication was truly committed to expanding internationally. The company signed a license with InfoPro, a publishing firm in Taiwan, to produce a weekly, Chinese-language publication that would launch in the fall. Similarly, *The Standard* made an agreement with the Jasubhai Group in India, which planned an English-language publication to launch at the end of 2000. In Israel, there were protracted negotiations with *Ha'aretz*, one of the nation's most respected daily newspapers, for both a print publication and a venture with its Web site, called Themarker.com. Weber would frequently say, in a semi-joking way: "Our goal is global domination."

And I would have a role in that, partly as an unexpected coda to the Boo.com story. Although I had been frustrated with the decision back in the spring of 1999 not to put Boo on the cover, in subsequent weeks I was thankful. Boo's launch date came and went. The ad campaign that I'd seen previews of began appearing on television (the spots were directed by the son of Francis Ford Coppola) and in glossy fashion magazines, even though there was no Web site yet for potential customers to buy from. The company wasted millions of dollars that way. Hugh Garvey was allowed to spend more than $1 million producing a single issue of Boom before that project was abandoned; he left the company and came to work at *The Industry Standard.*

Over the summer I met again with some of the top Boo staffers over dinner at a ridiculously trendy restaurant in Manhattan's meat-packing district. After several glasses of the signature Boo beverage—vodka and grapefruit juice—I began lecturing them about their site. They simply had to launch something, I argued, because they were damaging their reputation with the constant delays. This was unusual advocacy on my part; I suppose I felt burned by the fact that my story had been a relatively favorable account of a firm that was rapidly becoming the poster child for Internet excess.

Needless to say, they did not take my advice. The Boo site did not launch until October, by which time *The Standard*'s newly placed London correspondent, Polly Sprenger, had already done a piece asking where the hell the site was.[16] There was quite a bit of excitement in our New York office that afternoon; a friend who worked for a Net start-up sent me a note saying the site was the coolest thing he'd ever seen. I decided to give it a test drive by buying a pair of black Converse high-top sneakers. The experience was disastrous. The site had difficulty processing my order; I had to enter it several times, and just as often the screen would simply freeze. I tried calling customer service, repeatedly, and found that just as dysfunctional. In the end, it took more than an hour to place my order, and I still had to wait days for the shoes to show up. I wrote a merciless, minute-by-minute account of this experiment, which we posted on the Web site that afternoon. That was the last time I wrote about Boo.com.

But when I had come back from my initial trip to London back in the spring of 1999, I was convinced that *The Standard* needed a UK edition, and it needed it yesterday. I can remember taking Weber to a Knicks playoff game around that time and talking with him after the game in a bar. Fueled by London enthusiasm and an evening of beer, I made the case for a UK edition. This must have stuck in his brain, because in March 2000, he phoned me and said: "This is going to seem like it's coming out of left field, but do you have any interest in working out of London?" Michael Parsons was going to be moving back to the UK to work on a London-based version of the magazine, and the publication was planning a fall launch.

When I mentioned this offer to my girlfriend, Linda, she got very quiet; it was quickly clear to me that she was not keen to move to London. She had two principal reasons, both of which I understood and respected: (1) She held a very prominent position in the American book publishing industry and was unlikely to find a comparable slot in UK publishing; and (2) she would be moving to a city away from her family and friends, meaning that while I worked long hours to launch the European edition, she would be stuck at home knowing virtually no one. Without Linda's assent, I felt I couldn't make the move. I resolved to tell my bosses thanks, but no thanks.

But as I thought more about it, I realized I could be denying myself opportunities that don't come along too often: a move to London as a highly paid writer and editor, and the chance to run my own magazine. I began to think about compromises: What if I told *The Standard* I would do the job for a limited period of time? And what if I promised Linda that we'd see each other in one city or another every few weeks?

So that's what I did. I pledged to *The Standard* that I would give them eighteen months in London, or one year from the launch, whichever came first (part of me didn't believe we could actually get an edition out in the early autumn). I asked for a raise, increased stock options, and the title of editor-in-chief, all of which I got. Linda was hardly overjoyed with my decision, but she agreed that the job was too good to pass up.

It was part of my brilliant timing that I would be leaving for London just around the time the New York office was moving into its flashy West Broadway digs. The night before we moved out of our space on East 52nd Street, someone broke into the office across the hall where we had been leasing space and stole several computers. The building had a fairly advanced security system, and thus there was a lot of speculation that it was an inside job, though there was never any proof of that.

After more than a year and a half, I finally had the office I'd always craved. It was huge, with a window, plenty of file cabinets, drawers that locked, a big desk, lots of bookshelves, a phone that worked (well, sometimes). By the time it was finished, there was no time to move in; I never bothered to unpack all the boxes, because in a few days I had to move to London.

Flying Blind into Europe

I think there is a broad consensus in the Internet industry that the next big phase of growth will be in Europe. Some of these countries have thrown off the shackles of very strong regulatory governments and are now allowing the kind of telecommunications mobility that can make the economy really hum.

—Me, quoted in *The New York Times,* April 11, 2000[1]

The Hotel Arts in Barcelona is forty-four stories high and towers over the skyline of that charming Catalonian city. Sumptuously decorated with classic works of Spanish art, it is said to be the most expensive hotel in Spain. The hotel was the centerpiece of a waterfront renovation completed in time for the 1992 Summer Olympics, and everything about the Port Olimpic brims with uplift and optimism. In the hotel's shadow is the luscious, palm tree–lined beach called Platja Barceloneta, and nearby dozens of luxury yachts are moored. Most striking is a giant outdoor copper sculpture that glistens in the Mediterranean sun. Created by the American architect Frank Gehry, the work is officially entitled *Pez y Estera,* but it is better known for what it depicts: a huge, abstract, headless fish.

In May 2000, this was the setting for *The Standard*'s "Global Internet Summit," the first conference that the publication had organized outside of the United States. The Summit's goals were serious enough: *The Standard* was trying to take seriously the notion that the Internet, while still predominantly American in usage and content, would soon be a genuinely worldwide phenomenon. Battelle had issued a canned statement noting that by 2005, one-third of all Internet users would come from Europe and a quarter from the Asia-Pacific region. (There was a more calculated business goal as well; Battelle's statement also noted that the Summit was "setting the stage for future *Standard* ventures worldwide.") Entrepreneurs and investors from around the globe were invited to trade ideas and experiences. Former Israeli prime minister Shimon Peres was scheduled to deliver a special address.[2]

But if the conference had high-flying aims, it had absolutely stratospheric costs. Battelle booked a penthouse suite for himself, in which he hosted a reception where guests were treated to free cocktails and canapes; he apparently had a better room than John Travolta, who was staying at the Hotel Arts at the same time. More than forty members of *The Standard*'s staff attended the conference, most of them flying business class from San Francisco. The lineup included Chief Financial Officer Herb Montgomery (who surely should have been back home sorting out the planned IPO) and, inexplicably, two people from the publication's human resources department.

The attendees were treated to some of the city's most prized sites. The mayor of Barcelona hosted a formal reception in the city's Town Hall in a vast, vaulted chamber. In the room were several people painted ivory white and draped in outfits of red silk, standing still as statues. After a few minutes, this tableau vivant came to life, and the statues ran through the room. Meanwhile, four men began scaling down the walls on ropes, scattering rose petals onto the astonished crowd. What did any of this have to do with the Internet Economy? As one attendee recalled: "It was *Caligula*."

Not surprisingly, these displays of excess translated to the European audience not as evidence of *The Standard*'s power or wisdom, but as a kind of tacky cultural imperialism. Battelle did not help matters by insisting on dressing casually when he addressed the crowd—he did not even bother to wear socks—and by giving an improvised speech congratulating the attendees on how well they had "partied" in Barcelona. "I spoke to a Swedish woman after Battelle spoke," recalled Michael Parsons, who had just moved back to London to work with me on *The Standard*'s European edition. "She was appalled. To her he looked like a brash kid who didn't know shit."[3]

But that wasn't the moment in Barcelona that scared Parsons the most. It was at a cocktail reception at the privately owned Casa Battló, one of the most famous buildings in Barcelona designed by the Spanish architect Antoni Gaudí. Parsons and Herb Montgomery were sipping cava under a ceiling featuring Gaudí's signature undulating surfaces and Moorish-influenced tile mosaics. Parsons was doing his best to strike up a conversation, trying to pay Montgomery a compliment by saying that it was about time that someone with business experience was around to control Battelle's aggressive spending. And, given that a lot of money was about to be spent on the European launch, Parsons was seeking some reassurance that this lavish wining and dining made some kind of business sense, or at least was affordable. Montgomery's response was far from reassuring.

"We're flying blind," he said.

I CAN'T THINK OF THREE MORE BORING WORDS

I was unfortunately unable to attend the Barcelona Summit; it took place the week before I was moving to London, and there were too many details to be sorted out for me to fit two European trips into two weeks. I had also promised Linda that we would spend that final week together on the north shore of Long Island.

But I had begun my tenure as the editor-in-chief of the European edition the month before while still in New York, debuting with my foot firmly in my mouth. As soon as I accepted the position, our publicist decided to leak the news strategically. On the day before John Battelle was scheduled to announce the European edition before a cocktail audience in London, Alex Kuzynscki, the media reporter from *The New York Times*, phoned me. She is a notoriously peppery reporter, having made her name with a bitchy calendar column in *The New York Observer*. I had met her once or twice socially but had not had the privilege of being interviewed by her. She asked a couple of obvious questions about when we were launching, etc., and then lobbed one of the ruder queries any reporter has ever asked me: "Why are *you* qualified to do this?"

Unprepared, I stammered, "Um . . . well . . . I speak French."

No sooner were the words out of my mouth than I wished that I had not spoken them. I can't blame her for asking a legitimate question. And there was a good answer: I had been at *The Standard* longer than most senior staffers and had some experience both as a manager and a reporter for international stories; I think most of my colleagues felt I was a logical choice. But to outside eyes, there was no obvious reason why a former *Village Voice* columnist was the best candidate for this plum position. (Had *The Standard* had an infinite amount of time, it's likely its decision makers could have found some experienced foreign correspondent to edit the European edition—although I expect the outcome would not have been any different.)

I dreaded looking at the *Times* online that night, for fear that Alex would hang me with my own stupid quote. Thankfully, it was a short piece that left me sounding relatively competent: "I think there is a broad consensus in the Internet industry that the next big phase of growth will be in Europe," Mr. Ledbetter said. "Some of these countries have thrown off the shackles of very strong regulatory governments and are now allowing the kind of telecommunications mobility that can make the economy really hum."[4] When the article appeared, a fellow reporter teased me with an e-mail: "You sure are starting to sound like an editor-in-chief."

Another media encounter had a less benign result. I gave an interview to a trade publication, saying only things that to me were obvious. I compared what we were trying to do to the international editions of *Time* and *Newsweek*; that is, we would use a certain number of U.S. stories, a certain number of original, European-focused stories, and probably always have a different cover.

Apparently I used some dirty words. A mildly scolding message got back to me that the CEO of IDG, Kelly Conlin, saw and did not like the resulting story. In the view of IDG—a company that, after all, knew a lot more about international publishing than I did—the international editions of *Time* and *Newsweek* were not popular in their markets. They were read, I was told, only by expatriates and students, and what's worse, they weren't profitable. I knew a little bit about *Newsweek*'s European operation, and I thought this reaction smacked a bit of corporate jealousy. So I sent back to my superiors the *Newsweek* circulation figures; the four international editions supposedly have 750,000 readers, which sounded like an impressive number of expats to me. But I also promised never again to draw that comparison in public.

The incident underscored a trepidation I felt; because I was playing in the publishing world at a much higher level than ever before, and because I was living abroad for the first time, I was nervous about making mistakes without realizing them. Some of that came from simply being American; the British public, and certainly much of the British press, likes to see a little bit of American failure.

It would be a wild exaggeration to portray the country as anti-American. The British may criticize the domination of American mediocrity, but within a short walk from my London flat there is a McDonald's, a Burger King, three Starbucks outlets, and a movie theater that almost exclusively screens Hollywood's latest.

The salient issue is more subtle, which I think is just as true for

American sensibilities as it is for British. There is a kind of unconscious focus on the foreign. If you listen to a radio interview with someone not from your country who is ostensibly speaking your language, you are as likely to remember his or her accent as you are to remember what was actually said.

And our publication's "accent" had implications. By the time we launched our European edition, *The Industry Standard* was a magazine that was reasonably well known in the United States, at least among the potential target audience of media, financial, and technology professionals. But in Britain, it meant nothing, literally nothing. The name itself had no resonance, and more important, the concept of a broad-based newsmagazine reporting on "the Internet Economy" meant nothing. Nowhere was this gulf more visible than during the focus-group discussions we sponsored after the magazine launched. One participant said that he could not think of three more boring words than "industry," "standard," and "Europe." Behind the mirror I was crushed.

This was a difficult lesson for me to grasp, especially because my day-to-day exposure was with flatterers—company CEOs, publicists, potential partners—who said they loved us. But that was not the norm. To our readers—indeed, to my own staff—almost every aspect of the magazine had to be explained anew and often defended against the criticism: "That's not how we do things here." Those conversations yielded some hugely valuable tweaks to *The Standard*'s formula. They were also exhausting, and they pushed my patience above and beyond the boiling point.

NONE OF OUR BUSINESS

But in general, I arrived in London at the end of May 2000 filled with optimism and a sense that we were going to create something great. One reason for my optimism was that we felt certain that there was a need for the magazine, and we didn't see much by way of competition. It was something of a mystery to me that, compared to the United States, the United Kingdom has almost no general business media. Granted, America has been practically obsessed with business news in recent years, but *Fortune, Forbes, BusinessWeek,* and *The Wall Street Journal* have been around for decades and feature some of the best journalism in the world.

There were very few publications like these in the UK. In part because the country's economy was so stagnant in the postwar period, and in part because stock ownership in Europe generally was much less prevalent, the average reader was not expected to be interested in business. In the fall of 2000, for example, the BBC hired the editor of the weekly paper *Sunday Business* in a conscious attempt to bolster its coverage of financial affairs. An equivalent move would have gone largely unnoticed in the United States. But in Britain there was actually a debate, not only about whether this was a good idea, but about whether it could even be done.[5] Beyond the coverage of strikes and layoffs, it was felt that there was little public interest in business affairs. Those in Britain who really care about finance issues or specific business segments get their information from small, highly specialized publications.

The Economist may have begun life as a business-focused magazine, but it functioned primarily as an international newsweekly, with a plurality of its readers in North America. A UK monthly called *Management Today* looked at business issues in a serious but fairly popular way, and there were two personal finance titles, called *Investors Chronicle* and *Shares.*

And, of course, there was the *Financial Times,* the leading business publication in the United Kingdom, a venerable daily printed on distinctive peach-colored paper (and owned by Pearson plc, which owned a small stake in *The Standard*). From our point of view, the *FT*'s coverage of the Internet business only highlighted the need for a weekly magazine like *The Standard.* There were and are some very talented journalists covering the Internet business for the *FT*, but on an overall basis, the coverage seemed arbitrary and weak. You could never really predict on a given day whether the *FT* would cover a particular Internet story in depth, or, indeed, at all. (In fairness, I should say that we tried to recruit at least one significant reporter from the *FT* but failed.)

There were some other magazines that shared our space, notably a weekly called *New Media Age.* Like many trade publications, it had a lean staff and ran dozens of short articles a week, many of which were little more than rewritten press releases. We knew that we could produce more compelling content, and just to tweak it a bit, we hired the well-connected editor Mike Butcher as our news editor.

One advantage we thought we had was that we deliberately cultivated a pan-European perspective. Before moving to Britain, I was aware in a general way of some mutual dislike between the British and their continental counterparts. But I hadn't realized how much of British media life consists of taking potshots at Europeans. Shortly after I moved to London, the English soccer team beat Germany by a score of 1–0 in a hotly contested European Cup match on a Saturday night. The headline in one of the next day's tabloids read: "HUN NIL."

It may be classic American myopia, but I felt that such nationalism had no place in business journalism about a technology that is, after all, intrinsically international. And sure enough, when we began producing Web stories in the summer of 2000, our reporters were pleasantly surprised to have investment bankers in Germany and France call them back, saying they'd never been called by a British reporter before.

We also believed that our timing was ideal. The week I arrived in London, dot-com advertising was everywhere, just as it had been in San Francisco in 1998 and New York in 1999. The love affair with consumer Internet companies was in full swing. Supermarket giant

Tesco boasted that its Internet delivery service was actually profitable, and as I got on the tube the first week after moving into my Notting Hill flat, a woman handed me a card for a free delivery from Urban
Fetch.

The phenomenon was much broader than the expansion of a few
business-to-consumer businesses. It was apparent to me and *The
Standard*'s team that the Internet was becoming a truly global form of
commerce, uniting American and European businesses at a pace that
had been unimaginable even as late as mid-1999. One of the original
American online music retailers, CD-Now, was in the process of being
acquired by the German media conglomerate Bertelsmann. ExciteAtHome, the massive broadband portal, had announced a merger
with the Dutch broadband company Chello. And Lycos, for me so
often the benchmark of Internet companies, had been bought by the
Spanish firm Terra Networks, a subsidiary of Spain's communications
giant Telefónica.

Clearly, Europe was where the Internet story was heading, and we
were hardly the only American media company to recognize it. If anything, we were slightly late to the game. Neil Thackray, who became
The Industry Standard Europe's managing director, later recalled that
Battelle "was in a terrible hurry" to get the European operation
started. "He was worried the window would pass."

One of our principal print rivals, *Business 2.0*, was planning to
debut in the UK in June and in Germany in August. And on the Web
we were equally a few months behind; TheStreet.com had unveiled a
separate British site, TheStreet.co.uk, in January, and during the
summer, while we were gearing up for our launch, CBS MarketWatch
had launched a joint project with the *Financial Times* called FT MarketWatch, which had sites in both English and German.

The traditional media was chasing the Net story as well. Just as the
American press created dot-com legends out of Jeff Bezos and Steve
Case, the UK had for months been swooning over Martha Lane Fox,
whose travel site, Lastminute.com, had a much publicized IPO (the

preferred British term was "flotation") in March. The week I arrived in Britain, *Fortune* produced a "special report" with the headline "Europe's Got Web Fever." The cover featured the attractive face of Fabiola Arredondo, the managing director of Yahoo Europe. Inside, a series of articles laid out the European embrace of e-commerce and mobile phones; at times the coverage bordered on the breathless. "If it hasn't already," one *Fortune* writer said, "wireless Internet technology will soon be able to put the Internet in your pocket, replace almost all of your company's fixed-line phones, render your office superfluous—and then buy you a Coke. And of course, it will make a number of people very, very rich."[6]

My staff and I tended to scoff at such predictions. But it was impossible to deny that the prospect of the wireless Internet had gripped the imagination of Europe's markets and public policy makers. In April 2000, the British government had auctioned off five spectrum licenses to operate so-called "third generation" (3G) mobile phones. These phones were to operate under the standards of the Universal Mobile Telecommunication System (UMTS) and would theoretically be fast enough to provide a full range of Internet services through a mobile handset. The license starting point was £550 million; after 150 rounds of bidding, which took seven weeks, five companies (British Telecom, Vodafone, One2One/Deutsche Telekom, Orange/France Telecom, and Telesystem International Wireless/Hutchinson) agreed to pay a staggering £22.47 billion (or 36.8 billion euros) in cash for the licenses. In August, the German government followed up with a 50.4 billion euro auction.

As overwhelming as those figures seemed, most industry analysts believed that the telecom companies that managed to get the licenses would still have to spend that much again to build the network on which the 3G phones would operate. And all of that was being spent even though no one could guarantee that a significant market for 3G phones existed; indeed, it was spent when no one could even prove that 3G technology would actually work. It was impossible not to draw comparisons to the tulipmania that gripped the Netherlands in the early seventeenth century.

COFFEE AND BUDGETS

We didn't come into Europe completely unprepared. Jonathan Weber had met an extraordinary journalist named Bruno Giussani who had helped organize some of the sessions for the World Economic Forum in Davos. Bruno is an impressive man, with generous girth and hair the color of Alpine snow. Italian Swiss by background, he speaks six or seven languages fluently, and between his contacts at Davos and his work in organizing the Barcelona Summit, he seemed to know everyone in the European Internet business. He had agreed to edit and write the opinion columns for the European edition.

Since the summer of 1999, *The Standard* had also had an American reporter, Polly Sprenger, working full time out of London. Polly, a feisty and iconoclastic writer who'd come from *Wired News*, had established an impressive network of journalists and Internet sources, and I relied heavily on her.

Through one of her connections, Polly had found us office space inside an "incubator," a parent company that provided funding and logistical resources to Net start-ups in return for equity. We were in the very cool and central neighborhood of Soho, although the office space itself bordered on grotty. Our section of the floor consisted of long tables—no offices, not even cubicles—on which we put out laptops every day. A window looked out onto a noisy, dim alley. The most amusing part was that we worked in the belly of the start-up beast; we were cheek-by-jowl with a number of companies trying to strike Internet gold. One was a business-to-business exchange for the paper industry; one seemed to be trying to unite local merchants to get discounts on wine and spirits; another very earnest one, called Just Giving, was meant to be a one-stop Net shop for charitable donations. We often overheard these companies' telephone conversations and strategy meetings and had to stifle the urge to roll our eyes at their untested optimism.

During those months, I spent a lot of money on coffee. The office was not terribly presentable, and there were interviews to conduct, often two or three a day. A lot of these, therefore, took place at one of the expensive coffee shops near our building.

I felt like I had ceased being a journalist and had transformed into a salesman. Unlike the average traveling pitchman, I didn't even have a suitcase of wares to show off; my product, a pan-European Internet magazine and Web site, was entirely abstract.

What I did have was money. For better and worse, one of *The Standard*'s weapons was its willingness to pay high salaries to attract the right journalists. During The Fat Year, if we really wanted a reporter who had a lot of experience, we thought nothing of paying $100,000 a year in salary and bonus. And for a true superstar, we were prepared to go higher than that. Although the magazine was occasionally criticized for extravagance, I had no problem justifying high salaries for experienced and productive reporters and editors. The problems came either from over-paying middle-level and inexperienced reporters, or from hiring high-paid reporters who didn't pan out.

That money went a long way with the European staff. Compared to their U.S. counterparts, British journalists were significantly underpaid (although in some cases you get what you pay for: The reporting and accuracy standards in British journalism often leave much to be desired). If you pay a British journalist $60,000 a year, he is ecstatic; if you pay him $90,000 a year, he thinks he's getting away with something.

The pool of London-based journalists covering the technology business was fairly small; thus, news of the arrival of an American magazine with a big wallet had zapped its way through most of the relevant in-boxes by the time we got to town. Polly's network was invaluable, and the Barcelona conference had attracted some of the best business journalists on the Continent, and thus acted as a recruitment tool.

Of course, hiring employees on the Continent is no picnic. It's easy for Americans to underestimate the complexities of local workplace regulations and social security payments; our human resources department in San Francisco simply gave up and contracted out in order to handle our bureau chiefs in Paris, Stockholm, and Berlin. When I began the search process for the Paris position, Jonathan gave me a name of a woman whom he'd met at the Barcelona conference. She worked for *Les Echos*, and he said she was apparently the best journalist in France covering the Net business; other people echoed this opinion.

I was eager to meet her until I had a conversation with a friend of hers, who told me that in her current job she received twelve weeks of vacation time every year. I was aghast; to me that sounded like a part-time job. It was then explained to me that she had been getting ten weeks a year, but when France instituted a thirty-five-hour workweek, her bosses compensated by giving her another two weeks vacation. There was no way I could even come close to that; in addition to the fact that I wanted my reporters to be around more than forty weeks a year, it would simply have been unfair to the UK-based staff, who got five weeks a year, and the U.S. staff, who generally got two or three weeks.

Just as in New York, in Europe I had no problem in general defending the salaries that we paid our writers and editors. Indeed, in some areas I felt we were being outright thrifty; I managed to hire each of the bureau chiefs at a salary that was slightly lower than what I had been making in New York two years earlier. And I strove in Europe, as in New York, to hire people with different levels of experience, which helps keep the overall salary level reasonable.

Perhaps more telling, however, is that I essentially never had to justify any salary to anyone higher up. Until the launch of the European edition, we worked without a formal budget, just as we had in New York. Occasionally, someone from the human resources department in San Francisco might say something like, "That hire will come out of your budget." But such comments were rare and utterly abstract; there was never a point when I was given a figure and told: "This is how much you have to spend for the next six months."

In some ways, such fiscal freewheeling is a great advantage for an editor; if you don't have a budget, you can never be accused of spending outside of it. And to be fair to *The Standard*'s business staff, any annual budget produced during The Fat Year would have been rendered meaningless.

But as should be obvious, it's also a recipe for chaos. The biggest problem was not that a spendthrift would bleed the company dry (although no doubt that could happen); the biggest problem was that managers had no way of gauging whether a particular expense was appropriate, or even necessary. Also, without a centralized spending and revenue plan, it was essentially impossible to compare spending levels between departments (circulation, conferences, editorial, and so on). The business staff in the European office recognized more or less immediately that this was an amateurish way to proceed and set up a fairly rigorous budget procedure.

IT'S ALL IN THE BHAG

Toward the end of the summer, it became clear that the relationship between IDG and *The Standard*'s management had frayed. One of IDG's annual rituals is a Worldwide Managers' Meeting; in mid-September, this took the form of a cruise for executives and their wives that made its way to Nice, Portofino, and Monte Carlo.

From Battelle's perspective, this event should have been his Fat

Year coronation; after all, *The Standard* alone was accounting for more than half of IDG's North American revenues. But from the IDG trenches, no amount of financial success could erase Battelle's sins of arrogance. The business unit heads were established, lifelong players who valued corporate loyalty; on the ship they sang a mock anthem to the tune of "Only You." And a video was shown in which the top executives dressed as the characters from *The Love Boat*, which was capped off by Pat McGovern himself appearing on stage in the outfit of The Captain.

This was not Battelle's style. He needed the media spotlight, and he needed the world to understand that *The Standard* was his creation. "He just couldn't master their suburban deference," recalled one cruise participant. "There was so much animosity and hostility toward *The Standard*. When they gave out their awards, *The Standard* didn't win any."

Back at the home office, The Fat Year had reached its baroque period. There were two main topics of conversation at the end of the summer among *The Standard*'s employees; both had stupid names. One stemmed from a speech that Battelle had delivered to staff assembled in a hotel conference room—there was no room in any *Standard* office facility large enough to hold the entire staff. In it, he pledged that the company would have 900 employees by 2005, and a billion dollars in annual revenue. This projection was, as the screen behind him proclaimed, a "Big, Hairy, Audacious Goal"—or BHAG, as it instantly became known.

The second topic of conversation was known as the Trium project. Despite the mysterious name, everyone knew what Trium was, or thought they did. It was the name of an outside consultant, the Trium Group, that had been hired to take a comprehensive look at all of *The Standard*'s operations.

The head of Trium, Andrew Blum, had an unusual combination of experiences. A graduate of Reed College—by reputation an undisciplined, hippie-oriented school in Oregon—he had also been a first

lieutenant in the U.S. Marine Corps. Trying to understand from its Web
site exactly what Trium did was like trying to jog through quicksand.
"Trium worked hand in hand with the CEO and senior leadership team
to clarify the company's strategy and design an infrastructure that supported their vision of using the Internet to provide personalized-assis-
tant services to major corporations," the site boasted, I think, of its
work for one client. "Through a series of targeted, multi-day work sessions, Trium helped the team rapidly create and align behind a mission, vision and business model, and dramatically improved the
team's ability to communicate and work together."

Behind all this gobbledygook was a set of sessions held for *Standard* staffers at the luxurious Sonoma Mission Inn, about an hour
north of San Francisco. An editor recalled that his room "was a suite
with a fireplace, in-room jacuzzi, and a patio. It was probably one of
the best hotel rooms I've ever been in." Although staffers were told
they had to pay for their own massages, dinner expenses were paid for
by the publication, including a table of editors who consumed "four or
five bottles of $75-a-bottle wine." Sessions would last all day and oc-
casionally resembled EST-style exercises. In one session, *Standard*
staffers would tell a story about an encounter in the workplace that
made them feel victimized; they were then encouraged to rethink the
situation in light of their own responsibility. During one session, *The
Standard*'s president apparently told Battelle: "I feel like your wife."
Hence, to its detractors, Trium was a useless exercise in telling people
what they already knew, a parody of California's touchy-feely ten-
dency. It was also undeniably expensive: Trium was said to have cost
the company $1 million.

Yet many of the people whom I had expected to detest Trium the
most—notably Weber—came away impressed. I got antsy when I was
part of more than one conversation in which journalists who'd never
been anywhere near a battlefield were saying how much they admired
the Marines as an organization. A top editor later said that although
he'd never seen a copy of the final report, "I did hear that they found

us to be one of the most dysfunctional, skewed, managerially inept companies they'd ever worked with. Mostly because we had lots of managers who, in the end, had absolutely no power and no clue about what was happening in the company." Alas, Trium did little to change that.

SNAKE HEADS

Starting up a magazine involves a thousand tiny decisions, most of which have to be made quickly and without any guarantee of certainty. Some of those I found intellectually stimulating. My *Time*-and-*Newsweek* comparison had set off an alarm bell with IDG's Kelly Conlin because we had defined our publication in a peculiar, and arguably incoherent, manner. We wanted to be perceived as something different from what we were—the European edition of an American newsweekly. If we overemphasized our American character, we thought, then the British and continental audiences would spurn us. In a related dilemma that was repeatedly raised by Bruno Giussani, if we overemphasized British companies and British Internet personalities—a very real possibility, given our London headquarters—we would alienate the continental audience. The only apparent way around this dilemma was to say: We are a pan-European, English-language news publication.

There are a few problems with that definition, beginning with the fact that no publication of that type has ever worked. The newsstands of continental Europe are still stained with the blood of noble fools who have tried such ventures, notably *The European*, the ill-fated English-language daily launched by Robert Maxwell in the 1990s.

We were fully aware of such doomed precedents. I had an argument for why their fate would not be ours, which essentially boiled down to: The Internet is different. Of course, the bulk of our circulation would be based in the UK (an 80–20 ratio to start, I felt). But one reason that

British readers would lap us up was that we could keep them up-to-date on developments on the Continent. As for the rest, our niche was, I believed, important enough that the 5,000 people in France who needed to find us would find us, and I felt they would suspend any language objections in order to share the fruits of our knowledge. Down the road, if we proved that a European market for *The Standard* existed, then we should by all means publish local-language editions.

Based on its publishing experience, IDG (and even Battelle) never fully accepted this fudge. We spent weeks arguing about the URL for the European edition's Web site. IDG was adamant that the word "Europe" not appear in the main part of the Web address. It was willing to accept that we build a separate site as a subsection of the existing site, that is, at www.thestandard.com/europe. I argued that most Web users were not yet accustomed to finding domains that required an ending other than ".com," while others said our audience was sufficiently sophisticated.

Even after these tedious battles were resolved, Battelle and others continued to refer to us as the "UK edition," even though we were careful to call ourselves "European."

These arguments were like snakes that had swallowed their own tails: They went round and round without stop. It was impossible to tell the beginning of the argument from the end, or when the argument had actually been resolved. Absent any detailed market research, there was no way to know the right decisions, and even with market research, different people would still reach contradictory conclusions. I would sometimes emerge from a meeting with the distinct impression that I'd cut the head off the snake. Then the following week, I'd enter a meeting and bam! There was the snake head again.

This serpentine struggle of self-definition had subsections. Paul Mungo, whom I hired to be our managing editor, asked me over our first lunch at the Groucho Club whether we should use American or British spelling and grammar. A deceptively simple-sounding question.

The argument for American-style conventions appeared persuasive. *The Wall Street Journal, International Herald Tribune, Fortune, Forbes, Time, Newsweek,* and *BusinessWeek* all used American spellings. We also felt that in Britain there was an unspoken assumption that Americans knew more about the Internet business; hence there could be an advantage to highlighting our Yankee roots. And then there was the efficiency argument: If we used American spellings, then the articles we reprinted from the U.S. edition could be reproduced without being copy-edited a second time.

But as we stirred the issue around, the case for American became muddier. Because our edition was a different size than the American edition (the size of paper known in both countries as A4 is nonetheless slightly larger in Britain than in the United States, where it is 8½ by 11 inches), all the stories we picked up would have to be laid out anew anyway, thus eliminating the efficiency rationale. And our copy editors (called subeditors) were almost certainly going to be British. To have native British speakers enforcing American rules of spelling and grammar—especially on stories that had been written by British reporters—seemed clunky and likely to generate errors. In the end I felt that since we were trying to bend over backwards to be European instead of simply British, we should give the British the sense that we were part of their culture as well.

Other decisions were outright annoying. One maddening area was the question of self-competition. For some time, a very small number of copies of the U.S. edition of *The Standard* had been available in the UK. Over some objections, we made the decision to pull those copies. The European edition didn't want to lose any readers by offering them a choice. But more crucially, UK news agents, Neil Thackray insisted, would not stack two copies of the same magazine.

But the problem wasn't that simple. Internal competition is part of the IDG way of doing business. I didn't realize it until I'd already moved to London, but IDG had already licensed *The Industry Standard* name to several publishers in smaller European countries—including Sweden, Finland, Poland, and Switzerland—as well as Brazil and South Korea (Australia I already knew about). The basic agreement was that the licensees would have local-language rights to all stories published by the U.S. and European editions, and they could add on any material they felt appropriate. In return, *The Standard* would get a tiny percentage of their revenues.

This arrangement created two crucial problems. One was a straightforward newsstand issue: If we hoped to get any sales from newsstands on the Continent, those sales could obviously be thwarted by the existence of a very similar publication on the same rack.

The second concern might be deemed "brand protection." That is: Just how similar were those other publications? Several countries, for example, rejected the title *Industry Standard* and used the same logo with the words *Internet Standard* or, in one case, *Business Standard*. The most extreme instance was in Switzerland, where the licensee chose to abandon the very idea of a glossy-paper weekly magazine in favor of a thrice-weekly tabloid newspaper.

After a few weeks of fretting, I decided not to worry about these editions. For one thing, we seemed to have an understanding that there would be no licensing agreement in the Continent's largest markets: Germany and France. (I later learned that IDG saw this agreement as part of *The Standard*'s continuing arrogance: that is, you can have Bulgaria, we'll take the big boys.) More important, the quality issue would settle itself: If the editions were no good, they would fail. If they were successful, they might create better awareness of what we were doing. And above all, I was unprepared to argue with the IDG brass on this point. IDG had been signing international licensing deals for years; what the hell did I know about the best way for *The Standard* to capture the Polish market?

There were other decisions being made that I didn't happily accept. Prior to my moving to London, there had been an understanding that *The Standard*'s Web strategy had been flawed from the very beginning (or that we simply hadn't had one). With the opportunity to start anew in Europe, we resolved that there would be a separate position of editor-in-chief for the Web site. That was fine by me; I was certain that running the magazine would be more than enough responsibility. Somehow, though, that position was never budgeted, and so I had to take responsibility for the Web as well.

It was an exasperating experience. The problem wasn't personnel: We had relocated two first-rate people from *The Standard*'s Web team, Matt McAlister and Jen Marek, who had managed to build a handsome-looking and efficient site a few weeks before the magazine published its first issue. The problem was the perpetual inability to make the technology work. In our desire to appeal to the whole of continental Europe, we insisted that our version of "Media Grok" would cover the news in non-English-language newspapers as well (primarily the French and German papers and Web sites). Similarly, we struck a deal with a translation company to provide the weekly "Intelligencer" newsletter in German, Spanish, and French.

I was impressed with these efforts, but they were a nightmare to implement. Although obviously the European romance languages are similar to one another, the Continent's tongues present a dizzying array of punctuation problems, a thick stew of umlauts and cedillas. Think of an English-language typewriter or computer keyboard: It does not contain an easy way to make the symbols for, say, different international currencies. In the same way, Web browsers and e-mail editing programs do not have a consistent way to display some of the most basic accents and diacritical marks of European languages.

As we first began to send out translated e-mails in the summer and post stories to our site, I (as well as others) would see nonsensical marks in the middle of words and bring them to the attention of the Web staff. Usually they would get fixed, and the staff began compiling a list of the correct coding to make a particular accent appear on a user's screen.

But we never fully worked these out. It turns out that, for example, Microsoft Explorer and Netscape use different codes to make the same accent; worse, different *versions* of the same browsers use different codes. So there was no way to code a Web page to ensure that everyone who read it would see it punctuated correctly. The same maddening truth exists for sending out e-mail. Repeatedly I had readers send back copies of the translated Intelligencer to me with angry responses at the top indicating that they never again wanted to see their language mangled this badly. Instead of impressing our potential continental audience with our linguistic savoir faire, we were pissing them off.

There was also the question of what day of the week the magazine would publish. In the United States, we came out on Mondays, the same as *Time, Newsweek,* and *US News & World Report.* But in one of the early meetings we had with Neil, he said it was impossible to publish on Mondays, because the trucking unions refused to work on Sundays. I found this reason puzzling. For one thing, the Monday newspapers found their way to newsstands; I assumed that a truck brought them. And the next time I went to Paris I found I could buy a copy of the current *Newsweek* bright and early Monday morning on the Champs Elysées.

But again, Neil had been involved in British publishing for two decades, and I hadn't, so I had no ammunition. We chose Thursday as our publication day, meaning that the bulk of the magazine would ship to the printer on Friday and Monday, with the very last pages shipping Tuesday morning. This schedule was barely tolerable from my point of view, because the American edition closed its news pages on Wednesday, Thursday, and Friday mornings. Those articles would come in too late for us to publish in the same week, so the only news stories we could pick up would be a week old by the time we published them.

But a much bigger debate was going on through the spring and early summer, and that was whether or not *The Standard Europe* would be published in partnership with Pearson. Pearson already had a modest stake in *The Industry Standard,* and there was a personal relationship between Battelle and Pearson's CEO, Marjorie Scardino. Shortly after

I moved to London, Battelle contacted me and urged me to meet some Pearson executives. To preserve editorial independence—we had also talked about doing a tough story on Pearson's shaky Net strategy—it was agreed that these meetings would best be held with Parsons and Thackray, who had yet to start.

I thought Pearson had a lot to offer us, starting with office space, which at the time we lacked. Second, I drooled at the prospect of *The Industry Standard Europe* being bundled in with *The Economist* and the *FT*; their readers were precisely the audience we wanted to reach.

As it turned out, however, Pearson viewed us as occupying one of the least glamorous outposts of its empire: the Business Information unit. Even though Pearson had world-class holdings (including the *FT, The Economist,* Penguin Books, and the respected French business newspaper *Les Echos*), the Business Information division was a poky backwater essentially unknown outside Britain: It published a personal finance magazine called *Investors Chronicle* and two trade magazines, *Financial Analyst* and *The Banker*.[7] Regardless of how much money those magazines might make, they were irredeemably dull and simply had none of the Internet fairy dust that surrounded *The Standard*.

This contrast led to fireworks. Michael Parsons, who had the title of editorial director but functioned at the European edition more or less as a publisher, attended a meeting in Pearson's offices on Tottenham Court Road with a Pearson official named Michael Murphy, who was coordinating the business side of Pearson's various Web sites. Joining the meeting was Peter Martin, the deputy editor of the *FT*. After exchanging some pleasantries, Martin bluntly told Parsons that *The Standard* was going to "get creamed" in the UK market if it remained independent and that it needed the experience of the *FT* to survive.

Parsons was taken aback and made some comments about how he didn't feel that the *FT* had done a particularly brilliant job of covering the Internet business. Martin was a bit defensive but acknowledged that the *FT*'s coverage of U.S. companies had not been what it might. Parsons clarified himself: He had been talking about the *FT*'s coverage of the European Internet business. At this Martin became incensed and walked out of the meeting, saying snottily that he looked forward to *The Standard* showing Pearson how this could be done.

Despite such awkward moments, Pearson did come forward with an offer. I didn't want us to be lumped in with *Financial Analyst* magazine, but I knew that any argument based on magazine aesthetics was not going to carry the day with our board. Fortunately, Neil was against the Pearson deal for his own reasons. First and foremost, Pearson demanded what we all thought was an extraordinary chunk of *The Industry Standard Europe:* 40 percent. According to calculations that Neil presented at an executive teleconference, the value of what Pearson had to offer us—essentially real estate and subscription promotion—could be bought or rented for a lower price than what Pearson was demanding. Pearson was taking a hefty chunk of our business in return for subscriptions that would be brought in from promotions through the *FT.* But when Neil tried to set specific goals—for example, Pearson would get more equity based on actual subscriptions that their promotions brought in—they balked. (Of course, it's also treu that if we had gone in with Pearson, Neil's job might well have been eliminated.) As was often the case, Neil was much more agile with publishing numbers than anyone in our San Francisco office, including the CFO; no one tried to talk him back into the deal.

GOD SAVE THE EDITOR

By the end of September we had almost hit our publishing groove. Most of my hires had been made, even if not everyone had started yet. And it really felt like the business side people knew what they were doing. We had negotiated, on very favorable terms, a deal with the *Evening Standard,* London's premier afternoon newspaper. It was to distribute about 120,000 copies of a 16-page marketing "dummy" copy of *The Industry Standard Europe*, bundled into the October 5 issue of the paper. We worried slightly about the word "Standard" being in both the names but decided that any confusion would work in our favor. These copies would be concentrated on newsstands in the City, London's financial district, where, we hoped, a large portion of our natural readership worked.

Normally, dummy issues are filled with old stories or even nonsense language, but we had to put our best foot forward. One of our star British reporters, Rick Wray, had written an excellent feature story about the secondary effects of the tremendous sums that had been spent on third-generation mobile-phone licenses throughout Europe. Many of the big telecom players—Vodafone, Orange, Deutsche Telekom—had spent tens of billions for licenses, and since their shareholders couldn't or wouldn't absorb those costs, the firms were forced into massive bond issues. Those issues, in turn, were distorting the European bond markets in ways that were potentially disastrous.

It was a classic *Industry Standard* story—the intersection of technology and finance—and I wanted it as our first cover. But it was also devilishly abstract, making it hard to illustrate: Telephone licenses and bond debt are not exactly the topics that make magazine art directors salivate.

We ended up with a satisfactory concept: The cover line would be "Up in Smoke," and we would show a picture of a bond on fire. Not great, but on deadline, acceptable. Because of the size of the print run, we had to ship a copy of the cover to our printer by Friday afternoon, even though the issue wouldn't go out until the following Thursday.

Nicole Chiala, our art director, had arrived from San Francisco only a few weeks before we started producing the dummy. She had spent far too much of that time dealing with technology glitches and software snafus, and she was also under pressure to design marketing material for the business staff. As a result, I don't think she was able to give full attention to producing this cover. On Friday morning, she announced that she'd been unable to find an image of a burning bond (there was no time to even think about shooting one of our own). She had, however, found a picture of a five-pound note on fire.

I was not pleased. This predicament made an already tenuous cover image even more tenuous. But I had little experience ordering an art staff around, and Nicole seemed to be under a lot of stress; we still had nearly three weeks before the magazine launched. So I relented, with one question: Is it legal to show a five-pound note in flames?

"It's a stock image," Nicole assured me. "I'm sure it's been used a hundred times."

We shipped the cover that afternoon.

As it happened, Mike Bealing, our picture editor who had thirteen years experience at the *Daily Telegraph,* had sent a fax to the Bank of England that afternoon requesting permission to use the image in this fashion. He was absolutely right to do so; he was negligent not to tell me about it. Were there to be any future disputes about the propriety of using the image, that letter could be used to demonstrate that we knew we were doing something wrong.

Sure enough, on Monday, a fax arrived from the Bank of England's Banking Services Division. In beautifully bureaucratic prose, the fax said: "It is regretted that consent under Section 18(1) of the Forgery and Counterfeiting Act 1981 would not be given for your proposed reproduction of a Bank of England note. The concept fails to meet the Bank's requirements as set out in their Guidelines for Reproducing Bank of England Notes, a copy of which is enclosed for your information."

This response sounded ominous. Most, possibly all, of the covers had already been printed and were stacked up in Peterborough waiting to be bound around the rest of the magazine. We contacted our London solicitors to see if we might have recourse to a freedom of expression defense. After all, the Americans on staff argued, in the United States, showing money on fire is so common that it is practically a cliché.

The lawyers consulted for a few hours and came back with less than good news. Not only were we vulnerable to prosecution under the statute cited, but because the five-pound note carries a picture of Her Majesty the Queen, to depict the note in flames could be construed as a treasonous act. Treason, the lawyers reminded us helpfully, is one of the few crimes in the United Kingdom that is still punishable by death.

There was a lot of dark humor around the office that day. Over the summer, we had said that one mark of our doing a truly good job would be a lawsuit, but being sued by the Bank of England before we had put out our first proper issue was not what we had in mind. Neil told me that in his experience, it was the editor who went to jail. He was kidding—I think.

Under this extra bit of pressure, Nicole was miraculously able to assemble a picture of a bond, and using the visual software Photoshop, she made it look like it was on fire. We reshipped it to the printer. In the end we got a better cover, and we consoled ourselves with the view that this is precisely why magazines produce dummy copies: It's best to get the kinks out when you don't have to actually deliver copies to the newsstand. But it came at a cost: several thousand pounds to the printer, and a certain degree of credibility with the magazine's business staff. They were all British, and to them this mishap was a stellar example of what they would call an American "cock-up."

MY TURN TO BUY THE TOILET PAPER

There were also headaches a bit closer to home. Over the course of the summer, Polly Sprenger had become increasingly difficult to work with. Although she had been given the job she said she wanted—editing the "Posts" section—she was unhappy with it and seemed to resent the other reporters. I was sympathetic to a degree: It was no easy task to go from being the sole person in London to being part of a staff of dozens, including colleagues who didn't know the British Internet scene half as well as she did. At the same time, her misery was causing her to act out in the office, and other members of the staff began to complain. She was disrespectful and disruptive; at one point she and I were disagreeing over whether a particular story should lead the "Intelligencer" newsletter, and she thrust her hands out at me in a gesture of defiance and turned her back. In one meeting she plopped her head down on the table and kept it there.

Although there were times when I felt like firing her—and she nearly quit in the late summer—Polly was vital to the launch of the magazine. So we tried to rescue the situation in the fashion *The Standard* knew best: with money. She received a one-time bonus to compensate for the fact that the other Americans had been given generous relocation packages. We also agreed that we'd find someone else to edit the "Posts" section a few months after the magazine debuted. That worked—for a while.

The two weeks leading up to the launch of the magazine were a blur. I worked every day, including Saturdays and Sundays, as did key members of the production staff. On top of trying to finalize the first issue, we were also moving into our new offices. Michael, Neil, and I had chosen the facility over the summer in Southwark. The neighborhood, on the south side of the Thames, is not exactly London's most glamorous, nor its most centrally located. But we convinced ourselves that it was funky and on its way up; the Tate Modern museum had opened there, and nearby were several theaters and dot-com start-ups. Across the street from us was the Union Jack pub and a tiny fry-up café called City Snax, which was a huge hit with cab drivers. We joked that we'd know we'd had an impact on London's Internet Economy when an overpriced coffee bar opened up nearby.

When the offices were finally finished being refitted, Michael went down to check them out. Everything seemed fine except the color. Initially what we'd seen was an all white space, with some of the open pipes, columns, and door fixtures painted blue and red, which seemed adequate. But the architect we'd hired decided that this color scheme was insufficiently "New Economy." And so to capture the dynamism of our project, he painted the columns a pale orange, the walls of the offices and meeting rooms yellow, and the entire back wall green. It looked like an executive suite for circus clowns. After some dispute with a defensive architect, the walls were restored to white and we moved in.

The move could have been much worse—crucially, the computer network ran properly from the first day. But on some days the heat didn't work; on others, the electricity would go out on half the floor. There was also some unexplained electrical interference in the center of the room where we had placed the art and photo staff members; it caused their computer screens to flutter in a way that would have driven them mad if we hadn't moved them. And in the beginning, we had no janitorial services. Pitying my employees for coming in on a Sunday, I decided late one afternoon that the best way to boost their morale was to go to the petrol station next door to buy beer—and toilet paper. Ah, the glamour!

I began to realize that being editor-in-chief meant that you actually didn't edit very much. The physical editing duties you farmed out to staff, and hoped that the pieces were good and clear by the time they crossed your desk. The rest of the time you spent "managing," and that meant endless meetings with the other department heads.

I had mixed feelings about such meetings. In a pure church-and-state relationship—such as that practiced at *The New Yorker* through the 1950s and 1960s—there would be absolutely no overlap between the editorial and business departments. Let's say that I knew, for example, that Andersen Consulting was preparing a special 16-page insert explaining and extolling the virtues of Bluetooth technology (as it did). There would be a certain unspoken pressure on me in that week's issue to avoid publishing a story reflecting the magazine's actual position, that is, that Bluetooth is an unproven and overhyped format that is unlikely to live up to a fraction of the predictions made for it.

At the same time, it quickly became clear to me that if the editorial department hid itself away during planning meetings, then the marketing and advertising salespeople were bound to come up with plans that were truly horrendous. Just before our launch, we had a meeting with three companies we'd retained. One of these, Gnash, did traditional public relations (contacting the media about our launch, printing and distributing press releases, and inviting the press to our launch party); one did marketing for the news trade (the real nuts-and-bolts stuff, like designing flyers for news agents' windows and the little signs that pop out of the magazine rack); and the third was more along the lines of an image consultant, a company that tried to spread our name as widely as possible.

All three companies were pitching us their ideas for how to publicize *The Industry Standard Europe* at launch and immediately thereafter. Some of the suggestions I liked, such as sending out "teaser" postcards with provocative facts about the Internet Economy to a targeted audience. Others seemed useless, even crass; they proposed hiring people to carry copies on the London Underground during rush hour and conduct loud conversations about the salutary stories in the magazine. Michael and I shot that one down quickly.

I had only one agenda for the meeting. Back in New York, Bernhard and I had been burned by an outside PR agency on the Priceline story, and I wanted to ensure that something like that would not happen again. So I laid out the scenario for the representatives of the marketing firms and noted that one of them—Gnash—had many clients among the companies we covered.

"We would never do that," I was assured. "That's appalling," they said. "Unprofessional."

I was pleased to have gotten this issue out of the way. Or so I thought.

GET USED TO IT

The first edition of *The Industry Standard Europe* was published on October 19, 2000. When I got out of bed that morning, I could not stand up. For several days I had been experiencing an increasing pain in my right foot, and that morning it had reached an excruciating level. With Linda's help (she had come to town for the launch party), I took a taxi to a medical center in Waterloo Station. I was diagnosed with plantar fascitis, a fairly common condition among runners and joggers. Unfortunately, I am neither. Evidently I had been walking a great deal, wearing sneakers that were doing my arches no favors. I'll never know to what extent my suffering was exacerbated by the stress of putting out the first issue; a steroid shot in the heel eventually cleared up the pain. I was not the only one suffering; on the night of the launch party, Neil was practically incapable of speaking because a cold and too many sales pitches had rendered his throat raw.

The launch party had all the pomp and questionable taste one had come to expect from larger *Standard* events. It was held in a posh restaurant near the Bank of England called Le Coq d'Argent, which had a substantial roof area overlooking the Thames River. (Unfortunately, the weather in London is rarely as cooperative as in San Francisco, and for much of the evening's early portion the rain kept everyone inside.)

The U.S. marketing department had come with a plan to make a dramatic gesture: hiring a helicopter to hover above the roof and then drop down a stack of the first issues. We were saved from such atrocious symbolism when Neil pointed out that, because of restrictions put in place following various Irish Republican Army bombings, it is illegal to fly a helicopter over the Thames.

The compromise was only slightly less gaudy. As guests came in, they were greeted by a pair of actors on stilts wearing elaborate purple satin harlequin outfits. (One of our competitors, FT MarketWatch, actually hired people to hijack a bit of our publicity; they stood at the door wearing news ticker boards that advertised their site.) There was a live band, which, like all the bands at *Standard* events I attended, was overloud and undertalented. But the most memorable piece was a laser show featuring massive green rays that lit up over the Thames. They then converged on a rolldown fabric screen, scrambled around a bit, and began to form the image of the initial cover. Some people like this sort of thing, but many of our British guests looked on with equal bemusement and contempt.

Still, the turnout of more than 350 people was impressive, and it didn't cost very much, since Chase bank had agreed to sponsor the laser show. Some of the brighter stars of London's business and media world turned up, including Stelios Haji-Ioannou, the founder of Easy-Jet, and Andrew Neil, the longtime editor of the *Sunday Times,* who was now publisher of the weekly *Sunday Business* newspaper. At least the rain let up long enough for Battelle to make a speech; he seemed highly agitated that night.

I didn't know it at the time, but the executives at the top were already anxious about the European edition, even on its first day. Earlier that afternoon, Battelle had given Neil some sobering instructions: not to hire any more people. He said that he shouldn't officially announce that Battelle had imposed a hiring freeze, but should act essentially as if there was one. Neil declared himself flabbergasted at how quickly the financial assumptions had shifted. Battelle's response was: "Get used to it."

Au Revoir to All That

The market we swim in today is far different than the one we anticipated when we first began planning this magazine one year ago.

—Final editorial, *The Industry Standard Europe,* April 2001[1]

As Neil Thackray learned the day we launched the European edition, the autumn had put a chill into the finances of Standard Media International. In October, Battelle received the monthly report detailing the company's financial position. He had gotten accustomed to the fact that even though the company was making a profit, the cash flow for any given month was often negative. But this report had something odder on it. For months, the cash statement had shown a balance of between $25 and $30 million. This month, however, it showed only $20 million. He was disturbed, and he asked Anne-Marie McGowan, the recently appointed chief operating officer, if she knew what had happened. She said she didn't know and recommended asking Herb Montgomery, who was, after all, the chief financial officer.

Montgomery did not have a ready answer. "That was not a good sign," Battelle later recalled. It took several days before Montgomery came up with an explanation, which was essentially: People are taking a really long time to pay us. There had been a huge increase in the category known as "accounts receivable," or, more plainly, money that other companies owed us. It's one of the oldest problems in business, and an especially difficult one in the media business: Your suppliers want to be paid within thirty days, but your advertisers have up to ninety days to pay. In order to pay the bills, we'd dipped rather substantially into the cash reserve.

What Montgomery didn't say, and perhaps didn't grasp at the moment, was that a good chunk of *The Standard*'s advertisers wouldn't pay up in ninety days because they wouldn't be around in ninety days. Over the next few months, the company would file dozens of lawsuits against advertisers who'd failed to pay, many for amounts in the six figures.

Battelle knew he was going to need more money. And there were venture capital firms out there that were dying to get a piece of what was still the hottest business publication in America. He took a proposal to the board that *The Standard* take on another $50 million in private equity.

Pat McGovern was skeptical. "Why do you want to raise more money?" he asked.

Battelle patiently explained that, primarily, he wanted to have money in the bank for growth and for a rainy day. Second, he wanted to make sure that IDG was insulated against any risk in case the business went sour. Of course, he was also anxious to reduce IDG's stake so that *The Standard* could make its own decisions, but that thought was not exactly fit for board consumption.

McGovern looked at him and said, "Are you afraid your owners are going to let you run out of money?" The proposal was shelved.

WHERE ARE THE HEROES?

The autumn chill had hit Europe as well. Even in the short stretch of time it had taken us to hire the team and produce the first European issue, the mood of the Net business had shifted. The unabashed optimism of the spring had evaporated, and by October we faced the bracing news that the sector shakeout we knew was coming was, in fact, upon us. The Nasdaq and its European tech counterparts had begun sliding in the spring and had not recovered in the fall as some had predicted (or perhaps simply had hoped) it would.

With the disappearance of the market froth came the disappearance of willing investors, and hence the disappearance of companies. The news sections of our first full-length dummy issue, published on October 5, and our first proper issue, published October 19, were energetic chronicles of decline. Boxman, the giant Scandinavian online retailer that had been the third largest in Europe, was on the verge of bankruptcy. Urban Fetch was shutting down its London operation after a meager four months on the job.

Most distressing to me was the fate of companies much closer to our own business. Microsoft had contracted with a young Labour Party apparatchik to produce a UK version of *Slate,* but he admitted in late September that his potential backers had gotten skittish.[2] In September, TheStreet.com announced that it was going to have trouble meeting analysts' estimates, an announcement that practically spelled out the death notice for its UK site, which closed two months later.

I honestly believed that TheStreet's troubles had no direct implications for *The Industry Standard Europe.* The problem with TheStreet.co.uk, I felt, was threefold: (1) The UK site was never quite as good as the U.S. product; (2) the UK site was launched with the expectation that Britain's stock-trading population would rise, which didn't happen after the market began going down, and (3) TheStreet felt it had to close its UK operation because the finances of its U.S. operation were in trouble. Surely that couldn't happen to us; magazine ad pages were still coming in faster than they could be booked.

Nonetheless, the new spirit of decline did affect the kind of magazine we were able to produce. A niche weekly like *The Standard* needs heroes—or at least celebrities—and where they don't exist you have to create them. Creating them in a market where unprofitable companies have multibillion-dollar market capitalizations is relatively easy. Creating them in an atmosphere where no one is investing money, stock prices are declining, and companies continue to bleed investment cash is significantly harder. No heroes meant no compelling cover stories; in the nine issues we published in the fall and winter of 2000, only once did we have the head of a British company on the cover.

In addition, the magazine I wanted to produce had stronger cultural and intellectual aspirations than the American edition. I felt the magazine could tap some of Europe's leading intellectuals and force them to apply their ideas to the Internet Economy, or vice versa. Through the aid of our European editor Bruno Giussani, we commissioned an article by Pierre Bourdieu, probably the most prominent French sociologist of our time. The essay that came in, a sweeping attack on venture capital and entrepreneurial culture, argued that the so-called New Economy was essentially propped up by a global conspiracy intent on weakening the power of the state. I thought it was powerful but very abstract, and couldn't stand on its own; we sought someone to write a counterpoint essay but never found the right author.

More successful was the piece we ran in our fourth issue, an engaging essay by the British novelist Jeannette Winterson. Partly, it was an essay on the power of the Internet, but it also attacked the "ignorance and fear" of writers like Martin Amis and Louis de Bernières, who declined to aid Winterson in her effort to win back the domain Jeannettewinterson.com from an academic cybersquatter who had registered it, along with about 130 other author names.[3]

To be honest, however, there was an unspoken premise behind such articles that the Internet would continue to grow and even drive the economies of Western nations. So long as that premise was intact, average Internet business readers who were not Winterson devotees could at least comfort themselves with the notion that their businesses were stimulating the intelligentsia. But as the premise of Net growth became increasingly shaky, such essays began to look frivolous, or worse, behind the curve.

BRILLIANT MOMENTS IN PR

There were many reasons to be proud of the first issue, but one story in particular had been a genuine scoop that I had discovered by accident. In June, our old friends at Priceline had announced that they would be launching their European services—starting with Britain—in the fall. To the British press, this move was practically a declaration of war against the locals; "US e-commerce giant Priceline to invade Europe," read the headline in *The Evening Standard*.[4] Specifically, much of the press predicted that the main competition for Priceline's name-your-own-price travel services would be Lastminute.com, the local dot-com darling headed by Brent Hoberman and Martha Lane Fox.

Out of curiosity, I looked up who had registered the domain name Priceline.co.uk—and lo and behold, it was held by Lastminute.com, which had reserved the URL back in 1998. The picture was much more complicated than Lastminute.com and Priceline being the rivals that most (but not all) of the British press believed. Actually, Priceline had invested $5 million in early 2000 to acquire about 1.5 percent of Lastminute.com—a strange move for a company that wanted to launch a separate European business.

I knew there had to be a story there, so I gave this tip to Bernhard, who'd done strong work on Priceline in New York. It turned out that in

September, Lastminute had actually forced its investor Priceline to buy the domain name back. With its launch in the UK imminent, Priceline was effectively blackmailed into paying to get its own name. Bernhard asked Dennis Malamatinas, the CEO of Priceline Europe, about this demand, and he said: "I didn't appreciate that. Let's put it that way. I don't know their motives. I was, to be honest with you, quite irritated when I heard about it. When it comes to business ethics, how could they do this?"[5]

It's not every day that you get a CEO to dump on a partner like that. I felt certain that some of the daily papers would pounce on this quote, and so I made certain that our PR team at Gnash wrote a press release featuring this story. But the launch came and went, and no one in the British media cited our Priceline scoop. I forgot about it for about a week, and then I asked our in-house publicist why she thought it went unnoticed. She told me that a Gnash publicist wrote the release but never sent it out. Why? Because Gnash also handled the Last-minute.com account and thought that the story made that company look bad.

I was livid. I could barely break it to Bernhard that, just as in New York, we'd been screwed by our own publicity firm on a scoop about the same company! Toward the end of the month, Gnash's founder Narda Shirley apologized to me in a pub near the company's Notting Hill office, calling the incident a "total fuck-up." But it was too late to regain the momentum; a news magazine can hardly go around publicizing a story that's several issues old.

Stop the Presses

For all of my professional writing career, I've worked for weeklies, so I'm very familiar with their rhythms. You'd like to sit around and plan long-term coverage, make structural changes to

ease the workflow, really concentrate on getting even the smallest details right. But always a deadline looms. George Bernard Shaw once
likened writing a regular column to standing under a windmill; a vane
comes down and knocks your head, and by the time you stand up
again you can see the next one coming down.

Moreover, we had a lean staff; we were responsible for about 60 editorial pages a week, with only eight full-time reporters, who also had
to crank out breaking stories for the Web site. (Ideally, I would have
liked twice as many.) Some of that space, admittedly, we filled with
stories that had run in the U.S. edition. Still, because of the time lag
between editions, and the need to localize the subject matter and get
our own art, preparing the American stories was sometimes as taxing
as creating our own.

This pressure was particularly hard on our reporters. I began to
hear some grumbling that they felt like they were merely filling space
and not being given the opportunity to pursue unique or especially interesting stories. I was worried that even some of the best ones would
burn out.

Still, there were plenty of small triumphs to keep us going. The last
day of October was a Tuesday, the day we shipped our final pages to
the printer. I was pleased with that week's issue, which had a cover
story about Manchester United's transformation into a media company, and a fascinating story reported from Russia about taking
Pravda online. Most days I got a sandwich and ate lunch at my desk,
but on that day Michael Parsons and I decided to take a rare leisurely
lunch at a nearby Turkish restaurant.

When we came back, there was an urgent e-mail from Boris Groendahl, our Berlin bureau chief, who actually wasn't scheduled to start
work until the next day. He had discovered a not-yet-issued press release on the Bertelsmann Web site indicating that the company was
about to buy a piece of Napster, the renegade song-swapping site that
had been sued by all the major music labels—including Bertelsmann.
The release was in German and wasn't scheduled to go out until later

that day in Bertelsmann's New York office, after it had been translated into English.

I immediately realized that this was a huge story, but we had already closed the magazine hours before. Thankfully, Michael and managing editor Paul Mungo advised me that we could reship a page at essentially no cost as long as we didn't change the artwork. By coincidence, we had a story in that week's news section about the popularity of Napster in various European countries, particularly Britain, Germany, and Sweden.

We grabbed the reporter, Michael Learmonth, reopened the file, and wrote a new headline, deck, and lede, putting the news of the Bertelsmann deal in the first sentence. Paul called the printer and, presumably, someone there actually said, "Stop the presses." We reshipped the page, and Boris was already at work on a Web story. Thanks to our newfound international muscle, we were at the very top of one of the year's biggest stories before the San Francisco office was even open for business. I rounded out the afternoon by going to meet a particularly cybersavvy Member of Parliament. I felt elated.

TILTING AT WINDMILLS

The business side of *The Industry Standard Europe* never had quite the same triumphalism, even though there were many encouraging signs prior to launch. We had struck a deal to have the magazine distributed in every first-class seat on the Eurostar, the high-speed train that shuttles between London, Paris, and Brussels, and which had become the transportation method of choice for deal-happy Net executives. I negotiated a content deal with a new, impressive Web site called BreakingViews, which had been founded by the longtime *Financial Times* writer/editor Hugo Dixon. And the first issue exceeded its advertising targets by a wide margin.

But there were a number of early bad omens as well. One of the most significant business tweaks we made was the decision to run many more recruitment ads than the U.S. edition did. Such ads made up a vital part of the revenues of the UK's trade publications. But recruitment ads are much more accountable than display ads; if a company doesn't fill a job, it can conclude that the ad was ineffective. And so recruitment ads were very weak in the beginning; it takes more than a few weeks to establish a new title as a must-read.

Behind all of this the sales force of *The Industry Standard Europe* was fighting a protracted and complex battle—against IDG. Even before the magazine launched, we knew that IDG was at best skeptical about a European edition. What we didn't know was why. Some of IDG's arguments had merit, but there was also a baser self-interest involved. Because IDG had magazines across the globe, it also had a global ad sales force, called IGS, which sold ads for the entire range of IDG titles. There were two chief reasons to have a single sales force. First, it saved money: The hundreds of IDG titles would not be sustainable if each one had to pay an ad sales team. Second, it insured that each advertiser had a single point of contact with the company; if an advertiser was constantly pestered by a series of ad reps for different publications under the same corporate roof, he or she was likely to turn nasty.

That's all reasonable, except: Where did that arrangement leave *The Industry Standard Europe*? Neil's conception, obviously, was that we would have our own ad sales team to sell ads for our magazine, period. If the IGS team in, say, Germany, was able to sell an ad for us, Neil would be thrilled, and happy to pay a commission to the IGS salesperson. But given all the other magazines the IGS people had to represent, that scenario seemed likely to be an exception; the rule would be our team, our ads.

IDG executives did not see it that way. From their point of view, we had arrived on IGS's turf and represented, at best, an annoyance to their advertisers, and at worst, a drain on their revenues. IDG proposed a deal whereby our salespeople could never undersell IGS's rates and would have to send reports of all the sales calls they made. There was an attempt to split up the territories, but the way that Thackray read the proposal, potentially every customer who advertised in *The Industry Standard Europe* could be construed as an IGS customer, and thus he'd have to pay a 20 percent commission, even if no IGS person was involved in selling the ad. Thackray described the plan as "loony." He was going to have enough trouble making ends meet as it stood; if 20 percent of the advertising revenue was siphoned off, then the entire European operation was a suicide mission.

There was only one person capable of resolving this dispute independently: John Battelle. But Battelle was in a delicate position at this stage and, indeed, was on the brink of quitting his own company. His top priority was independence from IDG. That could take the form of outside investment, an IPO, or an outright sale, but it had to happen and it had to happen fast. The paradox was that in order to break free from IDG, he needed IDG's permission. And so the last thing he wanted was an intractable dispute over an issue that was relatively minor. Indeed, if the entire European edition had to be sacrificed in order to convince IDG to free *The Standard* as a whole, he was willing to accept it.

And so Battelle, always impatient with the present, made his argument based on the future. The arrangement with IGS was impossible, he told the board, because it would never be tolerated in a public company. Investors would immediately see the arrangement for what it was: a favorite-son contract with the principal shareholder.

His line of reasoning was accurate but was based on one mistaken premise: Standard Media International was not a public company, at least not yet. As long as IDG was our majority owner, favorite-son contracts were business as usual. In an appropriately European allusion, IDG president and *Standard* board member Kelly Conlin described Battelle's speech as "tilting at windmills." When Thackray heard that comment, he thought to himself: "Oh shit."

COVER ME

A bigger disappointment on the business side was in sales revenue. We had set our rate base at 30,000 copies, which was deliberately low. The first issue got a promotional bounce, but the sales figures for the next few issues were scary. Because of the system of newsstand returns, it takes months to get an authoritative, precise count of individual copy sales, but the early indications were that we were moving only a few thousand copies of each issue. Worse, the number seemed to be going down each week.

This data put a great deal of pressure on me, particularly concerning covers. I thought I had a good eye for covers and for which stories belonged there. And for many of the early issues I was deliberately trying to appeal to as wide an audience as possible. In the third issue, our cover story on Manchester United was an ideal way, I thought, to demonstrate that we weren't just about dot-coms, and so we graced our cover with David Beckham, the Manchester United player who is one of the UK's biggest celebrities and a worldwide star.

In retrospect, decisions like that were spectacularly wrong. We were a brand new magazine whose title was less than descriptive. Far from trying to prove to the world that we were bigger than the Internet, we should have been bending over backwards to show that we owned the Internet. News agents who weren't specifically paying attention to us looked at covers like that and scratched their heads; they couldn't figure out where to rack us.

Of course, the psychology of magazine covers is a bottomless debate. It's unlikely that different covers would have helped, because the market itself was falling apart. We'd had some sense of this downturn before we launched. One of our most direct competitors, *Business 2.0*, had launched its UK edition as a monthly in June, pledging an aggressive circulation of 70,000. (Its U.S. circulation as a biweekly at the time was more than 200,000.) Wendy Sly, our circulation director, got word from her newsstand sources that the first UK issue of *Business 2.0* had sold just 17,000 copies and that the magazine was at risk of being removed from the shelves of WH Smith, Britain's largest magazine retailer. We thought it was good that our competitor was suffering, but we soon concluded that the same readers who weren't buying *Business 2.0* weren't buying us either.

NO MORE ALLOWANCES

Back in America, the financial situation was beginning to look precarious. The cash position was not getting any better, and Battelle knew that bodies were going to have to disappear. Not just from the bottom, either; some of the people responsible for getting the publication into this mess were going to have to go. He started with some of the easiest targets: *Grok* was going to close up shop, after just four issues.

Another target would be Europe. On November 22, Battelle sent Neil Thackray a rather dire e-mail that said: "I am afraid we are in pretty significant downturn land here, and we need your help. Your budgets and your actuals are coming in over original expectations. We need to slow down your expenses, quickly. How can we do this?"

Neil had already pared down projected marketing expenses, and he had delayed hiring some key staff members (the European edition never had a publisher or a chief technology officer). He turned reluctantly but inevitably toward a cost that no one had told him he had to absorb: the Americans. When we started the European edition, a total of eight employees from the U.S. publication were relocated to London: four managers (Parsons, McAlister, Chiala, and me), one Web producer, an assistant photo editor, and two reporters. Moving to London is a disruptive and expensive proposition, and since the arrangements were made for our moves during The Fat Year, *The Standard* was quite generous to its expatriates. Based on a package put together by Ernst & Young, moving expenses were covered up to a certain amount. The company hired a relocation firm to help us find flats quickly (and that firm just happened to steer us to some of the city's more expensive neighborhoods). Each of us received a housing allowance and a cost-of-living allowance to ensure that we were not spending more to live in London than we had been in New York or San Francisco. Our taxes, made exceedingly complex by having to comply with federal, state, and UK laws, would be handled by Ernst & Young. My contract even entitled me to a company car, a privilege I never bothered to exercise.

Not long after I arrived, Neil began making occasional cracks about how expensive the American employees were. Evidently the living allowances were being deducted from his hiring budget; I was told that each expatriate cost the company twice as much to employ as a comparable UK hire. I found this hard to believe, since my own housing allowance was only a couple of hundred dollars a month—how much could this really have cost?

I learned the reality in November when I began discussing the possibility of a raise with one of the American reporters, Michael Learmonth. In my view, he had been doing excellent work and had been hired at a relatively low salary, and I wanted to boost his pay. But when I looked at his overall compensation, I discovered that his housing allowance was seven times the amount I had been getting! Ostensibly, the reason for this was that I am single and he had moved with his wife. Even so, he had only *one* wife, not six. And though personally I didn't begrudge him the sum he was getting, it seemed ridiculous to me that our personnel department would sign off on a pay scheme that rewards a reporter wildly more than the editor-in-chief.

Possibly if *The Standard*'s finances had continued to balloon, such anomalies could have been tolerated. But with cost-cutting pressure coming from San Francisco, by the first week of December Neil couldn't take it anymore. Even though the international assignment letters guaranteed that the housing and cost-of-living adjustments would be paid for as long as five years, we had to gather the expatriates on our staff and tell them that the publication could no longer afford them.

I felt tortured and guilty; some of these employees had agreed to come to Europe based solely on the fact that their cost-of-living would not be affected. Here we were less than a year later going back on our word. This put me in the tortuous psychological position of the angry parent; I was literally taking away their allowances!

At the same time, the need for belt-tightening had become obvious. Just before we had to tell the staff about it, Parsons was able to cushion the blow somewhat by getting the allowances extended for one more year. The expatriates were not happy about the prospect of losing their allowances, although it dawned on them that some of their colleagues in the United States were about to lose their jobs.

IF HE WANTS TO MAKE THINGS UNPLEASANT FOR YOU . . .

That was far from my only December headache. In fifteen years of professional writing, I had never been sued for libel, even at the *Voice*, where we published pretty tough stories. There had been a few threats, including one over a column item I'd written based on internal corporate documents that I technically should not have had access to. Thankfully, New York state has a strong "shield" law that protects a reporter in such a situation as long as he or she did not steal the documents.

Alas, from an editor's perspective, British libel law is painfully weak. In the United States, a successful libel action must prove that a reporter acted with malice, which in practice means being grossly and willfully negligent or using reporting and writing procedures far outside the norms of the profession. If the subject of an article can be construed as a public figure—and most can—the protection for the publisher and reporter is especially strong.

Not so in the United Kingdom. The standard that a complainant must prove is not malice, but simply that the subject was harmed in some substantial and demonstrable way. That standard often holds even if the material published is true. Furthermore, internal corporate documents are, as a rule, not publishable. In extreme cases, the subject of an upcoming news article can even get a court order preventing its publication (a high-risk maneuver, but still an incredible power). It's true that libel judgments in the UK tend to be much lower than in America, but at the same time, a publisher who loses a libel case must pay the legal fees of the claimant, which will frequently be higher than the judgment itself.

Suffice it to say that we didn't want to be sued for libel in the UK. And that's why I was so anxious about our coverage of a company called Efdex. Although largely unknown in the United States, Efdex was a high-profile business-to-business Web exchange for the food and drink industry. The man behind it was Tim Carron Brown, a former magazine ad salesman who had gotten into the food-purchasing business in the mid-1980s. Carron Brown was a consummate salesman; our feature story on him quoted a colleague who said he could "sell sand to Arabs."[6]

Carron Brown gathered around him an impressive list of investors and board members for Efdex, including Ian Molson, the heir to the Molson Breweries fortune; William Cox III, whose family owns a majority of Dow Jones; and Laurence Isaacson, deputy chairman of Groupe Chez Gerard, which operates restaurant chains throughout Europe. In 1998, he had secured a £10 million investment from the giant Japanese investment bank Nomura.

The company hired a staggering 300 employees and went through the motions of trying to build an Internet-based exchange system. Yet by early 2000, the company had failed to make its payroll. And when the liquidators arrived in September, they found that not only did the company have no revenues and no product, but it had somehow managed to run up £30 million in debt.

This was a juicy story of the dot-com bust, with more than a suggestion of improper conduct. We had difficulty illustrating the story; it was not the kind of piece whose subjects were going to sit for a portrait. We had one good black-and-white shot of Carron Brown; we also had some interesting stills from a corporate promotional video that Efdex had made during its heyday. As we had the piece reviewed by our attorneys, however, we were told that using the images from the video could land us in hot water; they were technically copyrighted, and we didn't have permission to reproduce them. This view was extremely cautious; at worst, we would have been committing a tiny infraction against a company that legally no longer existed. Still, we didn't want anyone affiliated with Efdex to have any valid reason to sue. In the end, we settled on a timeline and pullquotes to break up the dense text.

Polly's story was the most complex investigative piece *The Industry Standard Europe* had ever published, and I was quite proud of it; although it merited a cover, we went with a more photogenic news exclusive. In the first ten days or so after it ran on December 7, we heard nothing. When I arrived at our office Christmas party and went over to Neil, he congratulated me on a terrific piece. It turns out he had met Carron Brown while Neil was selling ads for a British publisher. Carron Brown had set up a meeting under the pretext of taking out an ad, but instead he was seeking investors for Efdex. Neil had told him the idea was stupid and wouldn't work.

Then one day I overheard Polly on what seemed to be a contentious phone call. While grimacing as she listened, she held up a piece of paper on which she'd written "BILL COX ON THE WARPATH." This news was worrying, since Cox was one of the major, on-the-record sources for the story; if he had trouble with what we wrote, it could mean larger problems for the story's credibility.

Not long after that, Carron Brown himself phoned me. He said he couldn't believe that we had published what we had, that the story was wrong from top to bottom. "Was it even edited before it ran?" he asked, incredulous. I assured him that it had been and asked him to cite any examples of errors. I believe in maximum exchange of views; if we'd made factual errors, I wanted them corrected. And if Carron Brown wanted an extraordinary amount of space on the letters page to air his objections, I was prepared, even eager, to give it to him. Frustratingly, he refused to point to any single thing that was wrong in the story. He kept saying, "It's the whole thing from top to bottom." He said he was meeting with attorneys to decide his next move and tried to menace me with the fact that Cox was upset with our story. "He's a very powerful man, and if he wants to make things unpleasant for you, he can," Carron Brown said.

This distressing situation was made worse by what was going on with Polly herself. She had already announced her intention to leave the magazine; if a libel suit were to be filed, *The Standard* would be in the undesirable position of having to defend a reporter who no longer worked for the magazine.

As I explored further, however, I found reasons to be reassured. Although Polly over the past few months had at times seemed drained, she had attacked the Efdex story with a military sense of mission and organization; her notes were voluminous, intact, and thoroughly supported what she'd written. And when I spoke to Cox, it quickly became clear that his problem with the story was not that we'd been inaccurate, but that he was embarrassed to be publicly linked with Carron Brown. He never said that the conversation I had with him was off the record, and so I took and kept notes: He admitted that Carron Brown had a "checkered past at best" and said that for Carron Brown not to have paid his employees was "unconscionable." I thought that if Carron Brown was considering calling this guy as a character witness, we were in good shape.

Still, I was nervous as I left for home for Christmas, and I left instructions with the features editor to check the mail carefully for any possible lawsuit and phone me immediately if anything turned up. Personally, it was not a great Christmas; among other things, my laptop was stolen somewhere between London and New York. The distance between Linda and me had taken a heavy toll, and our relationship had all but collapsed. Professionally, the two best Christmas presents I got were a framed issue of the premiere European issue from my Mom—and no lawsuit from Carron Brown.

"THE DAY THE MUSIC DIED"

The new year did not begin auspiciously. On January 4, I got a call from our U.S. publicist, Alissa Neil, my old *Voice* colleague. She was feeling anxious about announcing the upcoming layoffs. It's among a publicist's most joyless tasks, but for Alissa it was made more exasperating by the fact that she knew that her own boss, Chief Marketing Officer Kerry Zeida, was going to be let go, and she was pretty sure he didn't know yet.

I tried to talk her through her dilemma, but I was stunned that someone as high ranking as Zeida would be laid off. That was only the beginning; Alissa told me that two other top executives—Chief Financial Officer Herb Montgomery and Publisher Steve Thompson—would also be among those leaving.

Alissa asked me what I thought the media reaction would be to lumping these three dismissals in with the staff layoffs. I told her I thought any reporter paying attention would find that very strange. Company officials that high up don't get laid off; they make cryptic announcements about wanting to spend more time with their families, but they don't get laid off. By including their departures in with the three dozen other layoffs, mostly of low- to mid-level employees, we risked making it look like we were trying to hide something. She agreed.

As we finished the conversation, it dawned on me just how odd this situation was. Three of our top executives were on their way out, obviously involuntarily. What kind of magazine breaks an all-time annual record for selling ad pages, and then in a matter of days fires its publisher?

As for the rest of the layoffs, I allowed myself to believe that the first round of cuts, while painful, was necessary, and that it would not substantially affect the European edition. First of all, no purely editorial jobs were affected. Second, many of the jobs eliminated were Web producers who'd been brought on to build specific parts of the site. Once those functions were up and running, their services were less necessary; perhaps some of them should have been hired on six-month contracts in the first place. And finally, we had some two dozen people on staff with the word "marketing" in their title; if such an army was ever needed, it sure wasn't needed now that our Web and conference operations were slowing down.

Those observations, while plausible and comforting, added up to a conclusion that was nonetheless wrong. I began to learn over the next few weeks that the layoffs among Web personnel grew out of severe internal conflicts among the staff, and that many of the Web projects had been abandoned before they worked as planned. That would cause big problems in a few months.

On January 8, the layoffs were officially announced. Thirty-six employees were to be eliminated from the payroll. That would have been pretty much the whole company two years before; amazingly, that figure now represented a mere 7 percent of *The Standard*'s workforce. We had reached the inflated point of having 470 employees. The only mild comfort was the knowledge that we were hardly alone; on the same day, the digital division of *The New York Times* announced that it was eliminating 69 positions, or 17 percent of its workforce. The Associated Press story carried a comment from Martin Walker, the veteran magazine consultant. Walker summed it up pithily: "The party has ended. Reality is setting in now and I wouldn't be surprised to see some of these technology magazines fail this year."[7]

That was certainly the feeling on the inside. One daily task that fell to Bill Brazell, a Web editor who had been with *The Standard* from the beginning, was to send out an e-mail summarizing all the stories that had been published on the Web that day or were in the editing process. He always tried to enliven this slightly tedious communication by opening it with an interesting literary quotation or a rock lyric. On January 8, his missive included this slightly altered lyric from "American Pie," Don McLean's anthem of loss: "But January made me shiver/With each paper that I'd deliver/And something touched me deep inside/The day the music died."

The mood in Europe was not quite as somber as in San Francisco. Virtually no one in the European offices had ever met any of the people who'd been laid off, or even really had much contact with them, and so there was no personal sting. On top of that, there was a slight undercurrent of resentment at just how huge the U.S. operation had become. After all, the magazine that it was producing was increasingly shrinking to one not much bigger than our own, and it had about ten times the editorial staff that we had.

For a few more weeks, we were able to maintain a sense that the cutbacks were a necessary medicine happening in a sick land that was far, far away. It could even be amusing, as in early February when the vice president for finance sent out this company-wide e-mail: "Effective immediately, no employee is authorized to use Boston Coach or any other Limosine [*sic*] Service without prior written approval of [various department heads]. Taxicabs are about 50% the cost of limos. Our limo bill runs at least $15K a month. Use of Taxis or rental cars will cut this expense in half."

Fifteen grand a month for limos? I hadn't even known we had access to limos.

THE *FT* STEALS A STORY

Frankly, I had more than enough to deal with without thinking about layoffs. Journalistically, the magazine continued to impress me, but in some ways good journalism creates more work for the editor. One of our British reporters, Chris Nuttall, had been the first online journalist at the BBC, and he retained a number of strong contacts there. Toward the end of 2000, one of his sources told him about a simmering internal debate about the BBC's Internet strategy: There was a proposal to sell ads on the BBC's news Web site. In many ways the BBC is a thoroughly commercialized enterprise: It produces a large number of commercially successful magazines and makes millions of pounds a year selling rights to its original broadcast material. But it has always had strict rules about advertising; specifically, it has always protected its news operations by not selling ads against news broadcasts.

Now the Web was threatening to overthrow that historic arrangement. Not surprisingly, the commercial media saw the BBC as the recipient of a massive public subsidy and was furious about the prospect of competing with it head-on. That made for a feisty, exclusive story, which the British press treated in its customary fashion: They stole it. Six days after our story appeared, the *Financial Times* ran a news story saying, "The BBC is considering plans to introduce advertising to one of its public service websites, risking the wrath of commercial rivals who oppose the move."[8] The pink newspaper even went so far as to quote a "statement" from a BBC official that was, in fact, a quotation given directly and solely to our reporters. I found this conduct indefensible, if rather typical. Our publicist called to complain and was told that if I wrote a letter to the editor, the *FT* would publish it. I did; the *FT* didn't.

The controversy continued when Parliament announced that it would hold an inquiry into whether or not the BBC could get away with this policy change. We solicited a formal response from the BBC, which came in the form of a very thoughtful letter from Caroline Thomson, the BBC's director of public policy. I thought this was a major coup; we were right in the center of a major political debate about the Internet, media, and business. Somehow, even though that letter was addressed to me, a report of its contents ended up on the *Guardian*'s media site—before I'd even received the letter! I think I could be forgiven for concluding that the British press was not out to do us any favors.

Then, on January 19, Tim Carron Brown again phoned me. I wanted to keep our conversation to a minimum, but I wasn't prepared for his opening remark: "I've got some papers I want to send to you. Should I post them to you or to your solicitors?"

I took a breath, and I told him he should send them to our managing director. That was the end of the conversation.

I was in dread—not because I lacked confidence in the story, but because I did not want to go through the stress of a libel trial. Drearily, I told Neil that he should be expecting a package from Carron Brown or his lawyers. He was reasonably good-humored about it, but I sensed he was worried. Even a frivolous lawsuit could end up costing us a lot of money we could hardly afford.

Amazingly, the feared lawsuit never arrived. I subsequently came to think that Carron Brown had called me with at least one of two goals in mind: (1) to find out who our solicitors were, in case he might have some influence at the firm, or (2) to intimidate me into running a retraction of some kind.

WE'VE GOT A PROBLEM

At any rate, it only took a couple of weeks before it was clear that no one would be immune from the San Francisco cutbacks. With Polly now gone, we had an opening in editorial, and I found a candidate, Wale Azeez, whom I really liked. He was energetic, knew his beat, and was already on good terms with a few people on staff. He was also black, which was to be a start toward building a more diverse newsroom. I made him an offer that he accepted on January 18; he was to start a month later.

On Friday, February 16, the day before Wale was meant to start, I was on a trip for a few days to New York when I got an e-mail from Michael Parsons with the subject line "Bad News," and instructions to phone him as soon as possible. Neil Thackray had just returned from a three-day trip to San Francisco. On his last day, he finally got to see Battelle, who wouldn't look him in the eye. Battelle hemmed and hawed and said: "We've got a problem. We need to figure out how to run your business with twenty people." Thackray made some calculations and concluded that: (1) it wasn't possible, and (2) if it was possible, it would have to be without him, because Thackray was too expensive. They spent some more time poring over figures and couldn't find a way to make them meet; then it was time for Thackray to leave. He got to the airport, ordered a $15 glass of Chardonnay, and tried to reconcile himself to the prospect that *The Industry Standard Europe* was going to fold.

Neil had told the gist of this to Michael, who in turn interpreted it for me as an immediate hiring freeze. I had to call Wale on Saturday from New York and tell him he no longer had a job. Although he took it reasonably well, it was one of the most difficult and depressing phone calls I've ever had to make. And one of the downsides about working in the journalism business is that, if you tell a journalist that you can't hire him because of a hiring freeze, the next person he tells is likely to be another journalist. So still jet-lagged on Monday, I had to deal not only with the staff who had been looking forward to Wale joining us, but with persistent queries from Amy Vickers, a fierce reporter from *The Guardian*'s media Web site. The story she published the next day did not boost our morale.

Drop the Pretense

But the fate of the European edition was probably sealed even before the layoffs were announced in the United States. And that's because the edition had acquired a very powerful detractor: Pat McGovern. On January 2, he wrote a note to Battelle regarding a conversation he said he'd had with "a number of high-tech industry executives who are based in the UK." He had discussed our magazine with them, and the feedback was not good. One of the biggest problems, he claimed, was the European focus, which made our potential UK readers think they weren't going to get important news from America from us. But neither were we focused tightly enough on the UK for them to get their essential industry news. McGovern's supposed feedback group also said that "they miss not being able to buy the 'Mother Ship' edition of *The Industry Standard*." Therefore, he argued, UK readers who wanted to read about developments in the U.S. Internet business were picking up copies of *Red Herring* and *Business 2.0* instead.

McGovern recommended that "the UK team drop the pretense of being a European regional publication and take the position that they are the most in-depth, insider reporting on what is happening in the Internet economy in the UK." He also said that the U.S. edition should be restored to newsstands throughout the UK and Europe, "so as not to subsidize the paid circulation of our US competitors."

For a publishing company that prides itself on a decentralized structure, this certainly looked like management on a molecular level. These were not only questions that could best be resolved by the team on the ground, but they were the same serpentine battles that we had fought—and thought we won—back in the summer. The snake heads had returned, and this time with venom. It was clear that McGovern's objections were not intellectual jousting points; they were preliminary excuses to shut us down.

This was especially frustrating because many of McGovern's criticisms seemed plain wrong. From an editorial perspective, a narrow concern with the UK missed the point: The Internet story was part of the broader picture of European and British economic integration. Just a few weeks before McGovern sent his note, for example, the UK's largest Internet service provider, Freeserve, had been purchased by its growing French rival, Wanadoo.[9] I found it impossible to believe that a publication that had staff only in London could do a better job covering the implications of that deal than we did with a reporter in Paris.

On the business side, there was absolutely no evidence that our U.S. competitors were benefiting from any newsstand weakness on our part. As best I knew, *Red Herring* was all but eliminating its presence in the UK. It had quietly laid off most of its staff, and its well-known London-based editor Kenneth Cukier was on his way out to take a position in Hong Kong with *The Asian Wall Street Journal*.

Similarly, *Business 2.0*'s UK edition—which adopted the localized approach that McGovern recommended, albeit on a monthly basis—was suffering. Two days after McGovern's e-mail, *Business 2.0*'s parent company, Future Network, announced that not only would it miss its projected profit for 2000, but it would actually lose a million pounds; this statement sent its stock down 41 percent in one day's trading.[10] By May, the company would close its UK edition altogether.

It's also unlikely that McGovern had churned the numbers on putting the U.S. edition on European newsstands. Even if McGovern's highly optimistic projection that the U.S. edition could sell 5,000 to 7,000 copies per week on UK newsstands turned out to be accurate, it would still be expensive to do so. And if, as we suspected, such circulation would simply be shaved off the sales of the European edition, then the company as a whole would probably be worse off.

That said, there are aspects of McGovern's critique that had an intuitive truth. A few friends and acquaintances had, in fact, told me they wished they could still buy the U.S. edition on London newsstands (some chose to subscribe to both, but that was purely a junkie's strategy).

And I took seriously the criticism that we weren't putting enough U.S. news into the magazine; I had heard the same complaint, mildly and indirectly, from Weber himself. The biggest reason for that deficiency was the problem with the lag in deadlines, a seemingly insurmountable problem. Most of the news we were rejecting fell into this category; it would have been stale by the time we could publish it.

THE PRINGLES FACTOR

But another reason we weren't picking up a lot of U.S. stories was that the American edition had fully entered a new stage, becoming a kind of hyped-up *BusinessWeek*. Sure, there were still moments when we could flex our dot-com muscles like no one else; in the fall of 2000, when Gary Rivlin wrote his groundbreaking expose on AOL's arm-twisting business tactics,[11] I picked it up for our edition and made sure it got the cover. But more and more, the editors in San Francisco were looking beyond the dot-com and computer-networking companies that had historically given *The Standard* its best material, striking out instead for broader stories about technology and business. Some of that redefinition stemmed from necessity: To stick to the traditional *Standard* role of tracking the Internet Economy would have been a relentless chronicle of layoffs and bankruptcies. The editor-in-chief had taken to saying, "There's no point in being the bible of the Internet industry if increasingly there is no Internet industry."

Some of the resulting pieces were intriguing, if not always right for the European audience. During the Christmas shopping season of 2000, the U.S. magazine ran an interesting story about how The Gap chain of retailers had made a bet—that it had lost—that leather pants would be the fashion hit of the season.[12] Not typical *Standard* fare, admittedly, but the story explained the kinds of problems that retailers, online and off, have with controlling their supply chains. It discussed the abilities and limitations of Internet technologies to manage these problems. This seemed like a reasonably good example of using our technology base to expand to more general topics. (Since The Gap had a substantial UK presence, I would have considered reprinting the story, but by the time it appeared we had already put out our year-end issue.) Another sharp piece exposed the striking number of companies that were technically on the verge of being delisted from the Nasdaq, primarily because their stock prices had stayed too low for too long.

Other attempts at refining our mission were simply confounding. The worst was in late February, following the announcement of a massive joint venture between Coca-Cola and Procter & Gamble. A *Standard* article maintained that this alliance was a natural fit and attempted to prove this view via a 650-word history of Pringles, the ersatz potato chips. Why was this an *Industry Standard* story? The story offered only this facile connection between our territory and canned chips: "Made of reconstituted potato flakes that are molded, fried, seasoned and packed in space-age containers, the brand was born of what later became new-economy hallmarks: proprietary technology, easy distribution and branding to die for."[13]

This piece struck me as, at best, a sidebar to what could have been a larger story, and at worst, a thin cover for the fact that we didn't have reporters who were expert at covering old economy companies like Coke and P&G. If this was the only contribution *The Standard* had to offer about a $4 billion venture that had no practical connection to technology, then it would have been better to use the page for another purpose. I suspect the magazine's core readership looked at that story, wrinkled their eyebrows, and turned the page. My European colleagues were less charitable; one writer asked the staff via e-mail for its views on the story, causing the picture editor to crack: "Next Week: The Truth Behind Pickled Eggs."

OUT OF FOCUS

I couldn't imagine that McGovern wanted the European edition of *The Standard* to be publishing more stories about the likes of Pringles. But debates about our editorial mix were always useful, and we continued to have them, internally and even externally—in the form of focus groups.

The focus group is an inherently controversial form of market research, and especially so for a new magazine. Weber had vigorously opposed using focus groups in *The Standard*'s early days, and his argument seemed airtight to me: Magazine audiences often can't tell you what they want until you give it to them. Any start-up magazine that based its offerings on the desires of a focus group of readers will only end up reproducing the parts of other publications that readers already like, leaving little room for innovation.

But by early 2001, we were no longer truly a start-up, not even in Europe, because we were still a transplanted version of a larger U.S. magazine. Focus groups had become part of our makeup. And so on a very rainy February evening, a group of us set out on a little adventure to an office on London's Savile Row. We sat in a darkened room behind a two-way mirror and had to talk in whispers while watching a group of prospective readers in the next room. It was kind of like being at a cinema where you are the movie, as in the scenes from Albert Brooks's *Defending Your Life*. The temptation to shout out responses, to walk through the door and defend yourself, is immense.

We also found ourselves asking who would volunteer to do these things, and why. True, the participants were paid a nominal amount and fed a decent dinner with wine. But the group that I saw, at least, consisted entirely of middle-aged professionals; surely they weren't there for a free meal. Maybe they were looking for dates?

One participant clearly knew more than the average person about magazine publishing; another rather pushy man seemed to consider himself a bit of an Internet expert, even though he persisted in garbling the names of popular Web sites. Nonetheless, I was encouraged by some of their comments on the magazine. They found the articles, headlines, and design to be interesting and creative. But the maddening truth was that we were losing the sale long before people picked up the magazine to read it: The cover snakes reared their heads again. Several members of the group expressed disbelief that a single publication could have put such a diverse group of images on its cover. One of them said that this disparity reflected the fact that magazines and their covers were always put together by two different companies!

And I had to reconcile myself to the fact that these readers truly disliked the word "Europe." Some of this was simply national prejudice. When one participant was asked what he thought about a story we'd run on the difficulties of implementing France's controversial thirty-five-hour workweek, he replied: "I didn't read that, because I don't like French people." But mostly it wasn't European subject matter, per se, that they objected to; it was simply the use of the word "Europe."[14] Just as McGovern had argued, there was something about having the word "Europe" in the title that made readers think they were getting a subsidiary, perhaps even inferior product. And so, beginning with the first issue in April, we dropped the word Europe from our logo. Of course, it made no difference whatsoever.

SACK ME, PLEASE

By this time, talk of layoffs and hiring freezes had become incredibly common—and not just at *The Standard*. The downturn had become part of the dot-com culture, the way that all-nighters and stock options had been during The Fat Year. In late January, Bernhard Warner and I had a fun, freewheeling dinner with Amy Shapiro, the head of public relations for DoubleClick with whom we'd both worked in New York. She brought along her boyfriend, Brett Morris, who'd done some work for the troubled online division of Virgin. Brett told us a hilarious story about the day when the managers had gathered about half the employees in a room and told them that staff cuts were necessary. They described what kind of compensation package they were willing to give and tenderly asked for volunteers. Almost every single person in the room raised his or her hand; they were all enticed by the cash package and confident that they could find new work as soon as they needed to. In Brett's case, he was actually hired back that same day as a freelancer for the same company, for higher pay and work closer to the kind he wanted to do.

Bernhard and I had been hearing stories like this; his wife had volunteered to be laid off at CNBC. We decided to do a seriously reported, but somewhat tongue-in-cheek article for the "New Gig" section about the joys of being laid off; it was the first time we put a "New Gig" story on the cover (which made the recruitment advertising team happy). The image was of a man photographed from the nose down and carrying a box of various effects from his desk; you could see that his tie was loosened and he was grinning, and on the box was written: "SACK ME, PLEASE! Why today's workers love being made redundant." It had the potential to be mildly offensive, but I thought it had the right amount of cheek for a British audience.

Unfortunately, Amy did not see it the same way. In an e-mail to Bernhard after the story came out, she admonished him: "I'm disappointed that you thought it was necessary to compromise Brett to give your story the edge you wanted. He's lost his freelance job at Virgin." We'd given Brett the opportunity to speak without using his name, but he chose to go on the record. Still, we felt terrible: "Sack Me, Please" had actually gotten someone sacked. We offered to let Brett do some freelance writing for the magazine. But this was irrelevant, because after two more issues our entire magazine would be sacked.

THE BRIDGE GOES DARK

Toward the end of February, *The Standard* announced a second round of layoffs. This one was deeper and broader than the first—sixty-nine employees were removed from the staff—and editorial was not excluded. Actually, the drop-off in headcount was more dramatic than that, because quite a few people, knowing that layoffs were imminent, decided to quit or take jobs elsewhere.

In this climate of decline, other changes had to be made. The company scaled back the rooftop parties dramatically; it seemed perverse to be celebrating when so many were losing their jobs. And the contract for the billboard over the Bay Bridge—a pillar of *The Standard*'s overcommitment—was allowed to expire.

Throughout most of March, Neil was rarely seen in the London office. He thought he'd come up with a solution to the problem Battelle had presented us with: Sell *The Industry Standard Europe,* or at least find a partner willing to invest in us. Initially, this seemed like a perfectly valid idea. Only three months earlier, the European publishing giant Gruner & Jahr had plunked down a phenomenal $340 million to buy *Fast Company,* a magazine to which we were often compared. And so Neil spent his days in various meetings with media companies who'd expressed interest in investing in us, or at least sniffing around.

On the surface, it seemed like an attractive and easy deal. Neil had put together a summary of our business that, if you accepted the rosy projections, made us look like a big player. Our Web traffic was growing steadily, and at the rate we were going we'd be up to 4 million page views a month by 2003. We were looking for a cash infusion of approximately £4 million, for which we were willing to sell a substantial amount of equity in the European edition.

There were tons of qualified companies that could afford that price, but our timing was horrendous. Not only had the first quarter been disastrous, but the second quarter was showing few signs of picking up. Neil joked that in September 2000, before we had even produced an issue, he could have raised £20 million. Now, with nearly six months of a well-respected magazine behind us, we couldn't get £5 million.

Ironically, the other problem was that our deal was too small. For the companies that might logically have been interested in taking a piece of the European edition—AOL Time Warner, Pearson—we were a flyspeck. Our total circulation was never more than 32,000, with annual revenues projected optimistically at a few million pounds. Hence, any megamedia investor would have had its eyes on the larger prize: a piece of the U.S. edition. But the board was hardly disposed to give up its ownership.

I See Dead People

By the end of March it became clear that Neil was not going to be able to make a deal that would satisfy a new investor, IDG, and *The Standard*'s U.S. management—not in the four-week window he'd been given, and probably never in the dull atmosphere of the spring of 2001. A team at Credit Suisse First Boston was initially excited about pulling together a deal for us but wouldn't make it a priority without a substantial fee. Neil met with CNN and *The Economist*, but neither were in a hurry to make any decision.

There had been a substantial nibble from *Sunday Business*, a weekly financial paper that considered merging with us to beef up its tech coverage. My staff got wind of this deal and was nervous about the prospect of working with Andrew Neil, a Thatcherite publisher with a reputation for ruthlessness. But it was moot because *Sunday Business* was unwilling to put up any cash, which we needed to stay afloat. (Indeed, by the fall of 2001, *Sunday Business* itself had to merge in order to stay alive.)

IDG said that without a strategic partner in place, it was no longer willing to fund the European edition on a monthly basis. Instead, it would provide us enough money to live week by week. Neil tried to explain to the board that this strategy would mean that his company would go out of business. He had discussed the problem with an insolvency attorney and was convinced that UK law dictates that at the moment when you believe you can't meet your liabilities, you must stop trading immediately. Failure to do so, as he explained, "is a criminal offense, meaning that I could go to jail." He thought this bit of information might be a useful piece of leverage, yet Battelle and IDG refused to make a final decision.

Parsons, who was attending many of the potential investment meetings with Neil, was getting increasingly anxious and pessimistic. His weekly back-page columns became a regular surreal commentary on the state of our publication. In one, he described a fictitious encounter at the hospital with a child prodigy venture capitalist who had fallen ill. The reader slowly becomes aware that this is Cole Sear from the movie *The Sixth Sense,* who tells Parsons, "I see dead people." He means dead business people: "They're working. They look like business people. But they're not . . . Because their businesses have died." By the end of the column, you realize that the narrator is like the child psychologist figure who, in the movie, was played by Bruce Willis. That is, from the very beginning, he's already one of the dead people.

ANOTHER PRISON THREAT

On April 5 there was a birthday luncheon for Neil with all the department heads. Everyone was trying to act cheerful in the face of what was a decidedly uncertain future; it was of course pouring rain. Neil, somewhat drearily, noted that one year earlier, on his fortieth birthday, he had spent the day in San Francisco interviewing with John Battelle.

The most interesting part of the lunch was that the business staff had managed to get some top-secret newsstand sales figures out of WH Smith, the UK's largest magazine retailer. This was one of the only times that we had a direct way to gauge our performance against our competitors. Some aspects of the chart made me cheer; we were, for example, outselling *BusinessWeek* by a factor of 2 to 1.

But such bright spots were overshadowed by the fact that the entire sector was disappearing. The figures showed that for all business and technology magazines, newsstand sales had declined a massive 67 percent from the year before. Everyone was getting clobbered. Any projections we'd ever made about newsstand sales—or even who our readers were and what they wanted out of the magazine—were so far out of whack with the current market that they were essentially irrelevant.

That weekend I went to Florence for the first time to give a speech at a technology conference; in my spare time I found delicious pizza and made a pilgrimage to Michelangelo's *David*. The conference, held in a four-star hotel and sponsored by Compaq, had been built up to me to be a very big deal. There were only about twelve people there—not a sign of a healthy industry.

When I got back to the office on Monday, I knew within a few hours that there was a possibility that the plug would be pulled. Everything depended on a teleconference that would happen that evening. I went out to meet a friend for a drink, and I was smoking furiously and practically ranting.

I had to write two lead editorials for that week's issue: one that was business as usual if we were going to stay alive, and one that would function as the magazine's obituary. Both had to be laid out and sub-edited, meaning that a few people on staff had to be taken into confidence. Naturally, that confidence lasted at most a few minutes, and by noon on Tuesday almost everyone on the editorial staff knew there was a chance that we would be closing up shop. In the late morning, Parsons took me out for coffee to deliver the fateful news. Some people on the business side knew, but many went into the afternoon staff meeting not knowing what Neil was going to tell us.

In the meantime, we shipped the last pages of the last issue to the printer. The final editorial noted that we had always prided ourselves on being part of the story we covered: from scrappy start-up to bloated, would-be global player in just two years. "Now, like so many of the US-based companies we have written about, we are closing the chapter on our European edition."[15]

That task done, I went to lunch in the nearby Charles Dickens pub. A good portion of my staff was already gathered by a table near the front; they all knew what was coming. I tried to give them some kind of grateful encouragement, but I couldn't speak; I was overcome with sadness and guilt. At 3:30, Neil gathered the staff in our boardroom and officially delivered the news that we would no longer be publishing. Staff members would be able to keep their laptops. It would be pushing it to say that he was close to tears—he was British, after all—but he was definitely choked up. "Almost everybody was gifted," he said later of the staff, "and everybody had brought their passion into it. I almost couldn't do it that day."

More or less immediately, the staff relocated to the Union Jack, the pub directly across the street from our office. As everyone downed pints, Neil's mobile phone rang at about 5 P.M. It was a call from our publicist; she'd just taken a call from the printer, St Ives, an hour north of London in Peterborough. Someone there had read my last editorial, and the management had immediately decided to inform us that we owed the company about £70,000. (Neil later admitted that we'd been "deliberately not paying them, as part of managing our cash position.") Unless we wired the entire amount immediately, St Ives would not print the final edition.

It was too late to reach our bank for a wire, so Neil tried other means. Neil finally had to tell the printer: "Go tell your boss that the managing director says if he doesn't make the payment, he'll go to jail." They accepted this, and started the presses. I was amazed to learn that the printer read any of the magazine at all.

TAKING STOCK

Different people react to losing their jobs in very different ways. Some (especially those with young children) begin looking for work right away; some use the free time to pursue freelance projects; a few of *The Industry Standard Europe*'s staffers went on months-long worldwide treks. For those with a mild taste for revenge, however, it would be hard to improve upon Matt McAlister's parting gesture. Because he was the company's first hire (after Battelle), and because he was a high-level employee in charge of the Web team (first in San Francisco, then in London), McAlister had a large pile of stock options in Standard Media International. Those options had been a powerful anchor to keep him at *The Standard* at times when his heart told him to leave. But now the options were worth less than the $3 per share price he would have to pay to turn them into stock, and with the company clearly in trouble, they were on their way to being worthless.

And yet, in a counterintuitive act of defiance, McAlister chose to exercise his option—for a single share of stock in Standard Media International. He paid his $3 to the somewhat baffled finance department, hoping to receive a stock certificate. Partly, this was to have a physical, ironic souvenir of an era of false promises. But mostly, as he explained, "It was just to make them go through the paperwork."[16]

I was one of the few employees of the European edition not to lose my job. I had to make up my mind if I wanted to stay on with *The Standard* in London, move back to New York, or quit the publication altogether. The last option was made extremely tempting by an eight-month severance offer; Parsons, in fact, took the opportunity to quit altogether. Linda and I had broken up, so I no longer had a girlfriend in New York, and there was no genuine job for me there; the bureau chief position had been filled, and even if it had been vacant it would have seemed like a tremendous step down after editing my own magazine. And it irked me that this was happening in April; there aren't many months of pleasant weather in London, but the few that exist were about to kick in.

In the end, I found that the decision to shut down the European edition gave me a defiant boost. The decision to close was, I believed, unnecessary and premature. But to then just pack my bags and head home seemed to add premature defeat to premature defeat. I wouldn't do it; I'd be damned if I was going to leave London until I decided I was ready.

I made an agreement with Jonathan that I would stay on in London, with a reasonable pay cut, as the European executive editor. We would still have our own Web site, with one Web editor and one subeditor. I would still coordinate European coverage with one reporter in London (Rick Wray), plus Boris Groendahl in Berlin and Kristi Essick in Paris. It was a scaled-down version of what we had been doing, but I had at least the satisfaction of saving a few jobs.

That satisfaction would not last very long.

A Very Public Hell

I know my inexperience in running a large organization caused a lot of dysfunction at various periods. But we learned and we grew and we became one hell of a good team. At the beginning, we were kind of bluffing when we said we were going to play in the A-league of national journalism, but that wasn't true at the end.

—Jonathan Weber, August 2001

The Standard's Christmas party for the year 2000 had been a somewhat downcast affair. Although everyone on staff knew that the publication's general health was declining, only a handful of managers knew for certain that layoffs were coming in a matter of days. Reporter Jim Evans ran into Battelle and asked him how things were going. Battelle looked at him and recommended that they go to the bar for a drink. The bar was five feet away. Battelle took a step or two and began shouting "Beer! Beer!" at the bartender. Evans asked him what was wrong, and Battelle could barely grunt a response. Hoping to lighten the mood with a joke, Evans said: "Well, at least you're not a dot-com CEO." Battelle said: "It's worse. I'm a media CEO." He was, Evans said, practically in tears.

In the months before the layoffs and the shutdown of the European edition, *The Standard* still stood in an enviable position. But Battelle was carrying a burden of inside intelligence, all of it bad. Beginning in October, the monthly cash-flow reports had begun to show that the company was draining its savings account. Shortly thereafter, the publisher alerted him to the fact that ad sales were dropping badly. The final issue of 2000 was 132 pages thick, only a little more than half of the previous year's girth—and the staff had doubled.

The smaller dot-com firms were disappearing on a near-daily basis. That caused a classic breakdown of the digital food chain: The smaller companies were no longer buying servers and database software in droves. And thus the giants of the industry whom we'd always relied on—IBM, Compaq, Intel, Oracle—were slashing their ad budgets, sometimes in half or more. And neither were tech firms going public, which meant less work and less money for the big investment banks.

In the final weeks of 2000, Battelle had done what he could quickly to cut costs. And he'd tried to muster financial support from the outside, but found himself stymied by the IDG board members. "I should have quit then," Battelle later said.

Until the layoffs were announced in January, Battelle was living through what he described as "a private hell." But the layoffs came and went and did nothing to relieve the torture. Neither would the reports from the ad sales department. All that changed was that the hell went public.

FIFTEEN COPY EDITORS?

An editorial retreat was held January 16–19 in the skiing paradise of Lake Tahoe. It was an impressive display of Fat Year spending, and unfortunately timed for just a week after layoffs had hit the other departments. (Michael Parsons represented the European edition; I stayed behind in London.) Although the editorial department had been spared in the first round of layoffs, it was impossible for the bosses to promise that it would remain untouched. And thus apprehension invaded the editorial team's long-standing self-confidence.

For purposes of the retreat, some administrator had assembled a list of everyone in the editorial department, along with job titles and rough job descriptions. I was overwhelmed when I saw the list. The last time I had been in San Francisco, there were approximately 45 people on the editorial staff; this list had 129 names on it (and did not include the European staff).

I had not personally met the majority of the people on the list. A good number of them hadn't been on board for more than half a year, and their job descriptions defied the imagination. When *The Standard* started, there were two people who copyedited the whole thing. Now, according to this list, we employed fifteen copy editors—six of whom worked exclusively for online. Where we once had a "Metrics" editor, there was now a Metrics department consisting of seven staff members. Eleven people were listed as executive editors (I would have been a twelfth had I attended). There were full-time correspondents in Tokyo and Hong Kong, plus a Latin American editor.

The list was somewhat artificially inflated, because when *Grok* folded in December the parent magazine absorbed its employees. A staff of 130 was perhaps justifiable when *The Standard* was 250 pages thick, week after week. At earlier retreats, we'd struggled with how to fill so many pages with a limited staff; now the question was how a thinning magazine could justify a staff this large. The answer became obvious: It couldn't, and editorial was going to have to take its cuts just like the rest of the company. Thus the retreat, which was officially intended to discuss the publication's repositioning, took on the tone of an Agatha Christie mystery; who was going to get bumped off?

EVERYONE HAD THEIR DEAL

The top management of the company had become increasingly demoralized, as will happen if much of your day consists of drawing up lists of people to fire. Battelle was trying to find a way out. He had agreed with the board in the fall of 2000 to conduct a search for a strong number two position, someone who would handle the company's day-to-day operations. (Of course, we thought we were getting that with Herb Montgomery.) After a few months, that became a full-blown quest for a new CEO. The search went on for a long time; even Neil Thackray was asked if he was interested. After a quick look at the numbers, he decided he wasn't.

Unfortunately, such long searches at a high level are hard to keep a secret. On February 22, an item ran in Chris Nolan's *New York Post* column, headlined "Standard's CEO on Way Out," saying Battelle would be replaced by an outside CEO. Nolan is an infamous Silicon Valley gossip columnist. A few years earlier, she unwittingly grabbed a moment of national fame when her former employer, *The San Jose Mercury News,* disciplined her for having bought "friends and family" stock in a tech company as part of a freelance story she wrote for *Fortune* magazine. I had read her work in *The New York Post* and did not consider her a credible source of information. In her very first *Post* column in December 1999, she had written breathlessly that investment banker Mary Meeker was about to leave Morgan Stanley and move west to Silicon Valley. It never happened.

And so when the Battelle item ran, I sent out a wide e-mail to various colleagues, pooh-poohing the report. I wish I hadn't. Nolan had it nailed. The only detail she got partially wrong was that Battelle was planning to stay on as chairman (although that situation would reverse itself several times over the next few months anyway).

Battelle would later claim that IDG essentially sabotaged this search by rejecting any potential CEO who appeared independent.

And certainly the man who took the helm in March, Richard Marino, while qualified for the position, had IDG stamped on his forehead. Marino had worked nearly all his life for IDG and had risen to the prominent position of publisher and president of *PCWorld*. He had left the fold in the late 1990s, taking the chief operating officer position with CNET, but who is more loved than a returning prodigal son? By hiring him, IDG was sending a strong early signal that it wanted to rein in *The Standard*. It was not necessarily a signal that it was going to do so without spending money. In a highly unusual arrangement, Marino's pay package was guaranteed by IDG. He was to receive an outrageous salary of $400,000, with a guaranteed bonus in the first year of $350,000.[1]

The sad truth was that senior managers were being paid huge sums of money, yet they seemed to spend less time trying to figure out how to run *The Standard* than they did trying to figure out if they should leave—and if so, when and how much it would cost the company. When Marino was appointed, I immediately figured that Anne-Marie McGowan would walk out. A onetime investment banker, she had come to *The Standard* in the fall of 2000 to run the Web operation but quickly became the functional chief operating officer of the company. She was probably already doing at least half of what Marino's duties would be, and passing over her for the CEO hire was essentially a vote of no confidence. And, in fact, she threatened to quit. But by this time most of the top management knew that she played a vital and unique role and that the company was unlikely to match her skills anywhere else. She ended up agreeing with the board that she could leave at any time after the new CEO took office with a year's compensation. If she stayed until the end of September 2001, she was to receive a "retention bonus" of $200,000. Battelle, too, had negotiated an exit payment, and in the early part of 2001 he fully intended to take advantage of it. As Weber put it later: "Everyone had their deal."

FINANCIAL MALPRACTICE

The third anniversary issue of *The Industry Standard* featured a humble 80 pages, a shadow of the previous year's. The cover story, appropriately enough, was called "Revenge of the Old Guard." It was one of the only times the magazine used a substantial amount of text on the cover. "The 20th century began with the rise of the corporation and ended with the triumph of the upstart," read the cover copy. "At the beginning of the 21st, the establishment is roaring back, adapting to the new order much better than anyone expected." It was impossible not to read this as a comment on the upstart *Standard* being threatened by the likes of Time Inc.'s *eCompany Now*. The white type on black background conveyed a sense of urgency—or perhaps a wake.

In a way, the magazine was conducting a funeral for its own identity, both as a publication and as a company. For several weeks, the proposed solution to our financial problems was that *The Standard* would be reintegrated into the IDG fold. From a financial standpoint, this meant that IDG would buy out the 15 percent of the company owned by the "Series A" investors. IDG's plan, according to one *Standard* executive, was to pay "pennies on the dollar" for that share.

The re-embrace of IDG required using IDG's services, and thus returning to its fiscal-year structure. As a preamble to that arrangement, IDG asked Vicki Peilen, the publisher of *PCWorld*, to come in and assess what the company's financial situation would be if it were to be run purely as an IDG operation. She could not find a way to make the numbers work, especially given the company's long-term lease obligations. A *Standard* executive recalls her saying that she was "totally appalled" by *The Standard*'s books, especially the real estate and salaries. Peilen's motivations were questionable—it's more than possible that her comments were an early attempt by IDG to rationalize shutting down *The Standard*. But she nonetheless added to a sense of crisis, calling the company's financing "insane" and saying: "I've been in publishing for 22 years, and I've never seen anything like it."

According to *The Standard*'s official financial statements prepared by Ernst & Young, the company had $56,186,000 in lease obligations that could not be canceled. In 2001 alone, it was committed to $9,364,000, money that it surely did not have. One lease, which took effect in December 2000, was worth, over its ten-year lifetime, $23.8 million. Yet it had never been brought to the board for approval. When IDG executives focused on the real-estate obligations, they claimed to be shocked and appalled; an IDG official later referred to this $23.8-million lease as "financial malpractice."

The only solution was to abandon the real estate and hope that the landlords could be talked out of the leases. Functionally, this meant that employees would relocate into IDG buildings—even in London; I was instructed to meet with a top IDG representative who was willing to lend us some desk space for a few months. Also, my Web editor, Jamie Price, was moved off the payroll of Standard Media Europe and onto the IDG payroll.

It also meant that *The Standard* would abandon the more general-interest business direction it had been heading in since the middle of 2000 in favor of a more narrow focus on technology. No more Pringles; it was back to covering the nitty-gritty details of the technology and dot-com world. These midstream changes and the publication's uncertain future were especially frustrating to some of the top editors. Over the summer, Thomas Goetz and Bob Cohn (who had been editor of *Grok*) both announced they were leaving *The Standard* to take top positions . . . at *Wired* magazine, Battelle's alma mater. The story of *The Standard* had come full circle.

BRIDGE (NOT BRIDGE FINANCING)

In the immediate aftermath of the European edition's closing, there were three of us in editorial, one Web editor and one Web producer, two people on the business side (a Web salesperson and a financial administrator), and the Paris and Berlin bureau chiefs. It was better than nothing, but the London office got to be a lonely place. We had a massive open-plan floor, complete with desks, chairs, and matching file cabinets, but no one using them. It was as if a neutron bomb had gone off; the furniture was intact, but the people had evaporated. We joked about turning the space into a gym or a nightclub.

The only other office on the floor was a dot-com called The Auction Channel. It, too, had gone belly up; I think the landlord was pretty set against any new company having anything to do with the Internet. And yet, the only people our real-estate agent seemed to be bringing by to see the space worked for Net companies.

Months elapsed, and as the weather got warmer, the motivation in the office sunk lower and lower. In May, I had to lay off the copy editor, and it looked increasingly like I was going to have to get rid of either the Paris or the Berlin bureau.

The atmosphere felt like some slowly rotting colonial outpost from a Graham Greene novel. The American editors weren't all that keen on most of my story ideas, and the PR departments from the companies they did want covered—such as Virgin—were slow to get back to me. Our tech team had sold off most of the equipment, including the software that ran our voice-mail system. It rerouted the phone so that if someone dialed the main number or any dead extension, my phone would ring. This was annoying; sometimes I'd be getting calls every two minutes from people I had nothing to do with.

And yet, it's not as if the phone distracted me from pressing business. I took to playing CDs in my office for most of the workday, with the volume up high enough that my few remaining coworkers could enjoy them. I spent a lot of time playing computerized bridge; I even began writing a novel. We all took long lunches, especially as the weather encouraged eating a sandwich on the south bank of the Thames. The office smokers turned Michael Parsons's office into a smoking room. Just before Rick Wray left to take a job reporting on telecommunications for *The Guardian*, he had begun simply smoking at his desk. There was no one left who cared.

Psychologically, I had become a swinging pendulum. At one end of the arc, I was still furious with *The Standard* for closing down the European edition. At the other end, I was feeling guilty. After all, I was still making a high salary, plus a modest housing benefit and a cost-of-living adjustment. And because the magazine had so little space for extraneous topics like Europe, I wasn't turning out that many stories; by any standard of efficiency, I was a waste.

And, like just about anyone in a mass layoff environment, I could get paranoid. On May 24, only six weeks after the European edition closed, I tried to make a phone call from home using the corporate MCI card I'd been given in the fall of 1998. The call wouldn't go through. I phoned MCI, and the customer rep told me my card had been canceled. I panicked and assumed I had been laid off; Weber was traveling and I didn't know how to reach him. I fired off a bunch of e-mails to friends on staff and was assured that my name had never come up. It turned out that the company had canceled all calling cards for those who had company mobile phones. My card was restored shortly thereafter.[2]

I might have been able to control my paranoia—by lapsing into pure pessimism—if I'd known how bad things really were.

LEADERSHIP IS IN DENIAL

On May 3, Chief Operating Officer Anne-Marie McGowan dropped a bombshell on the board in the form of a very blunt two-page memo: "The business is in trouble," she declared, and was unlikely to improve because the organization was "paralyzed." "Leadership at *The Standard* is in denial about the dire financial and business situation," she charged.[3]

Among other things, she insisted that the editorial leadership had to change. She wrote: "Editorial leadership is in a power struggle with the business side. . . . Edit team resistance to company restructuring and repositioning is slowing our movement and driving internal and external confusion." Her recommendation was to "[bring] in new edit leadership."

Weber was in no denial about what this meant. "She was actively trying to get me fired," Weber recalled later. "I was stunned and hugely offended."

The irony was thick and sad. Of all the bold, sometimes improbable tasks *The Standard* tried to take on, from running international conferences to creating state-of-the-art CRM, the company did one thing consistently well: It put out a decent magazine every week. And now the person responsible for that found his head on the corporate chopping block.

This type of conflict is common in many companies, but in media firms it plays itself out in distinct ways. Weber had a great deal more leverage in this situation than, say, the head of marketing or conferences would have had. He had been at *The Standard* from before the beginning and continued to report directly to the CEO; he also had a direct relationship with, and a nonvoting seat on, the board. In addition, if he were fired or were to quit under protest, he could easily take key editorial staff members with him (including me, though I doubt that would have swayed the board very much). And even an outsider to journalism like McGowan must have known that if Weber walked out, "bringing in new edit leadership" to a publication in financial freefall that didn't even have a publisher would have taken a minimum of two to three months—time the company could not afford.

Weber decided to he had to protect himself and cut an exit deal like those held by other senior managers. He made a stand that if the editorial staff were to be cut below eighty people, then he would have the option to leave and receive a year's salary. Alternately, he could leave at any point and be paid six months' severance.

Even if McGowan's position was extreme (and she and Weber would later make peace), her broader points could hardly be ignored. She had based her five-alarm warning on a report from the company's Vision and Strategy Team (VAST), which had been appointed in late 2000 to look at the publication's long-term problems. The VAST report was devastating; from almost any publishing perspective, *The Standard* had become a wasteland. Everyone knew that the advertising had begun to decline; you could tell just by the magazine's new, slender appearance. The VAST report put frightening numbers on that decline. In October 2000, the magazine had sold just over $13 million worth of advertising. By February 2001—a mere four months later— the figure was down to $3.5 million, a drop of 74 percent. The Web site was similarly cursed; it had sold about $1.56 million worth of advertising in November 2000 and just $436,000 in February.

Of course, the advertising decline was not solely *The Standard*'s fault; every publication in its category was ailing. And the year 2001 did not get any better over time; according to one media trade publication, 2001 witnessed the largest decline in advertising spending of any year since 1933—the depth of the Great Depression.[4]

But *The Standard* was afflicted with a much worse disease: Readers no longer seemed to want it. Subscribers had stopped renewing at the rate the publishing industry considers a norm for this type of magazine, 65 to 70 percent; in fact, *The Standard*'s renewal rates had dropped to 35 percent.[5] That meant that more than six out of every ten subscribers did not consider the magazine worth keeping. Partly, this low figure reflected the fact that so many of *The Standard*'s readers worked for companies that were going out of business or shedding employees by the truckload. During The Fat Year, *The Standard* could send dozens of copies to dot-com companies, where employees would snap them up and subscribe in the office. But now, such issues went unread. IDG officials claimed that the 35 percent renewal rate may have been the lowest in IDG's publishing history. At that rate, it was simply too expensive to make an effort to gather new readers and keep the circulation intact.

And new readers no longer seemed enticed. *The Standard* had always prided itself on the subscriptions that came through the Web site, and in the first quarter of 2000, about 10,000 trial orders were registered online. That number plummeted; by the fourth quarter fewer than 6,000 trial orders came in.

With depressing numbers like these, *The Standard*'s budgets in early 2001 had to be substantially revised. It went from a growing, profitable publication in 2000 to one that, VAST said, would lose about $8 million in 2001 on about $90 million in revenues (the revenue figure was down 37 percent from the previous year).

McGowan recognized that the situation was even worse than that: *The Standard* was broke. "It is my belief that the business will not survive without immediate and drastic changes," she wrote in her memo to the board. "The company is effectively out of money, but still does not have a realistic financing plan and budget for 2001." She believed that the board needed to determine an acceptable level of losses for 2001 and that the company needed immediate bridge financing, a fancy term for a short-term loan.

McGowan's warning bell was intended to kick the board and the company into action. And yet in many ways, inertia reigned. She was correct in her criticism that the company lacked effective leadership. Battelle was still nominally the company's chairman, but to many observers he seemed as if he had checked out. He had been spending increasing amounts of time (and money) working on CRM issues, and since the end of 2000 he had had difficulty working with IDG because he resented it for not having invested more to grow *The Standard*.

And indeed, Battelle had already agreed with the board to leave the company by September. Ever since Steve Thompson had been forced out in January, *The Standard* hadn't had a publisher. There was no one at the top committed and powerful enough to represent *The Standard*'s interests, except, theoretically, Rich Marino, the CEO who had been installed by IDG. Alas, Marino barely cast a shadow. He was often silent in board meetings, and he refused to push vital issues even when he had made promises to do so. (*The Substandard* published a satire of his diary; in it Marino spent his entire day waiting for Battelle to return his calls.) But it seemed impossible to remove Marino, because IDG had signed him to a multiyear contract.

JOURNALISTIC LINES WERE CROSSED

As if fending off a suggestion that he should be fired was not enough, Weber spent May tackling a grave and semi-public challenge to his editorial leadership. Gary Rivlin, one of *The Standard*'s most prominent staff writers, had become disillusioned with the publication. He was paid well, and his stories almost always got top billing, but like many of the writers, he found the editorial process cumbersome and at times stifling. "I felt *The Standard* had lost its nerve," he recalled later. "We were so busy . . . trying to sound a certain way that we were bleaching out the voice that made me really like *The Standard*."

In the early part of 2001, Rivlin had taken nine weeks off to write an e-book about a prominent Silicon Valley venture capitalist. While reporting that book, his sources began telling him that one of Benchmark Capital's significant venture-capital funds, Benchmark III, was hurting because of overexposure to dot-com start-ups—such as Epin-ions.com and Respond.com—that no longer looked like they could possibly pay off. Benchmark was one of Silicon Valley's most cele-brated venture-capital firms, and a detailed story exposing its weak-nesses would have been a major coup for *The Standard.* He and Weber discussed a story on this, but Weber encouraged him to broaden his approach and look at a number of funds in similarly precarious states.

Weber was spending a considerable amount of time dealing with various issues on the magazine's business side, including preparing for *The Standard*'s 2001 Internet Summit. (Jane Goldman, who'd started as the magazine's features editor, had taken over the main ed-iting responsibilities.) As in previous years, the Summit's two "exec-utive producers"—responsible for planning speakers and topics—were Mary Meeker of Morgan Stanley and Bill Gurley, one of Amer-ica's best-known venture capitalists and a partner with Benchmark Capital.

Even before a single word had been written, Rivlin began to feel that the publication was out to protect Gurley. Gurley called Battelle, who in turn called Weber, who said to Rivlin: "I can tell this is already shaping up to be a real pain in the ass."[6] An e-mail circulated around to editors saying they should be extra careful with any story mention-ing Gurley. Weber acknowledged at the time that the prospect of a tough Benchmark story put him and the publication in "an awkward situation." But he insisted that no ethical breach had occurred, argu-ing: "Benchmark is not, never has been and likely never will be an ad-vertiser." Instead, Weber said: "Gurley is working for this company in something akin to an editorial capacity. I don't think it's so terrible for me to give a little extra scrutiny to a story focusing on that person."[7]

This was the perfect case of being a little bit pregnant. The publi-cation needed to hold its conferences and "Summits" in order to make money (although, ironically, at this point the conference portion of *The Standard* was losing large amounts of money). And what it had to offer paying attendees was its supposed editorial excellence, which is founded on journalistic independence. Editorial played a vital role in organizing the conferences and Summits. Weber may well have believed that a venture capitalist was acting in "something akin" to an editorial capacity, but the fact remains that if Gurley were to have pulled out of the Summit, *The Standard* would likely have suffered financially. That gave Gurley leverage that few subjects of other *Standard* stories ever had—indeed, leverage that almost no one in "an editorial capacity" ever had.

When the final edit was nearly done, the editors sought comment from Benchmark, because Rivlin hadn't included a response from the firm. A call was placed from Weber's office to a Benchmark officer named Kevin Harvey. There was a firm journalistic reason for this measure; the story relied in part on anonymous quotes, and it needed some official point of view, if only for perspective. Moreover, the subject of even the most damning piece imaginable—especially the most damaging piece imaginable—deserves an opportunity to comment. As it happened, Harvey denied that Benchmark III was in trouble.[8]

But it was too much for Rivlin. After a blowup with Weber the day the piece was sent to the printer, Rivlin walked out of the office and went to see a movie. On Monday, the day the story appeared in print, Rivlin quit. In a spiteful move, Rivlin forwarded his resignation note to eleven *Standard* colleagues across the globe, ensuring that the whole staff would be privy to his feud. "I've made no secret of my displeasure with your handling of the VC story, Jonathan," he wrote. "I believe journalistic lines were crossed—blatantly crossed, actually, with your decision to interview Kevin Harvey yourself on Friday, allowing Benchmark a back door into our newsroom."[9]

The notion that Benchmark had a back door into the newsroom is a stretch. A call for comment is hardly a measure of undue influence; it would have been less than fully responsible to run the piece without comment from every VC fund it discussed. But Rivlin had a point; the magazine had an overly complex relationship with Gurley and Benchmark, and some steps should have been taken to deal with that.

Ideally, Weber could have told Jane Goldman and others that the piece needed a fair and responsible edit—and then removed himself from the process. He later agreed that this would have been a wiser strategy.

The incident was made even more painful when, a few days later, Rivlin received one of the business press's most prestigious awards, a Gerald Loeb Award for Distinguished Business and Financial Journalism, for his story "AOL's Rough Riders," published in *The Standard* in 2000. Remarkably, even after Rivlin's fiery resignation, Weber was able to persuade Rivlin to stay on. In the end, the Rivlin affair was more than a clash about journalistic ethics; it represented a collective frustration that the company's financial decline was making *The Standard* a confusing, even unpleasant place to work.

RADIO SILENCE

Not only was there doubt about how the company would put money on the table in the future, there was even disagreement about how to count the money that was already there. During the summer of 2000, when it became clear that Standard Media International was profitable but not going to go public any time soon, IDG and the company had agreed on a tax allocation scheme. Because IDG owned more than 80 percent of Standard Media International, the publication was "consolidated" for tax purposes into their company. This practice had a potential benefit for both *The Standard* and IDG; even though *The Standard* was profitable, IDG could use *The Standard*'s operating losses to offset its overall tax burden.

Standard Media International paid estimated taxes to IDG every quarter. And for those periods when it had paid more than IDG actually ended up owing, IDG would repay that money, sometimes on a monthly basis, sometimes on a quarterly basis. (Such transactions, dubbed "intercompany receivables," are fairly routine for any company that has as many business units as IDG.)

There was a flip side, however. If *The Standard* stopped being profitable—as it did in the first quarter of 2001, and afterward—then it was actually entitled to a refund of taxes from IDG. And indeed, those refunds were delivered to *The Standard*. But some time after April 2001, IDG stopped making those payments. IDG's move was, as McGowan said drily, "a fairly unilateral decision,"[10] as it would be; *The Standard* desperately needed the millions that this payment represented.

IDG's argument, backed up by language in the tax agreement, was that its payments to *The Standard* were discretionary, at least until IDG actually got its refund back from the government. It simply exercised its option to cut that money off.

It was not long thereafter, McGowan said, that relations with IDG went from reasonably cordial to "radio silence." On the board level, IDG was trying to do whatever it could to avoid putting more money into *The Standard*. It no longer believed that *The Standard* could be saved simply by being folded into IDG's larger publishing empire. The magazine's short-term cash needs were dire, and the long-term obligations, from the staff to the leases, needed drastic restructuring. (In addition to that, all of IDG's publications were struggling from the tech slowdown.) To the great consternation of *The Standard*'s executives, McGovern's proposed solutions to the cash crisis consisted, in part, of loopy suggestions, such as charging would-be subscribers $1.97 for four introductory issues, instead of giving away four issues for free.[11]

It was almost as if McGovern was playing for time. Sure enough, a more serious proposal for a combination loan/restructuring emerged from IDG. The officials were willing to part with another $10 million, but it would come at the expense of the other shareholders, that is, the original outside investors. Not surprisingly, the board rejected those terms and asked for a new set. Instead of revamping its offer, IDG said it would ask the prestigious investment bank Allen & Co. to come up with a set of financing terms that both sides could agree upon.

That's when both sides crossed their respective Rubicons. Battelle and the non-IDG members of the board believed they had to neutralize IDG; in the charming parlance of investment bankers, McGovern had to be "crammed down." Battelle and J. P. Morgan's Jerry Colonna cooked up a plan that had, from their perspective, three virtues: (1) It would keep *The Standard* alive because it provided an infusion of up to $20 million in cash from Morgan, with a hoped-for $10 million to come from others; (2) it would involve removing Marino from the CEO position and restoring Battelle; and (3) it would reduce IDG's ownership of Standard Media International to below 40 percent, meaning that any future moves—such as a sale of the publication—could go through without having to convince McGovern.

IDG's position was far simpler. It wanted an excuse to get out of *The Standard,* at any cost. In a July meeting, IDG's board members rejected the JP Morgan investment terms, arguing that they undervalued the worth of the overall company. This was boardroom chicken: Each side was saying it would reject future funding proposals unless it got things its own way. If the company was going to survive, someone would have to blink.

FIRING BY E-MAIL

As all this fury churned behind the curtain, I was trying to continue as if little had changed. I'd done a cover story that lined up all the potential problems with the third-generation mobile phones in Europe, and I was pleased by the many positive responses I got. Continuing my fascination with developments in the arena of online music, I had proposed a feature story on an Italian online music company called Vitaminic, which had somehow managed to avoid the

Net stock catastrophe. When it wasn't buying every Internet music company in Europe, it was making deals with them. We had written a fair amount about Vitaminic in the European edition, and its colorful CEO, Gianluca Dettori, was always available for interviews. Alas, my colleagues in San Francisco didn't know much about Vitaminic, and the story ended up as a much shorter news piece.

At the same time, we were trying to get rid of our huge, mostly unused office space in London and find a new, much smaller place. Every time I got shown a potential office, however, the potential number of people who'd be working there was reduced. In the end, I was looking for a space for just two people; to save money, I was willing to accept a large space designed for one. In other words, I was back at the same place I'd been in the fall of 1998.

The next slice was that I had to turn our Berlin and Paris bureau chiefs into stringers. For a few months, this had been held out as a possibility, but I had resisted it, a task made easier by the fact that both Boris and Kristi did stellar work. I had always assumed that we could provide them with a base salary of somewhere around $20,000 a year, and enough work to bring them up to $40,000—a pay cut, but still enough to live on. Unfortunately, my mental figures were far higher than those *The Standard* ultimately offered: $500 a month, plus $1 per word for whatever stories they did for the magazines (and it would be unrealistic to expect the writing to add up to more than $10,000–15,000 a year). In essence, they were being fired, though of course you can't just fire employees in Europe.

This was yet another depressing cut. On the evening I was instructed to break the news, I had to leave the office by about 6:30, and I couldn't immediately reach Boris and Kristi by phone. So I ended up giving them notice of the arrangement by e-mail, definitely a low point for me as a manager.

WE ARE NOT GOING UNDER

Weber phoned me in early July and told me that IDG was going to stop funding *The Standard*. This prospect was, obviously, frightening, but both of us saw a potential benefit. IDG had not been treating us well lately, and if we could find a new buyer or investor who had a better grasp of how to handle the problems we confronted, then we might be better off in the long run. The publication would seek bridge financing to stay alive until the new buyer or investor was found, Weber said, but he did not say where the bridge financing was going to come from.

It was like hearing an echo. This was precisely what the European edition had experienced three months before, except that we hadn't thought about bridge financing (or couldn't find any). I was told to keep the information in confidence.

Which I did, mostly, though I shared it with a *Standard* colleague and old friend in New York, Matt Yeomans. I did my best to put a positive spin on it, as much to reassure myself as him. He immediately saw to the bottom of the situation, saying: "The worst case scenario is if they pull out before we find a backer, then we go out of business." I acknowledged that this was true, but insisted that it was extremely unlikely.

I was hardly the only person who was relaying the news. Over the weekend of July 7 I got a panicked phone call from a former *Standard* colleague who'd been laid off in January. She said she'd heard that IDG was pulling out and that *The Standard* would be shut down in a month. She was worried that the Web site would be shut down any day, and that I should print out any articles I needed. I thought she was being alarmist, but I sent Jonathan an e-mail warning him: "I think it's clear the story is out there, and realistically some version of it is bound to end up in the press pretty soon, I'd wager." He thanked me for the warning and said: "I'm highly confident we are not going under, we should have another $20 million in the bank fairly soon."[12]

That was reassuring, but the rocky relationship with IDG could not be suppressed. That same week, *Standard* executives got a phone call from a columnist at *The San Jose Mercury News*. Was it true, he asked, that IDG was "systematically purging" all references to *The Standard* from its Web site? Upon checking, the magazine's executives learned that, indeed, all references to *The Standard* were gone. An IDG publicist told the *Merc* that the problem was merely that pages needed to be redesigned to incorporate *The Standard*'s new logo. But, as the columnist noted, that excuse "hardly explains why text references were gone as well."[13] His conclusion: "IDG [is] getting ready to sever ties with *The Standard*." The truth was out there.

Shortly thereafter, on July 17, Weber sent out an e-mail that was intended to ease the staff's anxieties. "I know people are concerned about what's going on with the company," he told his staff. "Unfortunately there isn't really anything I can say at this point, we're continuing to work through various unresolved issues. As soon as I have something to share, I will. I know uncertainty is a big strain for everybody but we'll just have to hang in there a little longer. Thanks for your patience."

Somehow this was far less comforting than it was intended to be. Sure enough, the following morning, *The New York Times* published a short article about the doldrums of the magazine industry. It was surely the only story ever to mention *The Standard* in the same breath as *Maximum Golf*, a magazine edited by an old friend and colleague of mine, Michael Caruso. His publisher, Rupert Murdoch, was pulling the plug; *The Standard*, meanwhile, "plans to announce a third major round of layoffs, possibly before the end of this week," the article said.[14] Again, Weber tried to reassure the staff, sending out an e-mail saying his comments had been twisted beyond recognition. But no one doubted that the layoffs were already in the pipeline.

A PEAK AT THE SUMMIT

The Standard's annual Internet Summit on July 23–25, 2001, was not the lighthearted affair of previous years. The setting was stunning, as usual: the Four Seasons Aviara resort in Carlsbad, California. The list of attendees and speakers remained stellar: Gerald Levin from AOL Time Warner, Meg Whitman of eBay, Jeff Bezos of Amazon.com, Steven Ballmer of Microsoft. But the momentum had escaped from the ambience like helium from a leaky balloon. The bankers and venture capitalists who once predicted near-infinite growth in technology stocks were now backpedaling on estimates, wary of lawsuits and even law-enforcement investigations prompted by angry investors who had taken their recommendations literally.

And The Standard's executives had their own preoccupations. There was still no concrete agreement about how to fund the publication. On the day after the Summit, July 26, the board convened in an emergency meeting. At least some people who showed up for that meeting thought that one item on the agenda was going to be the removal of Marino as CEO; his performance was pleasing no one. But it never came up. Not that it mattered much; by August 2, Marino's attorneys would notify the board that he was leaving the company.

On the table was a modified proposal for a "bridge loan" from IDG. The goal of this "bridge financing" was to get the company on a more solid operating basis, with the aim of selling The Standard. It was never certain who, if anyone, wanted to buy it, but management believed that it could still fetch $50 million or more. But the "bridge" money was going to come at a very dear price, starting with further staff cuts. Weber had taken to telling colleagues that we needed to return to "start-up mode."

Still, Weber and Battelle insisted that the employees who stayed on be compensated—especially themselves, and Anne-Marie McGowan. They should be rewarded for staying on through exceptionally draining circumstances, they said, and more concretely, for taking a pay cut and watching the value of their stock options wither away; once theoretically worth $3 to $4 a share, they'd been repriced at 10 cents a share. That reward would come in the form of a bonus, to be drawn from a pool of money that would come from the sale of the company. Weber and Battelle came away from the meeting thinking that the board had come to a consensus that this bonus pool would be 15 percent of the sale price.

But lo and behold, in early August IDG announced that it had a different interpretation. The bonus pool would not be 15 percent of the sale price, but 15 percent of what was left over if the sale price was over $25 million. The terms were laid out in an e-mail from Colonna, who sounded resigned to letting IDG have its way. "We've all made extensive efforts, and attempts at compromise, in order to get this company financed so that we can effect a sale. While by no means perfect, the agreements we've struck and are attempting to reach, are a genuine attempt to be fair and find common ground."[15]

But there was a catch: Battelle and his team had less than twenty-four hours to accept these terms. Colonna said the offer would expire by 5 P.M. West Coast time the next day, August 3. Weber was incredulous at this demand, arguing that typically IDG would take weeks to do anything, and so for its board representatives to suddenly become sticklers for deadlines made no sense. "This ultimatum demanding that we accept entirely unreasonable and self-defeating terms in less than 24 hours was the height of cynicism and hypocrisy," he said.[16]

Battelle came back to the board with a further set of requirements. One demand was conceptual; Battelle recommended that "we not try to 'hide' or 'ignore' the fact that Rich did not work out. This will get out, and attempting to pretend that Rich is CEO will only harm us further."[17] Other demands were humane but relatively costly, such as continuing to pay severance to past employees. Battelle and his team also wanted to pay McGowan's retention bonus of $100,000 immediately, and another $100,000 on September 30. And they wanted to sweeten the bonus pool if the sale price went above $50 million.

Was this greed? It's a difficult judgment to make. It's not unreasonable for the founders and executives of a company to insist that they and the small remaining staff be rewarded by the company's sale. And the various sides were not that far apart; it was reasonable to assume that some kind of compromise was going to be found. Had Battelle, McGowan, and Weber been under the impression that the very existence of the publication hung on their requests about an employee bonus pool, then they might well have behaved differently. But to McGovern and IDG, the insistent request on a larger employee bonus pool looked greedy. It was one more instance where Battelle should have been grateful and humble, and instead he was sticking his thumb in the eyes of his benefactor.

IDG simply didn't respond to the term sheet. Colonna had put a specific deadline on his loan terms. In IDG's view, the terms sheet had expired, and there was no point in responding until another was delivered.

When Battelle realized that IDG was pulling an ultimate power play, he came back on August 6 and said he would abide by whatever terms IDG wanted to impose. He blinked. That took away IDG's objections, and IDG came back with a list of additional requirements it wanted to attach to any bridge financing deal—such as cash-flow projections that would have to be met on a weekly, even daily basis. Weber labeled this demand a "charade," because IDG had already calculated that it wanted to force bankruptcy. Weber said that IDG president Kelly Conlin specifically told him "that bankruptcy was a better option for IDG than the JP Morgan Partners offer."

Any such decision had to have come from McGovern, who later gave the following statement: "My overall observation is that only one factor caused *The Standard* to stop publishing. And that was the market collapse. The advertisers discontinued investing in the new economy publication category, and sales dropped by 70% to 80% within twelve months. Reader interest waned as well, and renewal rates dropped to 35% which meant the publication was not able to maintain contact with its target audience. The same market factors caused the collapse of *Business 2.0* and *Upside*."[18]

A board meeting by telephone was then convened for August 14. Marino was out, though there was still some talk about him possibly suing the company for "constructive" dismissal. There was no terms sheet on the table, and whatever efforts Allen & Co. had made to find a buyer had come up empty. Without immediate funding, the company had no legal option but to file for bankruptcy—the same scenario that had been forced on the European edition four months before.

The Standard's management believed—well, hoped—that the bankruptcy decision could be kept confidential until August 20. After all, almost the entire staff was on vacation until then, a holiday that had been mandated as a cost-cutting measure. But word leaked out from somewhere in less than a day. This created painful hours of work for department heads, who scrambled to find their employees in far-flung locations to tell them the publication was going under. The Web sites for *Advertising Age* and *The Wall Street Journal* were the first to print the news of our demise, and before long the story was covered by, among others, the Associated Press, *The Boston Globe, The New York Times, The New York Post,* Reuters, *The San Francisco Chronicle,* and *The Washington Post,* not to mention the British papers, who were hounding me for quotes. Even *The New Yorker* gave us a posthumous sendoff, reflecting a strange affinity between a technology magazine and the world of literature. PBS's *Newshour with Jim Lehrer* interviewed Battelle at length about the magazine's demise. This ending was like a window onto our overall marketing strategy. We had always treated the other media as one of our primary targets; if we succeeded in nothing else, we got them to give us one hell of a sendoff.

PROUD AND SAD

On Mondays, Jonathan had always tried to send out a note to the editorial staff with some observations about the issue we'd just closed, an update about a new hire, or something we should know about the business side. The final note was unusually personal. It is difficult to condense, so I have quoted it here at length.

> I feel terrible that things have turned out this way, I certainly did not expect it, and I will do anything I can to help in what I know will be a difficult situation for many people. I feel proud of what we've done, and profoundly sad that we won't be able to keep doing it. I have a lot of other feelings too—anger, for one, because I don't think it needed to end this way, and frustration that these last months were so consumed with doing hard things we needed to do for a future that we now do not have, and sorrow and guilt for leaving everybody in such a tough spot—but mostly I feel proud and sad.
>
> Through all of the crazy stuff, our basic goal was always very simple: to cover the story as well as we could, without pulling any punches, and to write it and present it in a clear, useful and engaging fashion. . . . There are a lot of good journalists and good publications out there who maybe could have and should have done this, but you are the ones who really did it. Be proud of that. It's a big deal.
>
> I'm also very proud of the way that many of us individually, and all of us collectively, matured and changed and became even better as we went along. A lot of people started here without a lot of experience. For some people it was their first real reporting or editing or designing job. For others, including myself, it was a far bigger job than anything that had come before. I know my inexperience in running a large organization caused a lot of dysfunction at various periods. But we learned and we grew and we became one hell of a good team. At the beginning, we were kind of bluffing when we said we were going to play in the A-league of national journalism, but that wasn't true at the end. . . . I think every one of us can look back at numerous specific stories and packages of stories and innovative features and designs and cov-

ers that we created and say to ourselves, "That was a great piece of work."

Finally, I'm very proud to have helped bring together such an extraordinary group of smart, creative, dedicated, charming, funny and friendly people—and this is where it starts to segue into the sadness part. There were not very many days when I didn't enjoy coming to work here, and that was mostly because I simply liked everyone so much. I know a lot of deep friendships have been forged here, and families of all kinds created. That is a beautiful thing. And once the noise dies down, I think that will be our legacy as much as anything else. I'm very, very sad that I won't have the opportunity to continue working with all of you, and to continue building those friendships—at least not in this context. I think all of us will take a lot of joy from those relationships for many years to come, yet I'm still heartbroken that most of you won't be here Tuesday morning.

Thank you, from the bottom of my heart, for making such a great publication, and for making everything about this experience so special. I will hold that forever, and I hope you will too.

Jonathan

Praise and disbelief came in from readers, too. More than 3,000 subscribers to "Media Grok" sent e-mails bemoaning the loss of our daily skewering of tech news. My favorite was the one that said: "I have read every issue of *The Industry Standard* from cover to cover from the beginning, subscribe to each of the e-mail newsletters and spend plenty of time on the site. You have no peer in industry journalism. I will sorely miss your voice, perspective and attitude. (There's a special fondness I must confess for Media Grok.) You deserve a white knight, a fat severance, and a month on the beach."

There might have been a few who could arrange a month on the beach, but for almost all of us, these were impossible fantasies. Unlike those who'd been laid off earlier in the year, we were not going to get any incentive for leaving. We wouldn't even get severance (with the exception of our one remaining British employee, who was legally entitled to it): just a laptop and a boot out the door. I wanted to kick myself for not accepting the eight months of severance pay offered to me if I'd quit in April. (My resentment subsided when I learned that, because of the bankruptcy, no such payments would have been made after August anyway.)

Others had it worse. Some contracted freelancers were never paid. In the case of our Berlin bureau chief, he was never even paid his salary for the month of July.

CRASS, CYNICAL, AND COOL

On Monday, August 21, the former staff members gathered to learn whatever they could about what had happened to them and why. Perhaps nowhere else in corporate America had an entire company been dismissed while virtually all of the staff had been on vacation. The crowd was mildly angry, but ultimately resigned. People were seeking not so much a severance payment—we knew that was unlikely or impossible—but an explanation. McGowan described what bankruptcy would mean for us: vacating the buildings, and the possibility that employees' health coverage would be lost. But the only full explanation could come from Battelle, who was in New York and had already given a performance to the staff there. The few of us left in Europe were dialing in on a teleconference line for the last time.

Battelle described himself as "deep into anger right now" but tried to give a narrative of what had occurred. "Why did IDG do what it did? So far, IDG . . . continues to claim that it didn't make this decision." But, he said, the death of the magazine was the obvious and inescapable result of IDG rejecting J. P. Morgan's term sheets.

Battelle laid out three reasons why he thought IDG decided to passively pull the plug. First was "the culture and psychology of the company we built," which, Battelle said, "is not one they know what to do with." IDG would prefer to see *The Standard* "wither and die" because "we have not created an animal that they know how to run." *The Standard*'s "high-quality business journalism requires relative advertising and marketing expense ratios that are very, very different from [the typical ratios at IDG magazines], and frankly are not consistent with it."

Then Battelle switched gears somewhat; he actually tried to give IDG some credit. "They would claim," he said, "with some reasonableness, that if they had funded [*The Standard* further], it would have been difficult to restructure the liabilities. And they didn't want to assume the liabilities." This observation was decidedly vague, and Battelle gave a nod to Anne-Marie for having fought *The Standard*'s battles over these balance-sheet arguments.

Finally, Battelle said it was possible that IDG had simply made "a crass, cynical, and cool spreadsheet calculation" that it as a company would be better off if *The Standard* went bankrupt. "I can't say it's the truth," he warned his former staff. "That would be irresponsible." But he said that he believed "IDG had decided that we were not a viable business. McGraw-Hill, Condé Nast, and Time Inc. all disagreed."

Once again, Battelle was dangling his East Coast media connections as if they would be possible saviors. But once again, no savior came forth.

WE CAN'T PAY THE RENT

Usually, when a magazine goes bankrupt, its largest creditors are the providers of obvious, publishing-related services: printers, paper suppliers, distributors. Not so *The Industry Standard*. When it filed for bankruptcy on August 27, the companies to whom it

owed money made it look more like a bankrupt dot-com. We owed a
staggering $2 million to Corio, one of the CRM companies that had
sold Battelle a fantasy it had never fulfilled. Similarly, we owed $1.5
million to Siebel Systems, another CRM firm. Another $310,000 was
due to the database firm Oracle. Nearly as much was due to the Four
Seasons chain of hotels, primarily for agreements to host future conferences and events at its facilities worldwide.

But the real killer was real estate. Nearly half of the twenty largest
creditors were landlords who had leased office space to Standard
Media International in New York, Boston, Dallas, Chicago, Washington, D.C., and, of course, San Francisco. A single year's rent to all of
them amounted to more than $4.3 million.

And even that figure did not include the rent that was still owed on
a ten-year lease for the right to occupy some 11,000 square feet in an
office building at 825 Third Avenue in New York. (The landlord was
Advance Publications, Inc., better known to the world as Si Newhouse's Condé Nast publishing empire.) Ostensibly, the purpose of
this rental—at the hefty price of $56 per square foot for the first five
years, rising to $61 per square foot after that—was for the New York
advertising and editorial staffs to share the same offices sometime in
the future. Although the lease had been signed nearly a year before
the magazine ceased publication, no one from *The Standard* had ever
occupied the space.

GOING, GOING, GONE

The auction of assets of Standard Media International took
place on the morning of September 24, 2001, in the unas-
suming setting of a bankruptcy courtroom on Pine Street in downtown
San Francisco. A number of former employees attended, primarily for
the theatrics; conspicuously, John Battelle did not show up.

The opening bid, for $150,000, came in from New Standard Acquisition, a company affiliated with the London-based tech-news Web site The451.com. Thematically, this was a sensible fit; there was substantial overlap between what the two publications covered. But financially, this was the bones of the dead being picked over by the near-dead. I'd hired one of the London reporters, Rick Wray, from The451.com and had interviewed two others from there; they were always amazed that the company was still in business. And indeed, just a few weeks later, British papers would report that The451.com was shutting down its UK operations (although the company survived in a different form with a vestigial London presence).

The opening bid was immediately topped by a bid of $200,000—which came from IDG. This turn of events threw the proceedings into a bit of a mess. To many, it seemed obnoxious—and possibly illegal—that IDG, having forced the asset sale by allowing the company to go into bankruptcy, would then end up buying the assets. There was a break in the session while this matter was discussed, but the judge was unwilling to interfere with the bids.

After the break was over, a new bidder emerged: a company called Futuredex, based in Los Altos, California. This firm was essentially unknown; its representatives described it as "a venture capital networking service."

A genuine war soon developed among the three parties, with bids coming in primarily at increments of $50,000. But of course it could not last: The crew from The451.com declined to go higher than $750,000. Futuredex issued its final bid at $850,000 (though later there would be a small dispute in which the company claimed it had said $815,000). When IDG topped that bid at $900,000, the offers came to an end.

There were times when seemingly rational people had contended that Standard Media International was worth $500 million, or even more. Now its pieces had sold for a combined price of $1.4 million (in a separate transaction, *Fortune* purchased the magazine's paid subscriber list for $500,000). That sum was less than the amount of advertising in any single issue the magazine published in 2000.

By the end of the day, Thestandard.com Web site published a story about the assets auction, the last story to be posted by the publication. The former staff members, still stunned and disheartened by the morning's events, gathered together at a bar. It was, aptly, called Grumpy's.

The Case for Murder

In a generally brutal publishing economy, special punishment has been reserved for the new-economy magazines. *The Industry Standard,* the sector's weekly bible—and ironically the most skeptical in its coverage—died an early death . . . that now looks like a mercy killing.   *—The New York Times*, March 4, 2002[1]

Shortly after I arrived in London, I had an exchange with my colleague Polly Sprenger about *The Standard*'s expansive plans. Having watched similar dreams for *Wired News* deflate, she was not a believer. "This sounds just like *Wired,*" she said to me. "How is this not going to end up just like *Wired*?"

I looked at her as if she were insane. Patiently, I explained: The market is much more mature today than it was when *Wired* first came along. We're a weekly and they are a monthly. And besides, Battelle saw the fate of *Wired* firsthand and had learned from its mistakes.

At least I was right about us being a weekly.

The parallels between the fate of *The Standard* and the fate of Battelle's previous venture are, in fact, striking enough to be painted in

Wired's signature Day-Glo colors. In both cases, a technology magazine quickly decided it needed to be much more than a mere magazine. Books, television, conferences, new titles, and a state-of-the-art Web site all took priority. An IPO was planned but couldn't get off the ground. A UK-based edition was hastily assembled and then quickly disbanded. The crucial difference is that *Wired* lived long enough to sell its pieces to Condé Nast and Lycos, which have seen fit to keep them alive.

Like Polly, I'd seen much-loved publications fall: In the 1990s, I watched *7 Days* and *New York Newsday* fold when everyone who read them believed they should live. So I don't enter into discussions of the closing of *The Industry Standard* as a naive partisan of editorial purity. I'm all too aware that quality alone will not guarantee the continued existence of a publication, and that from the investors' point of view, it often shouldn't.

At the same time, I don't accept the notion that media companies' decisions to close publications—no matter how prudent they may seem—are always the best way to protect the bottom line, especially in the long run. Among magazine enthusiasts, it's often noted that *Sports Illustrated*, started by Time Inc. in 1954, lost money for more than a decade after its launch. Today, however, it is consistently one of the biggest moneymakers in American publishing.

In the case of *7 Days*, I found it hard to believe that the magazine would not have thrived by the end of the 1990s. Had it stuck around, I think it would have continued to take some business away from *New York* magazine, and that the London magazine *Time Out* would not have bothered to enter the New York market. The long-term survival of the New York edition of *Newsday* is a tougher sell, because the losses it had to make up were so much larger, and because for decades the market for daily English-language newspapers in New York City has been stagnant at best.

BRANDING *UBER ALLES*

Assessing blame for *The Standard*'s demise is a difficult, Rubik's cube–style exercise—especially for someone like me who benefited from its phenomenal growth. Despite the many frustrations I experienced, I continue to think of it as a dream job. No matter what happened on the business side, creating quality journalism is its own reward, and we certainly did that.

So what exactly went wrong? It's tempting, given the *Wired-Standard* parallels, to lay the blame for *The Standard*'s demise at Battelle's feet. And certainly he bore some direct responsibility; obviously, financial management was not his strong point. But his cardinal sin was a failure of focus. Starting a weekly magazine is enough of a challenge for any professional, especially if you can make it profitable in two years. But sustaining it needs constant attention and strict focus, and Battelle's passions had left the world of print by the middle of 1999. He busied himself with financing the company and fantasies of CRM and let the magazine be run by others. (Indeed, based on comments he made when the publication began to fall apart, a few reporters questioned whether Battelle had even been reading *The Standard*.)

Battelle was well-intentioned: His emphasis was always to grow and build the company. Yet that strategy made sense only to the extent that it piggybacked on the magazine's growth. All the millions thrown at marketing may have helped raise *The Standard*'s "brand awareness," but was that enough? As noted, on the Monday after we ceased publication, Battelle insisted that *The Standard*'s "high-quality business journalism requires relative advertising and marketing expense ratios that are very, very different from [the typical ratios at IDG magazines], and frankly are not consistent with it."

That insight was true as far as it went, but it evaded the more salient issue: Were those "advertising and marketing expense ratios" working? Were they bringing in sufficient business to *The Standard* to justify their cost? The evidence for all of 2001 is that they weren't. A magazine can't live off brand awareness; it lives off readers and advertisers. We had the advertisers, at least during The Fat Year. We never really did have the readers.

The Standard never had a viable plan to sell copies on the newsstand. At its peak, the magazine sold perhaps 20,000 newsstand copies of a given issue. By January 2001, the average weekly figure was around 9,000 copies, and by March it had dipped to an average of about 7,000. This was a key area where the trade-publication paradigm limited what *The Standard* could do. Most trade publications have a design that could generously be labeled "functional," a polite way of saying that they are ugly. It's a chicken-and-egg standoff: If you think you don't need to sell copies on the newsstand, you don't invest in the art and design needed to make the covers attractive. And of course, if you stick that cheaply produced trade magazine on the newsstand, it won't sell very well because the cover doesn't stand out when sitting on the newsstand next to retouched supermodels.

Those staff members, on both the editorial and business side, who had come from more consumer-oriented publications used to complain about the covers, sometimes every week. Weber's response was that he wasn't going to make a priority of eye-popping covers so long as he knew that the company was not going to pay the money necessary to promote newsstand sales.[2]

The magazine's lack of newsstand presence needed attention far before the company's cash flow went sour. To a great extent, Battelle's hands were tied because IDG would not cough up the money for newsstand support. IDG's thinking was simple: *CIO* magazine didn't sell on the newsstand, either, and it seemed to be doing fine.

But it's also true that Battelle did not think it was a major problem. I recall discussing newsstand distribution with him once in 1999. He went into *Wired* mode, cursing the Post Office and the distribution business. "I could get the magazines in the hands of everyone who advertisers want to reach by Fedexing it to them every Monday," he said, shaking his head. The remark was not entirely serious; still, it was clear that building newsstand sales was going to be someone else's job.

And so it was: *The Standard*'s competitors', *Business 2.0* and, to a lesser extent, *Red Herring*, spent heavily to get prime placement on newsstand shelves. They could more readily afford it, as they published only once a month (until 2000 when they briefly went fortnightly). So *The Standard*'s reluctance to spend money on newsstand promotion and circulation-building was a false economy. Through the end of 1999, *The Standard* was growing at almost exactly the same pace as *Herring* and *Business 2.0*.

The Standard went from about 60,000 readers in the middle of 1998 to about 130,000 at the end of 1999. That put it within striking distance of *Business 2.0*, which reached a little more than 200,000 readers and had the luxury of being a relaunched version of an earlier magazine. But by the end of 2000, *Red Herring* had zoomed up to 300,000; *Business 2.0* was at a healthy 325,000, as was the recently launched *eCompany Now*. *The Standard* was still at about 200,000, a distant fourth place and with growth flattening.

By the middle of 2000, when *The Standard* was best poised to take advantage of its clout, the circulation stood at well below 200,000 readers (about 170,000 for the month of May). That readership might have satisfied the targeted advertising needs of technology companies and investment banks. But for the magazine to lock in its success, it needed consumer advertisers—the people who sell cars, clothes, booze, home stereos. For that group, *The Standard*'s circulation was way too low. Those advertisers could reach our readers by buying cheaper space (on a cost-per-thousand basis) in larger publications that our readers were already buying—such as *The Wall Street Journal*.

And that wasn't the only circulation problem. Of the 170,000 readers in May 2000, fewer than half—44 percent—were paying to read it. This was the legacy of the magazine's "controlled circulation" strategy. In its first year, *The Standard* relied heavily on giving the publication away to a desirable audience. It seemed to work, or at least the magazine was able to persuade enough advertisers that they were reaching a premium audience. But publishing a magazine this way rarely succeeds in the long run.[3] For one thing, *Standard* executives knew that potential public investors in the company might consider the strategy a major flaw. And some of the advertisers questioned whether the people getting their copies for free were actually reading them—or whether they were worth paying to reach. So in the second year, *The Standard* spent a good portion of its circulation efforts getting those readers to pay up.

But the hardest part was reaching out to new readers; that task *The Standard* never successfully tackled. There was a belief that the growth would occur organically, that readers would continue to find the magazine via the Web site.

And they did, for a time. But as traffic to the Web site started to plateau toward the end of 2000, so, too, did the Web-based subscriptions. *The Standard* effectively had no backup plan to get new subscribers. The direct-mail campaigns often garnered a very poor response. And by early 2001, existing subscribers were giving up on the magazine in droves.

WHO IS DAVID LAUREN, ANYWAY?

But isn't the falloff in readers merely one more reason that the magazine should have been allowed to continue publishing? After all, if they liked us once, they might like us again if the tech market recovered.

I'm a bit tougher on the magazine's long-term prospects than many of my former colleagues. Our management had always encouraged us to think big, to behave as if *The Standard* were not merely a weekly magazine and a Web site, but the kickoff to creating the Dow Jones or the Reuters of the twenty-first century. Not long after I started, I had periodic discussions with editors about the magazine's future trajectory. There was a general agreement that we would continue to focus on technology, new media, and telecommunications, and the changes they wrought on the business world, but we would broaden considerably the type of companies and businesses we covered. (There were parallel, fervent discussions about the kind of business research we could offer via the Web.)

In my mind, this was a sound strategy. My personal shorthand for this direction was: We become a younger, hipper *Business Week*. This broadening, I believed, would help us reach a larger audience—I had a target of 500,000 circulation in my mind—but still keep intact our insiders' sense of expertise.

I always assumed that we would embark on this strategy after we had proven ourselves to our existing readership and advertising base. Instead, buoyed by the glut of advertising pages that began to come in The Fat Year, and encouraged by the fact that all the major business publications began imitating our style of journalism, we began trying to shift strategy by the end of 2000.

In the early part of 2001, for example, we ran a cover story about David Lauren, the son of fashion designer Ralph Lauren, entitled "The Crown Prince of Seventh Avenue." It was an interesting and well-executed story. And the story actually had a strong Internet component, which put it squarely on our turf. But we didn't explain sufficiently to readers why this was an *Industry Standard* story. I suspect a lot of our traditional readers shrugged their shoulders and turned the page. (The headline alone is questionable: I doubt that many people among *The Standard*'s Silicon Valley readership would recognize that 'Seventh Avenue' is code for the fashion industry.) Other readers who might have enjoyed the story were never told that they should read *The Standard* for an article about the likes of Ralph Lauren.

In short, we failed to communicate the shift in editorial mission to readers, both existing and potential.

Magazine readers may be very intelligent on an individual level, but in the aggregate it's often necessary to treat them as if they're dim-witted. That is, if you're going to change a magazine's formula suc-cessfully, you need to broadcast this in a number of obvious and redundant ways. You've got to announce in advance that you're chang-ing what you do, you need the media to write about it, you probably need to change design elements, and you need to reach out to people who've never seen the magazine before. To do that job properly would require a lot of marketing and advertising money. By mid-2000 we had already spent a great deal in that area, with not too much to show for it.

Another part of that problem was staff. There was tremendous tal-ent at *The Standard,* but it wasn't limitless, and it wasn't uniform. Some of our best reporters and writers, such as Dan Goodin (who left for *The Wall Street Journal*) and Gary Rivlin, made gold out of any story they touched. Others could do a decent job covering a specific company or sector but had difficulty translating that skill to a more general business beat. Theoretically, they could have been trained by some of the more experienced editorial staff, but that staff was ex-hausted by putting out a magazine with 100-plus editorial pages every week. It's hard to blame the reporters for that situation; it's as if they were recruited for a basketball team and then told that the game was going to be track and field.

A similar gap evolved in the ad sales department. During The Fat Year, selling advertising for *The Standard* was not much more difficult than standing with a bucket during a downpour. But as the ad market dried up, we were left with a redundant sales force (separate teams for print and online, of course) that didn't have the experience to make the rain itself.

This may reflect some East Coast bias, but I think a big cause of the staff problem was the fact that the publication was located in San Francisco. You can count the number of successful, nationally known, general-interest magazines to come out of San Francisco on one hand—even if some of your fingers are missing. There's *Rolling Stone,* which decamped to New York in the 1970s. There's *Mother Jones,* which manages to defy many laws of magazine physics by the fact that it is funded through a nonprofit foundation. There's *Wired,* which sold itself to the New York–based Condé Nast conglomerate in 1998. And . . . well, that's it.

This isn't a putdown of the fascinating, dynamic city of San Francisco. And of course it makes sense for a magazine whose key advertisers, profile subjects, and readers are located in Silicon Valley to have a substantial presence on the West Coast. But over and over again in conversations, people from *The Standard* would say to me: "Wow, you sure hired a lot of great people in New York!" And over and over again in conversations with Weber and Battelle about employees who didn't work out, they would say: "There just weren't that many good candidates for the job" (Battelle would usually amend this with: "who we could afford.") Of course the talent pool for magazine employees is bigger and deeper in New York: That is where magazine people go.

The unpleasant truth is that, just like real estate, magazine staffers in San Francisco in the late 1990s were hard to find and overpriced. By the time *The Standard* needed to hire them, and fast, they were competing not only with the other West Coast tech magazines but with dozens of Web sites that had sprung up: CNET, Salon.com, and so on. The few thousand journalists and ad sales people in the Bay Area were now on top of the world.

This isn't to say that the magazine could have begun life in New York; its inspiration was purely a West Coast phenomenon. But it paid a price for hiring there.

LIVE BY THE BUSINESS MAGAZINE SWORD . . .

I think the bigger problem was whether *The Standard* truly had something unique to offer to the larger business audience. If you focus narrowly on the world of technology and its financing, your competition is fairly well circumscribed. But if you start writing about businesses that far outside of the technology and telecommunications area, you're competing in a much larger arena, with *Fortune, Forbes, BusinessWeek,* and *The Wall Street Journal.* Outside of our traditional expertise, I simply don't believe that in 2001 *The Standard* had very much that was unique to offer readers of those well-staffed and well-established publications. From time to time we could beat those guys with scoops and superior analysis, but we weren't ready to compete on that level every week.

This doesn't imply that the early implementation of this strategy was responsible for the death of the magazine. But I think the editorial leadership wasted a lot of time redesigning and redirecting the magazine without ever being told that its readers had begun to drift away.

With some success, *The Standard*'s executives insisted on being identified as a business magazine. That was where the glamour seemed to be, magazine glamour being, of course, relative; *The Industry Standard* was never going to be *Vanity Fair,* but it considered itself sexier than *Interactive Week.* And to aspire to be a financial magazine was a valid market position, especially against slower moving monthly competitors. The raging bull market that dominated the mid- and late-1990s was a godsend for all manner of financial media. It made CNBC, for a time, the most profitable cable channel in the world, more profitable than the major television networks combined. It helped solidify *The Wall Street Journal*'s status as the nation's leading newspaper. It created bumper year after bumper year for the established magazine players like *Fortune* and *BusinessWeek,* and allowed newer personal finance titles like *Worth* and *Smart Money* to flourish.

But if you live by the business magazine sword, you may also die by it.[4] As good as *The Standard*'s journalism was at times, it was never going to be good enough to transcend its publishing category. And the publishing category of Internet business magazines simply evaporated. In June 2001, the newly created Time Warner creature called *eCompany Now* declared itself null and void, choosing to merge with the rival title *Business 2.0*, which Time Warner bought for approximately $70 million. And in November 2001, *Red Herring* magazine laid off a good portion of its staff, reverted to a monthly frequency, shut down its conference business, and essentially gave up on its Web site. Even *Wired*, the granddaddy of the genre, saw its ad pages drop more than 40 percent in 2001. In July 2002, *Yahoo! Internet Life*, a monthly magazine in *The Standard*'s space that had built an audience of a million readers, announced it was folding, citing a 52 percent drop in "year-to-date market share." In early 2002, a *New York Times* article on the doldrums of New Economy publishing went as far as to declare that *The Standard*'s early death "now looks like a mercy killing."[5]

The devastation of the publishing category was not limited to the technology field; it affected nearly every publication that had anything to do with money and business. Business and finance publications are extremely sensitive to economic fluctuations, particularly dips in the stock market. It's almost ironic; one might surmise that in a bear market, the average reader needs more and better financial advice than in a bull market. But historically, that's not the way it works. When the economy recedes, institutional subscriptions to financial publications have a cruel habit of drying up, and more casual investors stay out of the markets altogether—or at least enough to curb their appetite for financial publications.

This trend is not a question of shaving copy sales by a few percentage points; when the demand for financial publications dropped, it collapsed as quickly and as steeply as it had gone up. In early 2001, we saw evidence of this in the UK; sales of financial and technology publications fell 67 percent in a single year. The two largest UK publications aimed at stock traders, *Shares* and *Investors Chronicle,* saw their numbers sink even further as 2001 dragged on. Established publications might be able to weather such storms, but it is simply impossible to launch a financial magazine into a trade wind blowing so hard in the wrong direction.

In the United States, *The Industry Standard* was hardly the sole 2001 casualty in the financial publishing world: *Individual Investor, Family Money,* and *Your Money* all closed up shop. Those publications that remained found a sharp drop-off in interest from both readers and advertisers. For the first six months of 2001, the newsstand sales of the four largest personal-finance magazines had declined precipitously from the year before: *Money* was down 25 percent; *Smart Money,* 30 percent; *Kiplinger's,* 42 percent; and *Mutual Funds,* 43 percent. And those declines took effect before the terrorist attacks of September 11; the subsequent drop-off in air travel only deepened the loss of readers, since those magazines tended to sell well in airports. Advertisers, too, disappeared, just as they had for *The Standard.* In their final issues for 2001, advertising pages in the four titles were down from the previous year's issue annual from 24.9 percent (*Money*) to 56.7 percent (*Mutual Funds*).[6] Any plan to save *The Standard* would have pinned maximum hope on the notion that advertising would rebound at some point in 2002. As of the middle of that year, no such happy event had occurred.

Could *The Standard* have anticipated the market drop-off and planned accordingly? Possibly. In a column published shortly after *The Standard* announced it was ceasing publication, the ubiquitous financial commentator James Cramer argued that back in August 2000, when the publication experienced a "revenue shortfall," it should have acted decisively. "Right then, [*The Standard*] should have reined in the spending, knocked off the acquisition plans and accepted the fact that it was never going to go public, so it had to get its finances in order. Instead, it went pedal to the metal."[7]

Of course, it's rarely that simple. A magazine publisher might be able to plan for a market drop-off of 20 percent, maybe 30 percent. But no businessperson can walk around acting as if there's going to be a 75 percent fall in revenues in a few months, citing a general-industry trend that hasn't shown itself yet. A certain degree of optimism, if not boosterism, is necessary; otherwise, employees will quit and associates will wonder why they should be doing business with you. As Battelle said in a qualified self-defense: "It's like telling people, 'I'm a priest, but I don't believe in God.'"

It's also worth noting that once *The Standard* did recognize its financial crunch, it managed to get costs down quickly and dramatically. Battelle claims that he brought the annual operating costs of the publication down from more than $200 million to $90 million in a matter of months.

Still, that's only part of Cramer's critique. It's hard to argue against his money-in-the-bank advice. He wrote, "If there's a moral to this story, put simply, it's that when a business is growing great guns, that's when you have to put the money away."[8] Standard Media International made a profit of more than $10 million in 2000, on top of the outside capital it raised of $30 million. If it had managed to hold onto half or even a third of that extra capital, it would not have entered the intensive care unit in which it found itself in the summer of 2001.

Could that money have been banked? Hell, yes. With crystal clear hindsight, you can save more than $20 million in a single paragraph. Spend half as much on marketing and public relations (savings: $6 million). Cut the Barcelona conference expenses in half (savings: $1 million). Don't sign a lease for a building in midtown Manhattan that you aren't going to use (savings: $1 million in security deposit, and untold millions in long-term obligations). Produce the European edition as a 50–50 partnership with Pearson or another company (savings: perhaps $3 million). Cap the total number of employees at 300 (savings: $5 million a year, conservatively). And forget CRM (savings: as much as $8 million).

Of course, that's kind of an easy and useless exercise. But it illustrates a vital point: *The Standard* had no built-in methods to control costs. It needed either a CFO who was willing to say no to some of Battelle's expansion projects, or mandatory board approval of all expenses over, say, $1 million—preferably both.

WHY NO IPO?

Even given the runaway costs, could the publication have been saved? It depends on what exactly was meant to be saved—and who did the saving. Certainly, in hindsight, a number of *Standard* executives wish that a chunk of the publication had been sold to the investment bank Thomas Weisel in the fall of 2000, valuing the company at a healthy $350 million.

The Standard's ultimate fate in such a scenario, however, is uncertain. Even if IDG had been willing to sell—which it wasn't—there's nothing that Weisel could have done about the plummeting market for tech journalism. Presumably, Weisel had little long-term appetite for running a media business, and it probably would have found itself in 2001 or 2002 trying to sell *The Standard* in the same depressed market with few plausible buyers.

The company might have been better off if it had proceeded with its public offering. This is far from an obvious conclusion, and there are at least four strong arguments against it. First, as a general rule, it's highly doubtful whether a small- to medium-sized media company should be publicly financed. All sources of media funding—including advertising—come with strings attached, but some conflicts are easier to prevent than others. There's something fundamentally incompatible about shareholders' quarter-to-quarter performance needs and the needs of high-quality, independent journalism. In addition, when the top managers are also major shareholders, the volatility of the stock price can be a tremendous distraction.

Second, it's debatable whether or not *The Standard* was ever truly ready to go public. Its internal financial management was weak, even chaotic. Its board structure would have had to have been changed, and investors may not have chosen to give a dot-com boost to a business that was fundamentally a magazine.

Third, the history of publications similar to *The Standard* that have gone public is tremendously discouraging. There are no perfect analogues, but certainly in investors' minds *The Standard* would have looked similar to CBS MarketWatch, TheStreet.com, and Salon. As of the end of 2001, the stocks of TheStreet and MarketWatch were trading below $2 a share; Salon was trading below 20 cents a share and had been removed from the main Nasdaq stock listings. Granted, during The Fat Year, *The Standard* had significantly higher revenues than any of those companies. That only meant, however, that as the company's revenues plummeted toward the end of 2000, investors would have punished *The Standard* all the harder.

The final argument was that a mediocre IPO would have shortchanged our private investors. Over and over, as the market dissolved in 2000 I heard the line from various companies that it is irresponsible to take a company public into a slumping market. It means the management is not doing everything it can to maximize the value it brings to its investors.

But that's precisely where the argument breaks down: irresponsible compared to what? As things stand, the initial investors lost all their money. It is absurd to argue that *The Standard* would be worse off today as a public company trading at $1 a share (or less) than as a bankrupt company and a nonexistent publication.

It's almost certainly true that if *The Standard* had gone public in mid-2000 that there would have been more layoffs earlier in the process. It's also conceivable that the European edition might never have launched at all. But if, collectively, those hardheaded decisions had been able to keep the company alive, I think most people would agree that they would have been worth the price. At the very least, it would have won the company's management independence from IDG's control, and *The Standard* would have been in a better position to determine its own fate.

DEATH AND TAXES

Therein, of course, lies the bind: It was essentially IDG that kept the company from going public. The IPO process is filled with technical questions that a majority owner, if it wants to, can use to stall for months or even years—and for good reasons or bad, IDG did. Which financial models should be used to determine the company's value? Which is the right auditing firm to use—and why shouldn't *The Standard* use the same one as IDG? What percentage of the stock should be offered to the public: 15 percent? 20 percent? What portion of the stock should IDG retain? Should there be a second (or "mezzanine") round of private funding prior to the IPO?

Which brings us back to the opening question: Was this a murder? Did the publication die because someone wanted it to die?

To prove a murder, a prosecutor needs at least four elements: a corpse, a suspect, a weapon, and a motive. Those who see the end of *The Industry Standard* as a murder have no doubts as to their suspect—IDG—or the weapon, the refusal to accept seemingly rational sources of emergency funding.

Yet viewed close up, the crime scene is not so straightforward. There isn't exactly a corpse—at least not one that has stopped twitching. A publication that has grown as high and wide as *The Standard* had doesn't die all in one swoop. In some cases, *The Standard* has continued to live in mutated form. In January 2002, some of the freelance team that produced the "Media Grok" newsletter relaunched the service (for pay) as "Media Unspun." The not-so-anonymous people behind *The Substandard* posted a number of its back issues on a Web site called Kersplat.com, though they were mysteriously yanked in the fall of 2001.[9]

Although the magazine ceased publication in August 2001, its Web site, Thestandard.com, continued to publish some fresh stories (as part of the plan to sell the publication's assets), even through the terrorist attacks in New York and Washington on September 11. By the end of October, the site had ceased to exist in any separate form. Although some of the magazine's archives could be found on the IDG Website IDG.net, Net users who pointed their browsers to Thestandard.com got a message saying the site could not be found, at least for a while.

Then, in mid-December, without explanation, IDG resurrected a Web site at Thestandard.com. To those familiar with the old site, this looked like some spooky parallel universe: Although the Web stories were organized into the categories that the publication traditionally used—Money & Markets, Policy & Politics, and so on—the stories on the front page were not newsworthy at all. The lead market story, for example, was a day's ups-and-downs report from three months earlier. And although the site indicated that it was intended as an online archive, it was initially launched with no search engine, rendering it useless (a search engine was later added).

But for a truly spooky, parallel universe, try looking at the bankruptcy papers. It's a funny thing about bankruptcies. Theoretically, they are designed as a kind of clean break that allows troubled companies to partially satisfy their creditors without being overwhelmed by them. But in practice, bankruptcies are anything but clean. For several weeks following the bankruptcy filing, there was anxious talk among *Standard* loyalists about a possible lawsuit against IDG. First, it was said that the non-IDG board members could sue IDG for financial irresponsibility. Then, following the assets sale, it was said that the creditors could sue IDG. Surely it was not kosher for a company to allow one of its business units to go into bankruptcy, only to repurchase that company for a fraction of what others might have paid pre-bankruptcy.

Yet no suit ever materialized. It was naive to expect the non-IDG board members, William Harding and Jerry Colonna, to take on IDG over a magazine that already folded. The institutions they worked for would not have allowed it; Harding's employer, Morgan Stanley, actually does banking work for IDG that it would have been loath to put at risk. As for the creditors, their primary concern was recovering some of the millions they were collectively owed. If IDG's purchase would help them achieve that, then they had little interest in stopping it, no matter how unseemly the deal appeared.

And so *The Standard* entered a pathetic twilight period, no longer a viable business but not quite dead. Through the early fall of 2001, mail and newspapers continued to be delivered to the building at 315 Pacific, most of it addressed to employees who had long since departed. A core team continued to report to work, to perform tedious tasks (like counting office furniture) or nearly hopeless ones (trying to collect unpaid bills owed to a bankrupt company). Through the summer of 2002, *The Standard*'s logo was still embossed on the door of the New York bureau on West Broadway, and on the lobby company directory of its office in London. Visiting these memorials was Parsons's scenario come to life: I see dead people.

The only real life left was in bankruptcy court, where the few remaining characters began squabbling amongst themselves. The bankruptcy motion carried a small but controversial provision that would set aside 5 percent of any asset sale to be paid out to John Battelle (2 percent), and Anne-Marie McGowan and Jonathan Weber (1.5 percent each). It seemed the ultimate irony to pay these sums to the principals of a publication that had failed; in the inverted lexicon of bankruptcy law, this sum was called the "success fee."

Of course, the fee was perfectly defensible. In larger bankruptcy proceedings that involve a sale of assets, the debtor is often forced to hire an investment bank, which in turn seeks a willing buyer. The investment bank could easily charge fees of up to 5 percent or more.

But in the context of *The Standard*'s abrupt closure, the 5 percent skim-off smelled bad. The e-mail chain of recently laid-off employees burned up with comments on the fee. For workers who were owed severance payments of thousands of dollars—and in some cases were owed actual salary payments—it was obscene to see the people at the top get an extra payday worth potentially tens of thousands of dollars.

For related reasons, the "success fee" also raised eyebrows among *The Standard*'s creditors. In a filing just before the asset sale, the creditors objected, saying that they were "concerned that the proposed 'success fee' to insiders and a key employee of the Debtor may be unwarranted." The creditors expressed their fear "that the success fee may be a disguised 'golden parachute' payment to these individuals, completely unrelated to services rendered in connection with the sale." (As of mid-2002, no such payment had been made.)[10]

What's worse, when Anne-Marie McGowan couldn't stand anymore to be one of the dead people, in late 2001, she quit. She then promptly filed a claim stating that the success fee was not only valid but should be much bigger.

The level of complication is downright byzantine: When it bought the assets, IDG not only became the debtor, but it claimed to be the company's largest creditor as well. That's because IDG's initial investment in *The Standard,* which had been valued at about $8 million, was still owed to the company in the form of a repayment note. It showed up as a footnote on the balance sheet. Even more dramatically, in the quiet that followed the assets sale IDG filed its claim with the bankruptcy court, asserting that it was owed an absurd $27 million.

But according to *The Standard*'s bankruptcy filing, IDG still owed *The Standard* more than $10 million in transferred tax payments. And therein lies the most plausible explanation for why IDG was willing to let *The Standard* die. IDG wanted to get its $8 million investment back; it always had. At the same time, it owed *The Standard* almost $10.4 million in tax refunds, money that would become due five days after IDG itself received a tax refund.

But there's another provision in the tax agreement that says that any tax money IDG owes to Standard Media International would be paid first by calling in the company loan, that is, the initial $8 million. So if there was no company to pay the $10.4 million to, then IDG in effect would have gotten its investment back.

Other signs of life can be glimpsed in the wreckage. Although some of the creditors raised questions about the European end of the business, the bankruptcy proceedings were essentially silent about it. Standard Media Europe is listed as a wholly owned subsidiary in the company's assets and assigned a value of "unknown." Yet it has not been liquidated; as of December 2001, Standard Media Europe was still registered as an "active" business with the UK agency Companies House. When I left the company in August 2001, there was still about £150,000 left in a bank account. Exactly two signatures were necessary to draw checks on it, one of which was mine; I haven't signed anything. The ultimate fate of that money is of some interest to, among others, the Berlin bureau chief, who is owed a month's salary.

IT'S STILL ALIVE!

But so many commentators on *The Standard*'s demise have missed one crucial fact: *The Industry Standard* continues to publish—outside the United States. Some of *The Standard* outlets that functioned purely as IDG creatures remained alive, at least in some form, through the beginning of 2002. In Sweden, *The Standard* continues to live on the newsstand, albeit as a monthly. That is also the case in Norway, China, and Taiwan.

Through the middle of 2002, the Australian Web site Thestandard.com.au still published as a news site and featured the magazine's logo (in June it was incorporated into a broader IDG site). And Brazil's *Business Standard,* which was one of the most attractive international editions, continues its life as a Web site. Battelle always spoke about the necessity of building a global brand. And, in fact, he did—one that outlasted even its progenitor. It's like the Cubans and North Koreans keeping communism alive long after their Soviet benefactors had given up the fight.

Viewed from that perspective, it should have come as no surprise that IDG bought the assets of *The Industry Standard.* Arguably, it had to. If another company had won the bidding, IDG would have risked losing the trademark rights on the various editions it continues to publish.

Although the tech-publishing world will probably never see another year like The Fat Year, it's a reasonable bet that the technology market will rebound. Typically, hypergrowth in a specific product —PCs, Web servers, mobile phones—is responsible for jumpstarting the market as a whole, and with that will come a renewed need for advertising. There's no reason why IDG couldn't relaunch *The Standard* in the United States as a tightly focused technology trade magazine with a small staff, modest editorial aspirations, and a worldwide licensing scheme. That, after all, is what IDG has always done—and what it wanted *The Standard* to do all along.

It's unclear what the value of such a magazine would be. For me, the ultimate sendoff for *The Standard* occurred when it received a distinct goodbye from the Internet culture. Shortly after the magazine ceased publication, someone on the West Coast put up for auction on eBay a collection of nearly every issue *The Standard* ever published (almost all in mint condition!). The final selling price was $20.50.

Epilogue:
Who Do We Shoot?

One of the most enduring movie scenes I've watched is in John Ford's adaptation of *The Grapes of Wrath* (1940). When the bulldozers arrive to evict farmers from their foreclosed land, the eldest man in the family comes into the field with a shotgun. But the bulldozer operators explain that it's not their fault; they're only doing what their bosses told them. And their bosses are just following instructions that ultimately come from the bankers back east. The old farmer, frustrated and confused, cries out: "Who do we shoot?"

This is roughly what it felt like when *The Standard* shut down. Vast sums of money had been spent and put the business in bankruptcy, hundreds of people were suddenly out of work, and it wasn't exactly clear who deserved the blame. Sometimes it feels easier to blame the people who are closest to you; other times scapegoating a distant financial villain makes more sense.

Looking at *The Standard*'s failure a year later, it's clear that the company's business side was mismanaged; in a limited capacity, I contributed to the mismanagement, or certainly did little to set things right at the time. I have no trouble accepting the death of *The Standard* as a media murder, but persistent financial neglect by the magazine's own executives provided an opportunity and an excuse for that crime to be committed. We fell prey to the rocket-fueled ambition and hubris of the dot-com companies we covered, and in short order we crashed with the rest.

That in itself is a sad story. It's sadder still because it's nearly impossible to see how the story could have ended differently—even if the company's management had been flawless. No matter how well the publication did during The Fat Year, there were structural contradictions in our financing that made it impossible for *The Standard* to adapt to overpowering changes. Looking back, the publication's top managers now see it as a mistake to have pursued an IPO strategy, even though we never actually went public. The inclusion of outside investors not only irritated officials at IDG, but it put enormous pressure on *The Standard* to grow very big very fast. We ignored any long-term consequences because we thought that in the IPO and aftermarket we'd have more money, individually and as a business, than we knew what to do with. We should have known that that was the wrong way to look at things—we published stories every week demonstrating the pitfalls of management-by-IPO, but it never sank in that those cautionary tales might become our own.

And while IDG's motives should never be taken at face value, their argument that the market evaporated is irrefutable. Those of us who worked on *The Standard*'s editorial side liked to flatter ourselves that the publication's outstanding journalism was responsible for its success. Maybe—but a bigger factor was being in the right place at the right time, at least during The Fat Year. It very quickly became the wrong place at the wrong time. Given the media market of 2001 and 2002, it is axiomatic that *The Industry Standard* would not exist in recognizable form today except as a money-losing operation, regardless of who owned how much of it. In a recession, people who want to run money-losing media companies become scarce. No matter how frustrating it may be, you can't shoot a recession.

By any measure, *The Industry Standard* is a tough act to follow. Many *Standard* employees felt burned by the company's management and premature closure, yet many others—myself included—feel as if they had the job of a lifetime. We were spoiled, not only by generous salaries and benefits, but by being given opportunities that exceeded our experience on paper.

And yet, when it all exploded, we discovered that being spoiled has its harsh side. More than a year after the European edition closed, several of my former editorial colleagues did not have full-time employment. I was pleased when a few who did find work told me that they were able to parlay their *Standard* experience, however brief, into higher salaries than they might otherwise have received. And a handful of colleagues in the States landed reasonably prestigious jobs at places like *The Wall Street Journal* and *The Washington Post*.

But a large number of laid-off *Standard* employees in the United States found themselves unable to get jobs. The media recession deepened through 2002, causing magazines and newspapers to cut back on their hiring and freelance assignments; at the same time, the job market became saturated with laid-off journalists. When I visited Los Angeles in April 2002, I swallowed hard as former colleagues— once among the best-paid journalists in America—made comments like: "Do you mind if we stop by the bank? I need to deposit my unemployment check."

With the Internet bubble having burst, the value of *The Standard* as a calling card in 2001 and 2002 was a fraction of what it had been during The Fat Year. The world that we once inhabited had evaporated. Dot-com executives and the bankers who funded them are no longer respected self-made billionaires. As likely as not, they are in bankruptcy, or being hauled before congressional committees to explain dodgy financial packages. As he often did, Michael Parsons best summed the situation up: "I was in a boy band. Where do I take my solo act?"[1]

IDG continues on as one of America's largest magazine publishing companies, although the technology slump has hurt the company. It no longer owns the product line that was once its best-known, the *For*

Dummies books. The *Dummies* brand merged with an online portal called Hungry Minds and was sold to the publisher John Wiley & Sons in August 2001, the same month that *The Standard* declared bankruptcy. Although IDG continues to launch new titles and joint ventures across the globe, it experienced rare layoffs in 2002 and shut down a business-oriented technology magazine called *Darwin*. It also slashed circulation some 20 percent at *Computerworld* and *InfoWorld*, two magazines it sends out free to targeted subscribers, and reduced the value of employee stock nearly by half.[2] Clearly, the losses that *The Standard* experienced in 2001 were part of a broader publishing problem that IDG and others are still trying to solve.

Neil Thackray, who'd bought a new house when *The Standard Europe* was still publishing, rather quickly landed a job as the CEO of a UK trade publisher, Quantum Business Media. Its portfolio consists entirely of titles that have precious little to do with the Internet world, including *The Publican* (for pub operators) and *Meat Trades Journal*.

Jonathan Weber took a job teaching journalism for the first semester of 2002 at the University of Montana at Missoula. My impression was that, after the Herculean hours he logged at *The Standard*, teaching was close to a part-time job for him, a way of decompressing after the publication's demise. In mid-2002, Weber joined a small, targeted financial information service called Off the Record Research. Their headquarters, bizarrely, are in *The Standard*'s old building on Pacific.

Herb Montgomery, *The Standard*'s CFO, went on to become the CFO of a curious company called Media Arts (on whose board he sat while he worked at *The Standard*). Media Arts is the online sales arm for art based on the work of an artist named Thomas Kinkade, a kitsch painter whose nostalgic landscapes have made him one of the best-selling American painters of all time. Yet Media Arts has suffered as a business: As of the middle of 2002, the company had reported losses for five consecutive quarters. In January 2002, as a way of demonstrating his company's appeal, Montgomery encouraged a newspaper reporter to visit a Kinkade "Signature" Gallery in the San Francisco neighborhood of Fisherman's Wharf. The reporter found that the gallery had closed a month before.[3]

One optimistic note has come from editor Jane Goldman, who by the summer of 2002 had made great strides toward starting up a new magazine. She had recruited a number of former *Standard* employees—including me—both on the business and editorial sides to help get it off the ground. Tellingly, however, Jane's magazine has nothing to do with the Internet or business: It's a populist food magazine with the working title of *Chow.*

As for me, I spent the better part of a year writing and revising this book, which is a decent way to deal with forced unemployment. I've been able to do some freelance writing on a variety of topics, from business regulation to the details of newspaper obituaries, and now work for *Time.*

I wish that *The Standard*'s story had had a different ending, that we had been able to survive until the advertising economy recharged itself. But I'll never regret choosing to work for *The Standard.* I'm proud of what we accomplished journalistically, and I think we prodded the rest of the media world to look at the technology business through a more rigorous set of filters. The experience taught me tons, not only about business reporting and managing a staff, but also about the importance of not buying too much hype, even when it comes from the people running your own company. Something about watching a good publication starve to death on $200 million makes you highly skeptical of any business, media or otherwise, that promises to change your life, through either technology or stock options.

Just about the only person who still seems to believe in reproducing some version of *The Standard*'s territory is John Battelle. When I last saw him, in January 2002, he was far from settling on a career path. He'd been teaching some at the respected journalism school of the University of California at Berkeley, and he said he was in the midst of several magazine consulting gigs, which he declined to discuss in detail. Yet he continued to hold out a dream of founding a new, perfect magazine. He envisioned a monthly magazine to be guided by the principle that culture in America is driven by business culture. (This notion became more tenuous as the year wore on, with every passing week revealing a new scandal in corporate earnings and/or accounting.) He was convinced that he could get the most talented and respected business writers in America to contribute, recruiting from the ranks of *The New Yorker* and *Fortune* and *Wired*. All he needed was someone to put up the money, and there are always plenty of people like that.

We briefly discussed the pros and cons of such a magazine, and then his wife Michelle came into the room for a moment. I jokingly told her we were discussing Battelle's next magazine. She turned to me with a smile and then placed her fingers in the shape of a cross, as if warding off a vampire.

Notes

Introduction: An Overdose, or Murder?

1. Elizabeth Angell, "Upholding the Industry Standard," *Brill's Content,* June 2000.
2. "The Industry Standard, Unplugged," *New York Times,* Aug. 18, 2001, p. A14.
3. There were, of course, other assets besides the bank accounts, including $7.6 million in accounts receivable and, the company maintained, about $10.4 million owed to it by IDG.

1. Impatient with the Present

1. Louis Rossetto, quoted in Elizabeth Angell, "Upholding the Industry Standard," *Brill's Content,* June 2000.
2. Interview with the author, 1998. Mitchell later became a top editor at *Business 2.0.*
3. In the summer of 1998, that business was spun off as a separate, publicly traded company called IDG Books Worldwide, although IDG retained ownership of nearly three-quarters of the stock. In August 2000, IDG Books Worldwide bought the online learning portal Hungry Minds, and shortly thereafter changed the name of the company to Hungry Minds, Inc. That business, in turn, was sold to the publisher John Wiley in August 2001, following a slackening of sales.
4. Chana Schoenberger, "Relying on Self-Reliance: IDG Chairman Has Built a Global Publisher on a Foundation of Local, Independent Units," *Boston Globe,* Sept. 6, 1998, p. E1.

5. But not to New York: Corporate legend holds that McGovern had a bad business experience in New York and therefore shuns that city. As a consequence, I did not meet him until I moved to London.

6. Jackie Bannon, "Great e-scape," *The Guardian*, April 27, 1998, p. 8.

7. Excerpt from the business plan for Thestandard.net, February 1998, p. 7.

8. "Architects of the Internet Economy: Redesigning the Rules of Business," an IDC White Paper, sponsored by *The Industry Standard*, 1998, p. 1.

9. *The Standard*'s internal lore holds that Battelle specifically demanded a separate building from IDG in order to preserve an independence from the owner. But in fact this was not unique; many IDG publications in San Francisco work from separate locations. More significantly—as would become clear during the bankruptcy proceedings—the lease for the building at 315 Pacific was signed by IDG.

10. Williamson left the publication on good terms and continued to make valuable contributions as a freelance writer and editor.

2. THIS WEEK'S BILLIONAIRES

1. In fact, most people use IT to abbreviate "information technology."

2. Jim Clark with Owen Edwards, *Netscape Time: The Making of the Billion-Dollar Start-up That Took on Microsoft* (New York: St. Martin's Press, 1999); Michael Lewis, *The New New Thing* (New York: W. W. Norton, 2000).

3. George Anders, "Resistant Strain: Healtheon Struggles in Efforts to Remedy Doctors' Paper Plague," *Wall Street Journal*, Oct. 2, 1998, p. A1.

4. Mark Gimein, "How Morgan and Goldman Caught a Cold," *The Industry Standard*, Nov. 2–9, 1998, p. 20.

5. Clark's book does not address the failed Healtheon IPO. Lewis's account essentially blames the poor IPO market of the fall of 1998. His account of the deal's dissolution mainly concerns the reactions of Clark and Healtheon's management; he doesn't address the relationship between the bankers themselves.

6. The editors of *PR Watch*, John Stauber and Sheldon Rampton, published a blistering book called *Toxic Sludge Is Good for You: Lies, Damn Lies and the Public Relations Industry* (Monroe, Maine: Common Courage Press, 1995).

7. In March 2001, About.com was bought by the magazine publishing group Primedia for an astounding $426 million in stock.

8. Lisa Bransten, "Two Popular Web Sites for Women to Merge," *Wall Street Journal*, Jan. 28, 1999, p. B4.

3. THE FAT YEAR BEGINS

1. Typically, Time officials do not comment on potential investments or purchases, but these negotiations were reported in the media at the time. See, for example, Mary Huhn, "Time Inc. in the Hunt for Cyber Title," *New York Post*, Feb. 2, 1999, p. 28.

2. Interview with the author. Huey declined a request to be interviewed for this book.

3. The figure comes from Competitive Media Reporting and is cited in Devin Leonard, "Is This the Next Tech Bubble?" *Fortune*, June 12, 2000, p. 145.

4. Suein L. Hwang, "Sick of So Many Dot-Com Ads? Click Here for More," *Wall Street Journal*, Jan. 21, 2000, p. B1.

5. *San Francisco Business Times*, Nov. 15, 1999.

6. Nola Sarkisian-Miller, "Radio Stations Raise Rates as Dot-Com Advertisers Pile On," *Los Angeles Business Journal*, Dec. 27, 1999, p. 4. Nationwide, the increase in radio advertising for 1999 was about 15 percent, to approximately $17.7 billion. Radio executives cited the dot-com explosion, along with other factors, as a cause of the boost.

7. James Ledbetter, "Jonathan Bulkeley's Book Values," *The Industry Standard*, March 15, 1999, p. 33. Bulkeley did not remain at the helm of Barnesandnoble.com for more than a few more months.

8. Lisa Granatstein, "IDG Title Surfs the Rising Tide of E-commerce," *MediaWeek*, Sept. 20, 1999.

9. The *Financial Times* used the figure $125 million (Alice Rawsthorn, "Online Fashion Retailer Sets European Start-Up Record: Arnault and Benettons Back $125m Launch of Boo.com," May 10, 1999, p. 25). That figure was widely reproduced in part because Boo's publicists steered reporters toward it. However, Boo.com cofounder Ernst Malmsten has written that "the correct figure was still only $75 million" (Malmsten, *Boo Hoo: A Dot.com Story from Concept to Catastrophe* [London: Random House Business Books, 2001], p. 177). To the best of my knowledge, the *FT* has never corrected its inaccurate report.

10. Malmsten, *Boo Hoo*, p. 180.

11. *The New York Review* article, published on August 24, 1967, did not itself discuss how to build a Molotov cocktail. It was a challenging review of a book by Martin Luther King, Jr., written by the late Andrew Kopkind.

12. Amy Harmon, "Stocks Drive a Rush to Riches in Manhattan's Silicon Alley," *New York Times*, May 31, 1999, p. A1.

13. The Bain & Co study is detailed in John A. Byrne, "Capital Gets Antsy," *BusinessWeek*, Sept. 13, 1999.

14. Cynthia Cotts, "Press Clips," *The Village Voice*, Jan. 26, 1999, p. 34.

15. Drudge's ranking is cited in Frank Rich, "Bob Hope Lives," *New York Times,* June 10, 1998, p. A29.

16. James Ledbetter and Kenneth Li, "The Smoking Gun Shoots a Millionaire," *The Industry Standard,* March 6, 2000, p. 72.

17. John V. Pavlik, *Journalism and New Media* (New York: Columbia University Press, 2001), p. xi.

18. Leslie Walker, "Net's Great Minds Network," *Washington Post,* July 22, 1999, p. E1.

19. These figures come from an interview with David Evans.

20. In an interview, Battelle insisted that the company never lost more than a couple of hundred thousand dollars a year on its party business, a figure he considered a worthy investment in reputation-building.

21. "Before Hours," CNNfn, Aug. 16, 1999.

22. Bamboo.com later merged with another firm into the Internet Pictures Corporation.

23. Much of Atkinson's history can be gleaned from a reading of its file in U.S. Bankruptcy Court, Northern District of California (San Francisco), case 97-3-3694-R (the various Atkinson bankruptcies have since been consolidated). Another source is David Rosenbaum, "Innocent Victim? How Atkinson Fell," *Engineering News-Record,* Oct. 13, 1997, pp. 30 ff.

24. From a sworn declaration given by Martin Nachimson supporting the banks' objections to Atkinson's request for authority to use its cash collateral; U.S. Bankruptcy Court, Northern District of California (San Francisco), August 1997.

4. WE NEED MORE BUCKETS!

1. Battelle quoted in Devin Leonard, "Is This the Next Tech Bubble?" *Fortune,* June 12, 2000, p. 145.

2. The real-estate data and the "hypergrowth" characterization come from data assembled by the real-estate information group REIS.

3. Jonathan Weber, "Millennium Madness," *The Industry Standard,* Dec. 13–20, 1999, p. 13.

4. Howard Kurtz, "Point and Clique: At Inside.com, Media Superstars Hope to Out-Scoop Giant News Rivals and Put People in the Loop—For a Price," *Washington Post,* May 3, 2000, p. C1.

5. Maryann Jones Thompson, "Music Moves Online: Consumers Get in the Groove," *The Industry Standard,* Aug. 2–9, 1999, p. 80.

6. Michael Schrage, "Is Advertising Dead?," *Wired,* February 1994.

7. The best account of AOL's rise to prominence is Kara Swisher's *Aol.com:*

How Steve Case Beat Bill Gates, Nailed the Netheads, and Made Millions in the War for the Web (New York: Times Books, 1998). Occasionally Swisher's analysis spills over into cheerleading, but her access to principal characters is unparalleled.

8. Sanford C. Bernstein and McKinsey & Company, Inc., *Broadband! A Joint Industry Study,* published in New York on Jan. 13, 2000. A less publicized finding in this report was that two-thirds of Americans who were already online said they were not interested in high-speed Net access.

9. James Ledbetter, "Industry Standard Gets $30M in Financing," Thestandard.com, Jan. 19, 2000.

10. James Fallows, "Palm reading," *The Industry Standard,* March 20, 2000, p. 51.

11. Michelle Slatalla, "To Boldly Go to the Supermarket with Captain Kirk," *New York Times,* Jan. 6, 2000, p. F4.

12. The $5 million figure came from chief operating officer Anne-Marie Mc-Gowan. Kerry Zeida, the marketing manager, put the overall cost of the TV spots at a little more than half that amount.

13. These figures come from an internal budget prepared in 2001. Obviously, they do not reflect actual expenditures for 2001, because the magazine ceased publication in August of that year.

14. Julie Rieger of Carat Freeman, quoted in Lori Lefevre, "Put a Cap on It," *MediaWeek,* July 17, 2000.

15. These figures come from the June 2000 "Commentary," a monthly department-by-department report that circulated among senior *Standard* staff members.

16. Polly Sprenger, "Where Is Boo.com?" *The Industry Standard,* Sept. 27, 1999.

5. FLYING BLIND INTO EUROPE

1. "Internet Publisher to Start European Edition," *New York Times,* April 11, 2000, p. C10.

2. In the event, Peres canceled at the last minute, citing a flare-up in the *intifada.*

3. Interview with the author.

4. "Internet Publisher to Start European Edition," *New York Times,* April 11, 2000, p. C10.

5. See, for example, Maggie Brown, "Doing the Business," *Guardian Media Pages,* Nov. 13, 2000, p. 4.

6. Janet Guyon, "The World Is Your Office," *Fortune,* June 12, 2000, p. 52.

7. Pearson's Business Information unit eventually suffered from the advertising downfall; in early 2002, it was put up for sale. A few months later, the unit was withdrawn from sale because there were no buyers.

6. AU REVOIR TO ALL THAT

1. "The Final Countdown," *The Industry Standard Europe*, April 12, 2000, p. 3.
2. Surprisingly, a UK version of *Slate* did eventually launch, in January 2002. It lasted a little longer than two months.
3. Jeannette Winterson, "Stirred by the Genius of the Net," *The Industry Standard Europe*, Nov. 9, 2000, p. 77.
4. James McLean, "US E-commerce Giant Priceline to Invade Europe," *Evening Standard*, June 29, 2000, p. 39.
5. Bernhard Warner, "Priceline into Europe with Eyes Wide Open," *The Industry Standard Europe*, Oct. 19, 2000, p. 41.
6. Polly Sprenger, "A One Man Feeding Frenzy," *The Industry Standard Europe*, Dec. 7, 2000, p. 51.
7. Michael Liedtke, "New Economy Magazine Publisher Standard Media Fires 7 Percent of Staff," Associated Press, Jan. 8, 2001.
8. Andrew Ward, "BBC Considers Website Adverts," *Financial Times*, Jan. 24, 2001, p. 3.
9. Kristi Essick, "Wanadoo Steps out onto World Stage," *The Industry Standard Europe*, Dec. 14, 2000, pp. 24–25.
10. James Ashton, "Future Forecast Reduced to (GBP) 34m," *Business A.M.*, Jan. 5, 2001.
11. Gary Rivlin, "AOL's Rough Riders," *The Industry Standard*, Oct. 30, 2000, p. 130.
12. Jennifer Couzin, "Mixing Business with Leather," *The Industry Standard*, Dec. 18, 2000, pp. 60–61. The headline, in addition to being a clever pun, is an allusion to Beck's album *Midnite Vultures*.
13. Ethan Smith, "The Other Chip Wars," *The Industry Standard*, March 5, 2001. It should be said that Smith is a fine writer who wrote some of the magazine's most interesting, and funniest, pieces.
14. It's entirely possible that focus groups on the Continent would not have objected as much to the word "Europe" in the title. But with the bulk of our readership in the UK, we had to give priority to these objections.
15. "The Final Countdown," *The Industry Standard Europe*, April 12, 2001, p. 3.
16. The company declined to issue McAlister a stock certificate.

7. A Very Public Hell

1. IDG has confirmed these figures. In the end, Marino was on the company payroll for less than four months and received $141,308.85, plus reimbursements for expenses.

2. Ironically, the calling card continued to function until November 2001, some three months after *The Standard* went under.

3. Memorandum to SMI board of directors, from Anne-Marie McGowan, chief operating officer, May 3, 2001.

4. *Media Buyer's Daily*, Jan. 17, 2002.

5. The 35 percent figure comes from the VAST report. In an interview, *The Standard*'s circulation director recalled that it was 38 percent, still drastically low.

6. This quotation is according to Rivlin's recollection; Weber said later that he did not recall saying it.

7. E-mail from Jonathan Weber to Gary Rivlin and other editorial staff, May 7, 2001.

8. Rivlin says that Benchmark's Harvey insisted on conditions for being quoted that Rivlin found unacceptable, which is why his draft contained no quote for comment.

9. E-mail from Rivlin to Jonathan Weber and Jane Goldman, May 15, 2001. Despite his fury over the Benchmark story, Rivlin retains strong respect for Weber and considers himself lucky to have been his colleague.

10. McGowan made this remark during a bankruptcy creditors' meeting on October 2, 2001.

11. This suggestion was reported in Greg Lindsay's extensive post-mortem, "The Fast and Furious Rise and Fall of *The Industry Standard*," *Folio*, Sept. 10, 2001.

12. E-mail from Jonathan Weber to the author, July 9, 2001.

13. Peter Delevett, "Wiretap column," *San Jose Mercury News*, July 13, 2001.

14. Alex Kuczynski, "News Corp. Intends to Shed Its Magazine Unit," *New York Times*, July 18, 2001, p. C4.

15. E-mail from Jerry Colonna to SMI board members, Aug. 2, 2001. Colonna declined to be interviewed for this book.

16. E-mail from Jonathan Weber to the author, Feb. 6, 2002.

17. E-mail from John Battelle to SMI board members, Aug. 3, 2001.

18. E-mail from Patrick McGovern to the author, Nov. 2, 2001.

8. THE CASE FOR MURDER

1. David Carr, "Those Jaunty Issues of the New Economy Take a Sober Turn," *New York Times*, March 4, 2002, p. C8.
2. The magazine redesigned itself in the spring of 2001, but it was way too late to address these problems.
3. There are some exceptions, including, obviously, the supplements to newspapers, such as *The New York Times Magazine*. Also, in the past five to ten years, most of the nation's "alternative weeklies," such as *The Village Voice, Boston Phoenix, Seattle Weekly,* and the like have all moved to free distribution. However, this is not really the same as controlling circulation among a particular demographic; it is merely a strategy to get the circulation number as high as possible.
4. This isn't to imply that the trade-publication market is free from the pressures of market downturns. All the IDG technology publications suffered in 2001, as did their rivals. In January 2002, CMP Media, another technology-publishing company, shut down its title *Internet Week,* which in different guises had been publishing every week since 1983.
5. Carr, "Those Jaunty Issues."
6. Figures cited in David Handelman, "Bear Market for Personal Finance Magazines," *New York Times*, Nov. 26, 2001, p. C10.
7. James, Cramer, "Ignoring Financial Reality Killed Magazine," *Rocky Mountain News*, Aug. 25, 2001, p. 8C.
8. Ibid.
9. Scuttlebutt among former staffers holds that *Substandard* pages started showing up in searches done through Google, and that fear of trademark or libel violations led to their demise.
10. This was cited in a creditors' motion filed with the bankruptcy court on Sept. 21, 2001.

EPILOGUE: WHO DO WE SHOOT?

1. In fact, Parsons got a job as a London correspondent for *Red Herring*.
2. Ross Kerber, "Tech Publications Scramble to Keep Advertisers Happy," *Boston Globe*, May 13, 2002, p. C1.
3. David Lazarus, "Warehouse Full, Galleries Empty at Kinkade," *San Francisco Chronicle*, Jan. 27, 2002, p. G1.

Index